Interaction of Media, Cognition, and Learning

❁ ❁ ❁ ❁ ❁ ❁ ❁

An Exploration of How Symbolic Forms Cultivate Mental Skills and Affect Knowledge Acquisition

Gavriel Salomon

❊ ❊ ❊ ❊ ❊ ❊ ❊

Interaction of Media, Cognition, and Learning

 Jossey-Bass Publishers

San Francisco • Washington • London • 1979

INTERACTION OF MEDIA, COGNITION, AND LEARNING
*An Exploration of How Symbolic Forms Cultivate Mental Skills and Affect
Knowledge Acquisition*
by Gavriel Salomon

JACKET DESIGN BY WILLI BAUM

FIRST EDITION

Code 7908

The Jossey-Bass
Social and Behavioral Science Series

Foreword

This book brings to fruition over a decade of dedicated intellectual toil by Gavriel Salomon. It provides a theoretical language—a system of concepts—for the study of a field of problems that has always seemed to me devoid of, and badly in need of, an adequate conceptual base.

Much of cognitive psychology's focus in this century, and that of many related sciences as well, has been concentrated on the power of verbal processes. Verbal learning and verbal behavior in a print-based society has seemed to dominate our conception of human intellect as Mont Blanc dominates the French Alps, or Everest the Himalayas. The eyes of the human sciences were naturally drawn to such peaks in awe. But even a majestic mountain does not stand alone. Verbal language evolved from earlier forms; from pictures, through pictographic denotation, and ideographic symbols, to polysyllabic construction and discourse. Its evolution took different forms at different rates in different cultures. More or less in parallel, and in much lower profile, practitioners of the arts, and of emerging technologies, continued the development of the earlier forms. These arts, however, have been left largely to their practitioners. There is no complementary scientific understanding of these forms, even though fragmentary research on one or another isolated problem has persisted.

Modern media now offer rich arrays, and often complex mixtures, of verbal, paraverbal, and nonverbal communications. While there is continuing value in the intensive study of a single form of communication in a single culture, a full understanding of human intellect eventually requires a comparative, interactive, and transactive view. This is now seen to be as true in cognitive psychology as it is in art or anthropology. Further, the subtle power of these communications media in shaping educational and social effects is now recognized. So, the time is ripe for both an enlarged view of human communication and a deeper analysis of its fundaments.

Salomon has sought a deep-structure theory for these purposes, based in an understanding of the characteristics of symbol systems. He has sought further to show that these characteristics can shape not only knowledge acquisition and organization through a particular medium but also the differential development of cognitive skills. To my knowledge, no one heretofore has posed such a challenging hypothesis to educators, parents and producers alike; they can, and are, creating cognitive skills geared to the processing of messages in particular media. By so doing, they may also be unwittingly inhibiting the development of other cognitive skills. This is an imporant result for education, for psychology, and for the field of communication. It is an important insight for theoreticians and practitioners alike. And it sets the stage for an important new era of research, not just on media narrowly and traditionally defined, but also on symbol systems as they operate through all forms and media of communication to influence the learning and cognitive development of human beings, individually and collectively.

The book is but a first step in this direction. It sets out an agenda that could occupy teams of researchers for many years to come. I hope young researchers in educational psychology, in particular, will read it and be guided by it, for it poses the sort of question that educational research should be asking about fundamental educational phenomena. Too often today, in this field and others, the press of the present demands immediate answers to superficial questions and the young are drawn off into problems that are gone tomorrow.

Gavriel Salomon is a good friend and a long-term collaborator on questions associated with the themes of this book. I admire him for having had the talent and drive to write it, and I commend it to your attention.

Stanford, California   RICHARD E. SNOW
March 1979   *Professor of Education*
                    and Psychology, Stanford
                    University

Foreword

❊ ❊ ❊ ❊ ❊ ❊ ❊

Introductory texts in the social sciences present a neat but misleading view of the course of scientific progress. According to the section on research methods, characteristically tucked into the first chapter, the investigator begins with a well-articulated theory of the domain under scrutiny. From this theory he generates one or more hypotheses. Then an appropriate experiment is devised, data are collected and analyzed, the hypothesis is confirmed or disconfirmed, and, if necessary, suitable adjustments are made in the theoretical superstructure that inspired the original investigation.

    Turning to politically engaged governmental agencies, one encounters a flow chart that is dramatically different but perhaps equally simplistic. In such cases one begins with pressing practical problems that demand solution. The problems in turn suggest a kind of study—laboratory or field, experiment or survey—that will garner information relevant to a solution. There may be pay-offs for the theoretically oriented scientific community but such dividends are secondary; the research succeeds to the extent that it helps solve the problem that initially generated it.

For those who conduct research, neither of these descriptions rings true. To be sure, the occasional theory cries out for a crucial experiment, the rare practical problem translates itself neatly into operational terms. In general, however, the relations among theory, experiment, and real world application prove much more intricate and far more vexing. Indeed, the connections are more reminiscent of networks of neural cells than a unidirectional flow chart.

Interaction of Media, Cognition, and Learning is a very apt blend of the concerns of the theorist, the empirical researcher, and the classroom practitioner. It is informed by theory; it presents important experimental evidence; it is filled with implications for pedagogy. Clearly it has emerged from the hand of someone directly acquainted with the relevant issues, indeed someone who has himself toiled in the library, in the laboratory, and on the firing line.

Gavriel Salomon is admirably suited to write this book. This gifted investigator has been concerned for a decade with a host of issues pertaining to the media of expression and communication. He has been heavily engaged with practical issues, for example, the introduction of "Sesame Street" to Israeli television. He has made significant contributions to the study of media effects, for instance, in his elucidation of the manner in which media can supplant cognitive processes. And he has plumbed the theoretical literature on the nature of knowledge in such diverse disciplines as philosophy, psychology, and education.

These diverse interests have coalesced as Salomon wrestles with two problems of classic proportion: How can knowledge, however discovered, be captured and presented in various symbol systems? And how, in turn, do individuals come to apprehend such presentations of knowledge? In pursuing these issues, he has performed several crucial services: he has synthesized the

relevant literature; he has devised key experiments that tease
out the *modus operandi* of various media of communication;
and he has propounded a program of research that he and other
colleagues can undertake over the coming decade. Researchers
may quarrel with some of Salomon's points and may well prof-
fer alternative explanations of certain phenomena he has described. This is possible only because he has written with enviable
clarity, allowing the rest of us to assess the claims he has made,
the interpretations he has offered, the hypotheses he has formulated. Indeed, in a field too often marred by vague handwaving
or ponderous sermonizing, Salomon's refreshingly vigorous
statements may well exert paradigmatic effects on theorizing,
research, and practice. *Interaction of Media, Cognition, and
Learning* should prove a powerful and beneficient force within
the field of educational research, and I am pleased to have the
opportunity to introduce it to you.

Cambridge, Massachusetts   HOWARD GARDNER
Codirector, Harvard Project Zero,
Harvard University

Preface

❁ ❁ ❁ ❁ ❁ ❁ ❁

For several years I have struggled with two questions: What aspects of the communication media should an *educational* psychologist study? And how can the fruits of such study be related to the mainstream of psychological research? There are numerous sources for my interest in these two questions. As a short-lived artist, I became interested in the visual media, which in turn led me, while I was a graduate student, to study cognitive aspects of map reading in a cross-cultural context. Somewhat later, I became interested in uncertainty and in the structural properties of media that cultivate uncertainty in teachers. I was drawn to examine what educational research on media offered and found to my surprise that the field was generally atheoretical and far behind contemporary advances in psychological research. Metaphorically speaking, I felt (and to an extent still feel) that many a researcher in this area looks for the lost dime under the street light because it is a better illuminated spot.

The results of ten years of work, in which I have addressed myself to the two questions mentioned previously, are summarized in this book. *Interaction of Media, Cognition, and Learning* proposes the beginnings of an empirically based theory that relates media's most essential modes of presentation—their symbol systems—to modes of representation in thought and to the acquisition of knowledge. The general arguments I develop in this book are that symbol systems, including those used by media, differ because they call for different kinds of mental activity in the acquisition of knowledge (thus benefiting different learners) and because they cultivate different kinds of mental skills (thus benefiting different kinds of mental processes). The purpose of the book is to provide the foundations of a theory, not to offer a fully developed one, and to stimulate discussion and new research, not to hand down definite answers.

In this book I draw upon recent advances in such areas as the study of symbol systems, cognition, cognitive development, psycholinguistics, and mass communication. Since I am advancing an unorthodox approach to a complex topic and cross the boundaries of a number of fields, this book should interest researchers and scholars in educational psychology, cognition and cognitive development, instructional design, communication, media, and educational technology.

A number of general considerations have influenced my work and hence the nature of this book. The first and most important is the need to move research on media in education from an atheoretical, unsystematic, "isolationist" exploration to a more systematic, theoretically guided inquiry. In spite of its advanced age, research on media has not yet overcome many of its childhood diseases. And it cannot overcome them as long as the domain of media is undifferentiated and the research is based on somewhat questionable assumptions. Further, since communicational media constitute a subclass of societal educational means, one can not fruitfully study media as a separate entity. There may be many ways to conceive, classify, and analyze media, but each of these ways should relate media to other psychological constructs within a broad theoretical network. By examining media from the standpoint of their symbol systems, I try to relate them to mental symbolic processes and to learning, which leads to several other considerations.

The second consideration is the need to propose a new approach to media, as seen from an educational-psychological viewpoint. My argument is that the *essential* differences between media are the ways in which they structure and convey contents —and not their technological differences in communicating contents, although these do exist. If we are to study media's potential contribution, my claim is that we must deal with their symbol systems. This claim derives not only from the essence of media's nature but also, and to no lesser extent, from the possible interaction between symbol systems that figure in our environment and symbolic processes that figure in our thinking. As this central theme is developed in the book, media *per se* are gradually phased out, while considerations of symbol systems in general are phased in. Indeed, one conclusion I draw is that media's symbol systems are but a special case of a wider class— the class of *social* symbol systems. The fact that media are technologically evolved has little to do with the way they affect the acquisition of knowledge or the cultivation of ability.

The third consideration is the current paucity of interest in the symbolic modes of mental representation. Although symbols in communication have been dealt with extensively by philosophers and semioticians, they have not—until recently— been integrated into psychological and educational theories. And although one finds recent claims that symbolic forms used in communication evolve first in thought, there is not much research into how communicational symbol systems—save lan-language—*affect* thought. In this book I take the position, partly inspired by work on language and thought and partly supported by my own empirical studies, that thinking employs a variety of symbolic forms and that these are called on and evolve in interaction with communicational symbol systems.

The fourth consideration pertains to differences in the role of symbol systems in the acquisition of knowledge and in the cultivation of mental skills. Such distinctions cannot be easily and clearly drawn, however, because the differential roles that symbol systems play in both capacities are interrelated. Yet, distinctions are helpful insofar as they direct attention to the yet little-explored ways in which communicational symbol

systems function as mental skill *cultivators*. I describe some
research to show that such media as film and television can, and
do, affect the mastery of mental skills through the symbolic
modes they employ, thus suggesting that the various symbol
systems of media are more than simply alternative ways to
transmit information. The differences just mentioned serve, in
fact, as the major impetus of the book. Much of the discussion
is devoted to the questions of how differences among symbol
systems affect the acquisition of knowledge and how they affect
cognition.

   The fifth consideration is the distinction between what
symbol systems *can be made* to affect and what they *typically*
affect. This distinction is critical because not everything an edu-
cator can achieve by realizing *potential* attributes of symbol
systems is necessarily achieved "naturally." Since the skill-
cultivating potential of media's symbol systems has largely been
overlooked, it has never been realized. Much of what we know
about media concerns only their typical effects (usually as conveyors of content), but this tells us little about how they can be
made to serve education better. Studying what can be achieved
with symbol systems does not exclude the study of what takes
place typically. Although the former may be of greater interest
to educators and the latter to communicationists, the conver-
gence of the two approaches may be of even greater interest to
psychologists.

   The last, but not least, consideration is of individual
differences in skill-mastery and in learning. Including individual
differences when studying the effects of media, cognition, or
learning is by now widespread. However, more often than not,
it means that either some age-related or situation-related differences are measured or that aptitude-treatment interactions are
studied. In trying to interrelate media, cognition, and learning
through one set of constructs—symbolism—including individual
differences becomes an integral part of the undertaking. It
would be impossible to consider the *interactions* of media,
cognition, and learning without taking into account the variety
of mental representational forms, or the variety of ways in
which individuals extract knowledge from coded messages.

   Avoiding the position of unidirectional effects of communicational symbol systems on learning and skill-mastery, I find myself adopting a view of reciprocal interaction between symbolic environment, the learner's cognitive makeup, and the utilization of specific mental skills. These affect each other in reciprocal ways: Learners' abilities influence the kind of information they aim at extracting, which in turn determines what kinds of symbolic modes they encounter; the latter call for specific skills whose employement affects their abilities and the kind of information they can aim at later on. The consideration of individual differences within an interactional framework is as necessary as the consideration of interactions between humans and environments when individual differences are studied.

The book is roughly divided into two parts. Four chapters are theoretical treatments: Chapter One on media, Chapter Two on symbol systems, Chapter Three on symbol systems and cognition, and Chapter Five on the role of media's symbol systems in skill cultivation. Another four chapters describe empirical studies: Chapter Four examines the role of symbolic elements in knowledge acquisition, and Chapters Six through Eight look at their role in skill cultivation. Chapter Nine attempts to pull together, revisit, widen the scope, and summarize the preceding eight chapters.

The work described herein could not have been carried out, nor could the book ever have been written, without the help, encouragement, and inspiration of numerous colleagues and friends. Specifically, I am grateful for the unqualified encouragement I have received from Richard E. Clark, now at the University of Southern California; without his support, I would not have had the persistence to undertake such a project. I am equally thankful to Richard E. Snow of Stanford University, who introduced me over the years to his unique and exciting ways of looking at human skills and aptitudes and thus greatly influenced how I approached these aspects of my work. David R. Olson of the Ontario Institute for the Study of Education inspired my interest in the symbolic aspects of media through his writings and ongoing personal contacts. Howard Gardner of Harvard University not only stimulated me to explore new avenues of thought but also served as a never-tiring, never-too-busy critic whose suggestions I found invaluable; I cannot point to a single aspect of my work that he has not contributed to. David H. Feldman of Tufts University was in many respects my alterego, correcting my course of progress, sounding me out, reformulating ideas I could not yet express in articulate form; and, when it came to rolling up sleeves, he volunteered his valuable time and energy to carry out the American phase of the cross-cultural study. Olson, Gardner, and Feldman contributed most directly to this book. During the year in which I wrote the book, they maintained a vital support system of advice and inspiration, which culminated in two conferences we held in Boston.

Akiba A. Cohen of the Hebrew University of Jerusalem was my partner in executing some of the studies I reported here. Being a computer wizard and a mass communication expert, he was an indispensable part of the research. Albert Bandura and Eliot Eisner, both of Standord University, who represent two poles of a continuum ranging from hard-line empirical work to esthetic considerations, greatly influenced my thinking. Rivka Rimor, Dorothy Piontkowski, Andrea Lash, Dennis Cronin, and numerous others served as my graduate assistants at the Hebrew University and at Stanford. They are responsible for the actual administration of the studies, the collection of background material, and valuable editorial assistance. Helen Nash typed (and retyped) the manuscript tirelessly.

Most of the research was done at the Hebrew University of Jerusalem and began with a small grant from the American Psychological Foundation. But the main bulk of the work was later supported by grants from the Spencer Foundation, which was also generous enough to provide additional support for the actual writing and for the conferences in Boston. Inspiration is perhaps a necessary condition for such work, but the research would not have been possible without the Spencer Foundation's support, and I am deeply grateful. Finally, the writing itself took place during a sabbatical at Stanford University, where I was treated as a welcomed guest.

Stanford, California   GAVRIEL SALOMON
March 1979

Contents

❇ ❇ ❇ ❇ ❇ ❇ ❇

Foreword   ix
Richard E. Snow

Foreword   xiii
Howard Gardner

Preface   xvii

The Author   xxvii

ONE   Reexamining Educational Research and   1
        Conceptions of Media
        Prevailing Assumptions in Media Research •
        Another Conception of Media • Summary

TWO   Characteristics of Symbol Systems   28
        Symbols and Symbol Systems • Psychological
        Considerations • The Example of Film • Summary

xxiii

THREE   Relationships of Symbol Systems to Cognition   61
           Differences of Content and Ease of Processing •
           Differences of Requisite Mental Skills •
           Differences of Construed Meaning •
           Differential Cultivation of Skills •
           Summary

FOUR   Differential Uses of Mental Skills for Learning   88
           Rationale • The Television Experiment •
           Additional Considerations • Summary

FIVE   Cultivation of Mental Skills through   113
           Symbolic Forms
           Cultivation Through Skill-Activation and
           Practice • Symbols as Tools of Thought •
           Language in Thought • Internalization of
           Language and Other Symbol Systems •
           Internalization Through Observational Learning •
           The Mental Functions of Codes • Transfer of
           Cultivated Skills • Summary

SIX   Impact of Films Designed to Cultivate   139
           Mental Skills
           The Experiments: General Considerations •
           Experiment I: Zooming and Cue-Attendance •
           Experiment II: The Role of Verbal Mediation •
           Experiment III: Filmic Laying Out and Its
           Effects on Visualization Skills • Experiment IV:
           Changing Points of View • Summary

SEVEN   Effects of "Sesame Street" on Television-Naive   157
           Children
           The Longitudinal Study • An Experiment:
           Encouraging Mothers to Coobserve the
           Program • A Replication: "Sesame Street"
           Versus Adventure Films • Summary and
           General Discussion

Contents

EIGHT   Cross-Cultural Cognitive Effects of Television   187
         Exposure
         Method • Results • Discussion • Summary

NINE   Interaction of Media, Cognition, and Learning: 214
         Summary and Reflections
         *Media's Symbol Systems and the Acquisition of
         Knowledge • Media's Symbol Systems and the
         Cultivation of Mental Skills • Reciprocal
         Interaction*

         References   246

         Name Index   269

         Subject Index   275

The Author

❁ ❁ ❁ ❁ ❁ ❁ ❁

GAVRIEL SALOMON is associate professor of educational psychology at the Hebrew University of Jerusalem and also a faculty member of the Institute for Communciation.

Salomon was born in Tel Aviv in 1938, where he attended school and later graduated from an art academy. He was a member of a kibbutz (1957-1959) and a school principal in Ma'alot, a new immigrants' settlement in the northern part of Israel. He was awarded his B.A. and M.A. degrees from the Hebrew University of Jerusalem in education, geogrpahy, and psychology (1964, 1966) and was awarded his Ph.D. degree in educational psychology and communication from Stanford University (1968). His first teaching position was at Indiana University (1968-69), followed by a position at the Hebrew University, where he chaired the Department of Educational Psychology (1976-77). He has been a Visiting Scholar (1977-78) and Senior Research Associate (1978-79) at Stanford University.

During his studies in Jerusalem, Salomon served as a psychological tester in industry, as secretary general of the Israeli Student Organization, and later as the head of the In-Service Training Department for Teachers at the Hebrew University. In 1974–75 he took a leave of absence from the Hebrew University to establish a field psychological service with the Israeli Defense Forces.

Among Salomon's publications are *Commentaries on Re-Search on Instructional Media* (with R. E. Snow, 1970), *Communication and Education* (in Hebrew, 1979), as well as articles in the *Journal of Personality and Social Psychology, American Educational Research Journal, Journal of Educational Psychology, American Psychologist,* and *Review of Educational Research.*

Salomon is presently studying organizational psychology in schools, focusing particularly on modes of communication that interact with teachers' and principals' self-efficacy and control.

Salomon lives with his wife, Varda, in Jerusalem and is the father of two daughters—Tal and Mairav. His hobbies include painting and sailing.

To my wife, Varda Shoham-Salomon

Interaction of Media, Cognition, and Learning

❊ ❊ ❊ ❊ ❊ ❊ ❊

An Exploration of How Symbolic Forms
Cultivate Mental Skills and
Affect Knowledge Acquisition

ONE

Reexamining Educational Research and Conceptions of Media

This book is concerned with understanding media in education. It focuses on one particular dimension of communication media —their symbol systems—and the ways it relates to cognition and learning.

The reader may question the merit of approaching media through their symbol systems of representation. Media are, after all, complex entities that entail more than just symbol systems. An entity consisting of technology, contents, instructional situations, and symbol systems is qualitatively different from the sum of its components. Indeed, our awareness of the complex and multivariant nature of media's roles and functions in education perhaps should force us to take a holistic approach. Neither the practical selection of media for specific learning situations nor the description of their practical utility would be satisfactory without a comprehensive look at all the attributes—content, symbolic appearance, situation, management, didactics, and economics. Why then focus on one particular dimension of media, and why focus specifically on media's symbol systems?

The study of media in education implicitly assumes that each medium entails some particular, even unique, attributes that matter or can be made to matter in learning. The objective of the media researcher would then be to identify those classes of unique attributes and to examine within a theoretical framework the ways in which they can contribute to learning. Hence, the researcher's greatest attention would be given to the differentiating characteristics of media rather than to their commonalities. Unfortunately, this is not the direction that media research has generally taken, leading Oettinger and Zapol (1971) to state that learning, as usually measured, is independent of the "details of means." Jamison, Suppes, and Wells (1974), who reviewed the research on instructional media and technology, arrived at the same conclusion; and Leifer (1976) found that the only meaningful difference between media is their *content*.

Olson (1974, p. 6) summarized the state of the art most succinctly: "It is an indictment of our present state of knowledge that we know neither how to assess the psychological effects of these technologies nor how to adapt them to the purposes of education. *The impact of technologies both ancient and modern on children's learning is either negligible or unknown.*" Whether or not the potential effects of media in education are indeed negligible or unknown is still an unresolved issue. However, a *holistic* approach to media, in which all potentially contributing factors are lumped together, can hardly aid us in resolving it.

Equipped with the advantages of hindsight, we might say that research on media in education thus far can be likened to *exploration.* As with cognitive development, exploration needs to precede *search* behavior (Wright and Vliestra, 1975). Whereas exploration, greatly influenced by the appeal of external stimuli, is unsystematic and unconceptual, search behavior is better focused, goal directed, and conceptually guided. Indeed, this is the progression through which research on media is beginning to move. But if the field is to move toward search behavior, then it requires, quite clearly, a more focused, systematic, and theoretically oriented approach—an approach I will take in this book.

The shift from exploration to a more focused search does not explain why I chose to focus in particular on media's symbol systems. The reason for this choice is twofold. First, it can be argued that media's symbol systems or "modes of appearance" (Goodman, 1968) are the primary, most essential attributes of media. (Presently, let us consider symbol systems as "modes of appearance" consisting of sets of elements that are inter-related within each system by syntax and are used in specifiable ways in relation to fields of reference. Chapter Two will provide a more formal treatment.) Media are our cultural apparatus for selecting, gathering, storing, and conveying knowledge in representational forms. Representation, as distinguished from raw experience, is always coded within a symbol system. If one attempted to remove pictures from film, cartography from maps, or language from texts, what would be left? Media without symbol systems are as inconceivable as mathematics without numbers.

Second, all cognition and learning are based on internal symbolic representations. Cognition is conceptualized by most contemporary psychologists as the processes that enable an individual to represent and deal symbolically with the external environment (Rosenthal and Zimmerman, 1978). Some would even claim that cognition, learning, and internal symbolism are inseparable. As Anatol Rapoport writes (1965, p. 99), "Symbolism is not something that happens to man (as conditioning happens to a dog). Symbolism is something man does. It embodies the entire gamut of man's mental life. It is the mode of his mental life."

If symbol systems are central to media of communication and to thinking, then the interactions and interdependence between the two systems cannot be ignored. For instance, it is possible that symbolically different presentations of information vary as to the mental skills of processing that they require (Olson and Bruner, 1974). It is also possible that the major symbol systems of the media cultivate mental skills differentially and that one learns to use media's symbolic forms for purposes of internal representation (Eisner, 1978).

Thus, my decision to deal with media in a more focused, systematic, and theoretical way stems from the need to progress from exploration toward search so that the unique aspects of media can be studied. My choice of media's symbol systems as the focus for investigation stems from the potentially rich interactions among media symbols, thinking, and learning. In the following discussion, I will examine three major assumptions that underlie past research on media and will suggest a different conception of media. This examination in turn will lead us to look more closely at media's symbol systems and their psychological and educational implications.

Prevailing Assumptions in Media Research

After more than half a century of research, our conceptions of media are still fuzzy, and our understanding of their unique potentialities is still inadequate. Perhaps this is partly due to difficulties in formulating the essential questions (see, for example, Mielke, 1968). Research questions are often based on implicit assumptions, and shaky or untenable assumptions may block the formulation of fruitful research questions. We can see the role of such implicit assumptions in the following examples. If, for instance, one implicitly assumes that all textbooks are sufficiently different as a medium, from films, then a question pertaining to their relative effectiveness in teaching can be asked. On the other hand, if one has reason to assume that media as delivery systems do not differ, but that only content differs, then another kind of question would be asked. Until recently, individual differences in learning were regarded as "noise" in experimental psychology, an assumption that gave birth to questions about differences between averages. However, when a new set of assumptions was introduced, suggesting that media and individual characteristics interact (Cronbach, 1957; Snow and Salomon, 1968; Cronbach and Snow, 1977), aptitude-treatment-interaction (ATI) questions were formulated.

Might it be that some of the major assumptions underlying and directing past research on media in education were somewhat questionable? Three assumptions seem to have dominated research. First, it was implicitly assumed that each medium is a more or less invariant entity with fixed clusters of attributes. Studies of the differential effects of media were then expected to lead to better practical selection of one medium over another. Second, media's invariant entities were assumed to be alternative routes to previously fixed educational ends. Studies were designed to identify "better" media for teaching mathematics or reading or science. Third, an implicit assumption has been that research findings are immediately applicable to the solution of practical problems of the kinds encountered by communicators and educators. Each of these assumptions deserves some elucidation.

The Nature of Media

The first assumption implies that media are discrete, invariant entities—that all the manifestations of a medium are sufficiently similar to each other to constitute a distinctive category to be contrasted with other categories. Indeed, from institutional, political, or sociological points of view, media are appropriately conceived of as invariant entities. Newspapers are "an institution," and so is television. Similarly, publishing is an economic enterprise that differs from radio broadcasting, and both are invariant entities when considered as social or political forces. If the political, economic, or social power of television is described, the total system is to be considered. Minor deviations, such as educational use of closed-circuit television or content variations, are irrelevant. The contention that television's most important role is "agenda setting"—telling us what to think about (McCombs and Shaw, 1972)—is unaffected by local or production differences. Media in this sense are theorized to affect society in different ways regardless of internal variations. The conception of the medium-stimulus as an invariant, total system is then appropriate, and internal differences are irrelevant to the overall effects of one medium when contrasted with another.

However, such a global definition of the medium-stimulus is insufficiently differentiated for cognitive-psychological and educational purposes. A medium does not interact as an invariant system with a learner's aptitudes so that learning is facilitated for some but not for others. Rather, something *within* the mediated stimulus, possibly shared to some extent with other media, makes the presented information more comprehensible or better memorized by learners of particular characteristics. The factors within a medium that may facilitate learning are certainly not to be equated with the whole medium. Salomon and Sieber (1970) fround that students generated many alternative explanations about the nature of a randomly spliced film but performed less well when shown a straightforward version of the same film. The factor that accounted for such a difference was not the medium of film; rather, it was a particular attribute (in this case, structure) that could be present in film as well as in other media.

Nor are the factors of a medium that can contribute to learning always present whenever the medium is employed. But they are often available to a medium (or a number of media), and, given specific learning situations and learners, their employment could *potentially* contribute to learning. For example, slow motion is available to the medium of film, but it is not always present. To the extent that it is used and carries critical information to learners who need it, it can be expected to facilitate learning. However, not all films use slow motion, not all slow motions carry critical information, and not all learners need the slowed-down visualization. Hence, no generalized conclusion about the medium as an invariant entity is warranted. Rather, specific potential attributes of a medium may, under some circumstances, with some learners, matter in learning.

This distinction points toward a discrepancy between the results of media research in instruction and mass media research. The results of instructional media research lead to the conclusion that "learning seems to be affected more by what is delivered than by the delivery system" (Schramm, 1977, p. 273). On the other hand, mass media research confirms that individual media do have profound effects (Comstock and others, 1978), that they function differentially and in quite important ways. For instance, "Israeli and Australian studies . . . find that newspapers are seen as important links bewteen self and society, while books and cinema are more self-oriented—books for self-improvement and cinema for self-gratification" (Katz, 1977,

p. 47). Media can be considered as invariant, discrete entities in some social sciences when the overall effects of total systems are studied. They cannot be so considered when one examines subtle interactions among components of media, individual characteristics, and learning outcomes.

The argument advanced here parallels somewhat similar arguments in studies of personality and cognitive development. Empirical research has not succeeded in supporting the assumption of stability of personality traits across time and occasions (Mischell, 1977), nor has the conception of "stages" in development been upheld (Flavell, 1971). Similarly the differences within a medium, as Schramm (1977) notes, are as great as those bewteen media. How can we ask questions pertaining to the differences between whole media systems, if their conception as invariant entities turns out to be questionable? In personality research, it is claimed that some people may display a greater degree of stability of some traits under some conditions (Bem and Allen, 1974). Perhaps media also differ systematically in some respects but not in others. Thus, these differences may have important psychological consequences under some conditions but not others.

Print is one of the oldest technological media. It has traditionally been seen as *a* medium, to be distinguished from other media such as film, television, or computers. Film and television, and newspapers and comic books, are conceived of as pairs of different media. Note, however, that these media and these pairs of media differ from each other in some respects but not necessarily in others. For instance, printed books differ from newspapers along dimensions of timeliness, format, and typical content, but not in terms of the technology of print or the symbol system (language) they use. Similarly, film and television may differ in technologies and in the social settings associated with their use, but they differ far less in symbol systems. Television-computer games are "television" in nearly all respects *but* their symbol systems.

If media differ along specific dimensions (such as their technologies of transmission, contents, or symbol systems), then there are a number of possible ways in which media can interact with human behavior and learning. Not only do the sources of variance differ, but they affect different domains of outcome (Salomon and Cohen, 1978). The technology of a medium affects the modes of interaction with users (compare computer-based instruction with a television show of the same content), and the transmitted content affects the knowledge acquired. The social context in which a message is received affects emotional states, and the didactic mode of the message affects the ease of processing its content. It follows, then, that different aspects of media interact with different aspects of behavior, thus undermining a conception of media as invariant entities.

Means and Ends

Failure to acknowledge the differential sources of effects in media and their multiple domains of outcomes may have led both to the assumed invariance of any one medium, and to a second assumption—that media are but alternative routes to the same fixed ends. This assumption can be traced as far back as 1924, when Freeman (described by Saettler, 1968), one of the first researchers in this area, wrote of the "relative effectiveness" of film as contrasted with other visual materials. Freeman noticed the interactive nature of media's effects. Their effectiveness, he wrote, depends on the nature of the instruction and the learner's characteristics. In addition, he claimed, film produces unique kinds of experiences, which therefore also produce unique learning outcomes. Unfortunately, this view was generally ignored by most researchers. However, reinforcement for the view that media are but alternative routes to the same fixed ends came from empirical findings. The repetitive "nonsignificant difference" in media experiments communicated, in effect, the idea that it does not really matter what medium or medium attribute one uses. It can be seen how research with ambiguous results reinforced its own assumptions, thus turning them into self-fulfilling hypotheses.

What makes this assumption erroneous, at least in part, is that if some media, in some instances, have some unique characteristics, then unique learning-effects should be expected (see, for example, Pryluck and Snow, 1967). More specifically, if media carry any unique significance at all, it must often be in the way events and knowledge are differentially structured. In this way, different experiences are created, suggesting different meanings to be extracted and activating different modes of information processing. For example, the experience gained, meanings construed, knowledge acquired, and processing involved in viewing *The Godfather* on television are unlikely to be identical to those involved in reading the novel. As Ludwig Von Bertalanffy wrote (1965, p. 41), "If the meaning of Goethe's *Faust*, of Van Gogh's landscapes, or Bach's *Art of the Fugue* could be transmitted in discursive terms, their authors should and would not have bothered to write poems, paint, or compose, but would rather have written scientific treatises." But the possibilities of different experiences of different media (discussed further in Chapter Three) totally negate the assumptions that media are alternative means to the *same ends* or that they serve all learners equally well.

Marantz and Dowaliby (1973), to mention one study in a growing body of literature, have shown that when a film, audio lecture, or transcript of a lecture are presented to students, the student with high scores on the analytic-perceputal Hidden Figures Test does best. That test measures one's ability to single out an item from a dense background. When audio lecture and transcript of lecture are combined into one, it is the low scorer who benefits most. These authors claim that the latter mode of presentation directs the low scorer (hence, the more field-dependent person) to the critical details of the presentation. High scorers, on the other hand, do better when allowed to exercise their own analytic skills. Such findings suggest that specific media attributes, when used as carriers of the critical information to be learned, call on different sets of mental skills and, by so doing, cater to different learners. It becomes justified to assume that no medium, not even a specific medium attribute, is best for all learners.

Media can do more than serve the same educational ends for different learners through alternative means. Since different modes of packaging information create different experiences, there is little reason to compare media at the level at whch they converge—that is, transmit *common* contents. Rather, it would be of much greater promise to discover the areas in which media diverge and hence serve as means to *different* ends. Olson (1974, p. 8) comments on this possibility: "Perhaps the function of the new media is not primarily that of providing more effective means for conveying the kinds of information evolved in the last five hundred years of a book or literate culture, but rather that of using the new media as a means of exploring and representing our experience in ways that parallel those involved in that literate culture. In this sense, media are not to be considered exclusively as means to preset ends but rather as means for reconstruing those ends in the light of the media of expression and communication."

Accepting this possibility calls, first, for a new conception of media, one that does not define them as sheer technologies or invariant entities and that relates them to thinking and learning. Second, it calls for the identification of those characteristics of media that differentiate among them and thus are potentially important sources of influence. Third, it requires a more theoretical orientation to reserach on media. The latter argument leads us to the third assumption to be examined, namely that research findings will directly lead to better choice decisions among media.

Expectations from Research

When Levie and Dickie (1973, p. 958) wrote that "the demand for valid information upon which to base media choice decisions will become more pressing," they were reflecting a prevailing mood of expectancy—research on media ought to guide practice, and, as technological developments increase at a rapid pace, so should guidance from research. However, as Jackson and Kieslar (1977) observe, most practitioners do not turn directly to researchers for advice. They rely on their intuitions and common sense. The reasons for using television instead of, say, radio as a lever for massive educational reforms in Korea (Schramm, 1977) or in El Salvador (Mayo, Hornik and McAnany, 1976) are intuitive as well as practical, political, and economic.

Research was hardly involved in the decision-making process.

But even when researchers claim that their findings can be immediately translated into action, as media researchers in the past have claimed, the results simply do not measure up to the expectations. For example, in studies on color pictures or films (Katzman and Nyenhuis, 1972), the common finding is that color has little if any effect on learning as traditionally defined. The real questions are not only whether color matters to learning but *why* it should matter at all. Even if positive and systematic results had been found, how could they be accounted for? How generalizable would they be? Is there a theoretical framework in which color is studied that explains why color is functional? Practice-oriented research tends to be extremely limited in generalizability and therefore also in applicability. Knowing merely that some media-based project worked, without an explanation of how and why it worked, leaves other projects with little or no basis on which to estimate their own probability of success. Thus, the assumption that research can directly guide practice is, as Kerlinger claims (1977), quite false, and it creates expectations that cannot be fulfilled. The reason is that "the solution of a research problem is on a different level of discourse than the solution of an action problem" (p. 6).

The alternative, then, for research on media would be to try to understand and explain the relations between constructs, thus providing explanatory principles (Cronbach, 1966; Kerlinger, 1977). More specifically, one would need to study the nature of a medium's most essential attributes and the psychological functions that they can be made to accomplish under different conditions and for different learners. Such research will be able to "develop explanatory concepts, concepts that will help people use their heads" (Cronbach, 1975, p. 126).

But this is more easily recommended than done. We become increasingly aware of the fact that people, settings, tasks, and time interact in such complex ways that even yesterday's conceptions of first-order interactions now appear to be naive. Once interactions are invoked, one enters "a hall of mirrors that extends to infinity" (Cronbach, 1975). Acknowledging the overwhelming complexity of interactions in human behavior introduces a descriptive *science* of the behavior of *specific* people in specific settings. Even the classification of settings and situations into a single "basic" taxonomy is consequently being questioned (Mischell, 1977), as their descriptions are found to depend more on perceivers than on intrinsic attributes. Thus, instructional theories become increasingly more like intensive local observations, akin to historical rather than scientific interpretations (Cronbach, 1975), that apply "to the teaching of arithmetic in grades 1-2-3 in Washington and Lincoln Schools in Little City" (Snow, 1977a, p. 12),

Two implications seem to follow. One is that in the face of complex interactions between humans and environments (media included), practice-oriented research promises poor generalizability beyond the situation in which it is conducted. Second, the alternative cannot be the recording of "intensive local observations." These are conducive for the design of instruction, not for its theoretical comprehension. Rather, our research ought to aim at identifying "pertinent variables and to suggest possible mechanisms to study [them] in more general natural situations" (Cronbach, 1975, p. 124). More specifically, we should aim at formulating *skeleton hypotheses*, to which numerous specific instances would apply.

For example, a large number of studies in instruction have led Cronbach and Snow (1977) and Snow (1977) to a general hypothesis that increasing the information-processing burden in instruction allows high-ability students to capitalize on their ability while overtaxing the lower-ability students. Removing some of these burdens compensates for the lower students' weaknesses. In effect, the instructional treatment must do for these students what they cannot do for themselves (for example, organize the material). This is a *skeleton hypothesis* that applies to a diverse list of cases. Compensation for deficient mastery of relevant skills does not specify what skills are relevant, as they may be highly indiviudal-, situation-, and content-specific, nor does it say what in an instructional treatment can be made to compensate for learners' deficiencies. In fact, different kinds of instructional treatments do compensate in *functionally equivalent* ways. For example, the insertion of test-like events into a text seems to compensate the deficiencies of learners with poor memory-storage (Berliner, 1971). Similarly, using pencil and paper during problem solving compensates for memory difficulties of high-anxiety learners (Sieber, 1969). Snow's (1977b) hypothesis offers both an explanation of *why* entirely different instructional methods and stimuli interact with learners' abilities and a conceptual framework to be tested with new stimuli, new learners, and new situations. It cannot, however, be taken as an immediately applicable guideline for any practical purpose.

In sum, I argue that the three most typical assumptions about media (their invariant natures, their role as alternative means to the same ends, and media research as the basis for selection decisions) are wholly or partly invalid. Specific attributes of media can accomplish specific psychological functions of relevance to learning in interaction with learners and learning tasks. But before we learn when and under what conditions any particular functions can be effectively realized, we have to understand its nature. This analysis calls for focused, theoretically oriented research, which can provide us with skeleton hypotheses such as Snow's. This analysis also calls for another conception of media, a conception that promises to generate new kinds of questions.

Another Conception of Media

The conceptual definition of an entity or field of study depends on the perception of its most essential components relative to some criterion. As criteria vary, so may perspectives. Alternative perspectives can yield alternative insights. For example, a work of art can be described in terms of the attributes that distinguish it (for example, Langer, 1957), thus asking "what is art?"—or in terms of the situations in which it qualifies as art (Goodman, 1977), thus asking "When is art?" Different perceptions of an entity under investigation yield different distinctions. Hence, "The world is as many things as there are ways to describe it" (Goodman, 1968).

Media can be conceived of as invariant systems when

related to social, cultural, economic, or political structures. Psychological and educational examination of media require, however, more subtle distinctions. It is not a medium of communication that makes a difference in learning, but rather a specific attribute it potentially entails. But attributes of media do not exist as independent qualities. Each attribute (such as structure, color, concreteness, pace, difficulty) belongs to a *universe or class* of such attributes. Thus, for example, the king portrayed in an illustrated book belongs to the category of conveyed contents, and the contour lines in maps belong to the class of symbol systems.

The classes of media attributes that have the potential of affecting learning cut across the various media. Thus, all media convey *contents*; the contents are structured and coded by sometimes shared and sometimes more medium-specific *symbol systems*; they all use *technologies* for the gathering, encoding, sorting, and conveying of their contents; and they are associated with different *situations* in which they are typically used. Media, then, consist of these four (or perhaps more) classes of attributes. Although each medium consists of all four classes of attributes, not all attributes matter equally in learning. In some cases, a technological attribute distinguishes one medium from others in terms of the learning experiences it affords. Computer-based instruction is a case in point, as its technology allows the kind of individualization and interaction not permitted by other media. In other cases, it is the situation that uniquely facilitates learning, as is the (often overlooked) case with books. Or, it may be the medium's mode of presenting content—its symbol system—that permits the securing of meanings no other medium can allow.

The case of "Sesame Street" illustrates this point quite well. Given the shortage of preschool educational opportuniites that were available in the 1960s to inner-city children in the United States, "Sesame Street" contributed to learning mainly through qualities of its *content*. When the program was brought to Israel, where preschool education was already well developed, the same television program contributed mainly through only

the relatively novel *formats* of its contents. The contents themselves (numbers, body parts, basic spatial concepts) were
commonly taught in all preschools anyway. Thus, its contents
led to the acquisition of *knowledge* by American children, but
its novel formats developed *skills* in Israeli children (see Chapter
Seven). Let us briefly examine the ways that different attributes
contribute to learning in different situations.

   Technological Attributes.   Technological attributes
account for differences in the dissemination of information—its
availability and accessibility. Such differences, disregarding
variations of content or mode of presentation, may lead, for
example, to a gap between the "information rich," who succeed
in making use of what becomes available by media's technologies, and the "information poor," who fail to do so (Katzman,
1973). Other technological attributes may account for new
instructional possibilities, such as computer-based instruction
and pocket calculators, or for particular behavior patterns, such
as "shallower" viewing of television resulting from the availability of many channels (Cohen and Salomon, 1978). Under
some conditions, technological differences lead to impressive
consequences. The telephone, to use but one example, has
undoubtedly introduced great changes into our social modes
of interaction. In a similar vein, when educational television
is being introduced into a country with a poorly developed
educational system, great social and even political changes
follow.

   But note that, in all such cases, comparisons are of the all-
or-none nature. It is never *only* a technology that is being introduced. The introduction of a new technology is accompanied
by access to new contents, access to newly designed curricula,
involvement in new social situations, or the development of new
personal and social techniques. The introduction of educational
television into El Salvador had impressive effects (Mayo, Hornik,
and McAnany, 1976), which resulted from the general educational reform but not from the technology of television itself.
To the extent that a technological development is accompanied
by the development of (say) a new technique, the use of that

technique can be expected to have a cognitive effect (Bruner, 1964). Feldman (in press) also maintains that the acquisition of a technique that is associated with a technology or tool is likely to contribute to the understanding of specific concepts; it may also enhance understanding of certain rules and logical operations. Indeed, Jacques Ellul (Gordon, 1969) goes so far as to claim that all arts and sciences are doomed to the dominance of *techniques* that are afforded by technologies.

The impressive observable changes that follow a grand-scale technological change result mainly from what technology carries with it and rarely from the technological innovation *itself*. When only a technological change is introduced and everything else is held constant (for example, the shift to push-button telephones or from open-curcuit to closed-circuit instructional television), no great changes can be observed. This is perhaps best illustrated by research on instructional media, where many of the experiments, intentionally or unintentionally, compared one technology (television) with another (live teaching). As Gordon (1969, p. 118) notes: "Most research in this area has been designed merely to measure the influence of technology (not mediums) upon academic grades, rather than determine the real difference between the mediums themselves. That these experiments have shown that the same kind of teaching operates more or less the same way with and without technological aids . . . might have been anticipated before experimentation began." The study of technologies per se has been repeatedly criticized (Mielke, 1968; Salomon and Clark, 1977) on the grounds that when *everything else* is held constant, sheer technological variations cannot have any meaningful effect, aside from the self-evident and the trivial.

Contents. Contents conveyed by media are, of course, their primary purpose and researchers' major focus of attention.

Historically, criticisms of media were nearly always aimed at their contents, from Plato's comments on the contents of stories, through the criticisms of the horrors of children's tales, up to modern criticisms of television's portrayals of society. The identification of some media with their contents is perhaps best illustrated by the extensive study of aggression and more recently of prosocial behavior and drug advertisements on television. With a few exceptions that tend to focus on the *means* of structuring the content (for example, Singer, in press), most of what has been said about commercial and educational media pertains to their contents.

Such an identification of medium with content is sometimes justified, but in most cases it is not. Until quite recently, maps were devoted exclusively to the depiction of geographic terrains. However, developments in nonparametric statistics led to the utilization of maps to describe statistical relationships among variables (small space analyses). At the same time, new media (for instance, heat photography) are used to describe geographic terrains. Other media are even less closely associated with any give domain of content. Print, television, and radio clearly cater to a wide variety of contents, thus illustrating the absence of association between media and content.

Although it is clear that media's contents teach, inform, excite, or guide and that different kinds of content accomplish different functions, it is not clear how these relate to one or another particular medium. Consider the observation that television's news "sets our agenda" for priorities. Would not the same be true of radio or newspaper news? The answer is no, as each of these media can be expected to affect us differently. But then, since the contents are (relatively) common to all three media, it cannot be the *contents* that account for the differences. Rather, other classes of factors, quite independent of content, account for the differences, such as the social setting in which the medium is used or the way the contents are coded, packaged, and structured.

When, say, televised violence is studied, one gains better understanding of the effects of the type of depicted violence made accessible through the technology of television. But violence can be presented in tales, books, or comic strips as well. What then makes *televised* violence so particular? Easy accessibility is one factor. Would the effects of violence in books and violence on television be the same if accessibility were constant? One has reason to believe that it would not. Thus, there is an added quality to televised messages that transcends the obvious effects of technological accessibility or the particulars of contents. This quality is the mode of presentation, the symbol systems used. The effects of televised aggression would indeed be different if, instead of viewing such acts, children were only to listen to aggressive stories. Witness the reduction of postviewing tendencies for aggression in third graders when only commercials were removed from a television program, so that cause-and-effect relationships became more proximal (Collins, 1973, 1975). Consider, then, how much stronger an effect could be expected when the *whole* symbol system of a program is changed.

Underlying much of the criticism of media's contents and the investigation of their social effects are hidden assumptions about their unique symbolic formats. When television's violence is claimed to lead to increased aggressive or prosocial behavior, it seems to be implicitly assumed that not only the violent or prosocial contents account for the effects. The easily accessible technology and, more importantly, the vivid and realistic depictions (an attribute of the medium's symbol system) appear to contribute to television's effects as well. However, the relative weight of these factors is unknown, as they have not been seriously studied. The same is true of reserach on instructional media. Much research has been devoted to the teaching of specific contents via one medium or another, but the implicit assumption has been that the crucial factor is the symbol system that carries the content rather than the content itself. After all, if the same content is conveyed by two media in a comparative study, not much else *besides* the symbol system is left to vary.

Social Settings and Situations. Like contents, social settings are only partly associated with the use of media. Television is usually viewed at home, with or without the presence of other family members; movies are typically viewed at the theater hall; and newspapers, more often than not, are read over breakfast or on the way to work. However, in most cases, no particular social situation of media use corresponds in a one-to-one relationship to any particular medium.

It is true that some social situations facilitate (or interfere with) learning from a medium. Thus, it has been found that children learn more from television when their mothers watch programs with them (Chaffee, McLeod, and Atkin, 1971), and it has been hypothesized that people are less likely to inhibit their emotions in the anonimity of a darkened theater hall (Mialaret, 1966). Similarly, it has been claimed that one's freedom to determine the speed of picking up information from the print media results in better information processing than does watching television (Singer, in press). However, although situations can affect learning and attitude change, they are, like contents, generally independent of any medium. Not only movies are seen in a theater hall but also plays, ballets, and operas. Nor is the family gathering around a television set more unique to that medium than solitude is to map reading. Families also gather around a visitor, and one's solitude is used to read books or cartoons or to examine a stamp collection. The use of media correlates with social settings, but this correlation is rather low. Thus, although a medium is always used in some situations, siuations cannot define a medium or distinguish one medium from another. How then is a medium to be conceived?

Medium, Technology and Symbol Systems. A medium is closely related to a particular technology, but the medium is not to be equated with that technology, a particular domain of content, situation of use, or a specific symbol system. A medium of communication entails all four classes of components, but not all of them are equally critical in defining a medium. Both content and situational factors are usually only *correlates* of a medium. Replace one type of content rendered in film with another, or one situation of viewing with another, and the medium of film is still the same medium. (This flexibility is less true of maps; however, maps are the exception to the rule.) On the other hand, if we exchange one major technology for another, the whole medium changes its nature. Still, there is more to a medium than its technology (when seen in an educational-psychological context), mainly because technology per se does not affect learning directly. Rather, technology interacts with learning to the extent that it does because of other factors— notably the symbol systems that evolve from technological possibilities.

A symbol system, as suggested at the beginning of this

chapter, is a set of elements that refer in specifiable ways to domains of reference and are interrelated according to some syntactic rules or conventions. Some of these conventions are formal syntactic rules, as in arithmetic or language. Others are informal conventions, as in the arts. Symbol systems can be considered as *systems*, since each such class (or scheme) of symbols correlates with one or a limited number of fields of reference (Goodman, 1968). Thus, the field of reference correlated with musical notation differs from that correlated with cartography, and both differ from that typically correlated with language or pictures. More generally, symbol systems differ with respect to the aspects of reality each deals with. In this view, languages, pictures, graphs, the table of chemical elements, the theorems of Euclidean proofs, and the arts are all symbol systems insofar as they are means of reference.

Symbol systems can be distinguished from each other along a number of dimensions, a point that is further discussed in Chapter Two. Presently, it suffices to say that some symbol systems are more elementary than others. For that reason, De Fleur and Ball-Rokeach (1975) distinguish between premedia—such as dance, tatoos, or speech—and technologically evolved media. Such a distinction points in effect to the difference between symbol systems that have existed independently of the contribution of technologies and those that have evolved through interaction with technologies.

The more elementary symbol systems are perhaps universal and natural. The primary modes of symbolic behavior and the elementary symbol systems that correspond to them are, according to Gross (1974), the linguistic, the socio-gestural, the iconic, the logico-mathematical, and the musical. From these elementary systems, increasingly more elaborate subsystems are derived, which are fine specializations in nature as well as in relationship to fields of reference. The iconic system, for example, gives rise to such subsystems as photographs, drawings, caricatures, and sketches; the linguistic symbol system gives rise to prose, poetry, technical language, and so on. As we go "down" on this grossly sketched taxonomy, we find that the derived systems are often less "pure," and they increasingly overlap with each other (Gross, 1974). Most important, derivations that result in increasingly more complex subsystems (for instance, the symbol system of film) are often, although not always, related to technological means. Some derivations are completely unrelated to technologies. The notation used to describe ballet movements in graphic form and the sign language for the deaf are examples. Other derivations precede technological developments. For instance, although the introduction of copper engravings led to further developments in three-dimensional perspective drawing, the initial use of such a subsymbol system preceded the copper engravings, as can be witnessed in Dürer's woodcuts.

However, many symbol subsystems emerge in interaction with developing technologies. Film initially was static photography of staged plays, and television started out as a convenient distributor of films and photographed radio. Even literate language is claimed to have emerged first as a result of phonetic alphabets and later as a result of print (Olson, 1975).

When a new technology of communication is developed, it often borrows the symbol forms and typcial contents of a veteran technology. For example, maps, in their early development, borrowed from mythical drawings. Later in the process of development, the newly developed technology interacts with the existing symbol systems available to it, and new subsystems or new *combinations* of subsystems begin to emerge. The history of film is a relevant illustration. From a static recording of moving, short sequences of staged events, film has developed a unique blend of multi-level, multiple-coded languages (Kjørup, 1977). As will be discussed in more detail in Chapter Two, film's unique "language" consists of a special blend of symbol systems, its own unique systems, and its ways of combining nonunique symbols. The interaction among language, music, and the depiction of events over time exemplifies how film blends symbol systems. The filmic symbol system in which black hats represent villains and clocks represent the passage of time illustrates film's unique systems. The way real time is reduced to a few shots and causality is transformed into interchanging shots illustrates how film developed its own conventions of composition.

Thus, when examined from this point of view, *technology can be conceived of as a necessary but not sufficient condition for the emergence of a distinctive medium. The sufficient condition is the specific blend of symbol systems that is made possible by a technology and is available for expression and communication through that technology.* Photography could never have existed without the camera, but it is the specific mode of rendering events through use of the camera that gives photography its distinctive place among media. The development of copper engraving radically changed the way complex scenes were earlier rendered through woodcuts by allowing a greater and finer range of shades (Wolf, 1977); it is this characteristic that distinguishes copper engravings from older woodcuts.

Similarly, the development of print was a necessary condition for the development of text; the way linguistic messages were shaped by print was the factor that distinguished text from utterance (Olson, 1977a). Eisner (1970), following the same logic, argues that new materials and technologies available to an artist enable him* to create new symbolic modes of expression. Thus, for example, some new modes of expression through the medium of sculpture could only have evolved through the development of the acetylene torch. It seems that this added quality—the mode of expression that becomes available to a medium—is its most distinguishing character. As we shall see in the following chapters, it is also the quality of a medium that holds the greatest promise for learning.

The interaction between a technology (including its particular class of materials, such as prints or stone) and the symbol systems it uses gives rise to new modes of rendering information and experience, that is—to a *medium*. A new symbol system (actually, a new *blend* of symbol systems) evolves and creates a particular mode of expression that makes a medium distinctive. Thus, the medium is not the message in McLuhan's (1965) sense, but the new symbol systems that evolve through the interaction

*The pronouns *he, his,* and *him,* not having been superseded by convenient, generally accepted pronouns that include the female gender, will be used throughout this book with the understanding that they refer equally to *she, hers,* and *her.*

between the medium's technology and preexisting symbol systems *influence* the messages of that medium. As Carpenter (1960), McLuhan's predecessor, has pointed out, the symbol systems that typify a medium are not mere envelopes into which unaltered messages are inserted. The symbol systems affect the content and give it distinctive form. Indeed, as a medium such as television develops, it not only moves farther away from its next of kin—film and radio—it even changes filmic messages when these are transmitted through it. Certain television formats (commercial advertisements included!) are imposed on messages that were coded in another medium's symbol system. Ballet on television, although still ballet, communicates differently than ballet on stage; the close-up of a dancer's face and the juxtaposition of images are examples of television's unique mode of expression.

This conception of media leads to a distinction between the symbol systems (and their developing blends) that are *available* to a medium and those that are used in *actuality*. The former represent the prototypical case of the medium; the latter represent the actual use of the medium in daily life. A homemade, 8-mm film hardly uses the coding elements available to the medium, nor does an educational film that places a talkative teacher and blackboard on the screen. Similarly, a tourist map that shows enlarged, three-dimensional renderings of a town's monuments deliberately avoids using the cartographic symbol system available to it. Thus, while a medium's specific blend of symbol systems is potentially available to it, not all of the medium's messages (or "utterances") necessarily make use of all that symbolic potential. Consequently, we have "photographed radio" on television news as well as "television news." The latter emphasises the medium's essence and thus is closer to the prototypical case of the medium. Similarly, we have "televised instruction," which uses only the medium's technology as a passive recording and transmission device, and "television instruction," which capitalizes on the medium's symbolic capabilities.

The distinction between the potentially available and the actually employed symbolic capabilities of a medium is essentially a distinction between the prototypical and the variant.

The study of the cognitive aspects of category formation (for example, Rosch and Mervis, 1975) and of the qualities of prototypes in similarity perception (Tversky, 1977) can help us in clarifying this distinction. All products of a medium bear some resemblance to each other, if only because they share the same technology. But usually, different products will share also the symbol systems of which they are specific samples. To the extent that such products (films, texts, maps, television programs) share structural elements with each other and thus constitute networks of overlapping attributes, they can be said to have *family resemblance* relationships.

Family resemblances do not imply that all members of one category (say, all films or all representations of historical events) are exact replicas of each other. Rather, products or items become members of a family by virtue of sharing one or more critical attributes with some but not necessarily all other members of the family (Rosch and Mervis, 1975). It follows, then, that resemblances between family members form a distribution of shared attributes. Some members entail more of the common critical attributes than others. The prototypical or most representative case is that element or product that shares the most critical attributes with the largest number of other family members and has the least attributes in common with members of other families.

When applied to media products, this formulation of family resemblance and prototypes is somewhat difficult, since the number of attributes that products could share is very large. Thus, criteria are needed to distinguish between critical and noncritical attributes, lest we group together survey maps and films by the National Geographic Society on the basis of their common denotata, and statistical diagrams with electric circuit diagrams on the basis of their common label. What, then, constitutes the critical criteria?

The discussion thus far clearly suggests that neither contents nor situational correlates of media should be used as critical criteria. Media vary, of course, with respect to the contents they typically convey. But such variations are outcomes of the symbol systems involved. Different symbol systems comply or correlate with different fields of reference (photography with objects, graphs with mathematical relations). To the extent that media differ with respect to the symbol systems they use and emphasize, they also vary with respect to the contents they convey. Thus, for instance, the fact that television can depict visible aspects of events, and books can describe nonvisible ones, is the result of the symbol systems each medium makes use of, not of anything inherent in the medium. Types of contents are correlates of media but not defining attributes of media.

Only media's symbol systems can serve in this critical capacity. Symbol-systems dimensions—such as *notationality, density, digitalness,* and *analogy* (Goodman, 1968; see Chapter Two for elaborations)—could serve us best, as indeed they are the most essential attributes of media. A prototypical case, then, is that type of message that has the most *symbolic* attributes in common with other members of that medium family, when membership is determined by the same criteria. To summarize, I propose to conceive of media essentially as technologies plus the symbol systems that develop in association with them and to classify media and their respective prototypes as family resemblances based on dimensions of symbol systems.

Two implications follow from this proposition. First, families of media and of media products may not always be discrete categories. Distributions overlap and merge into each other. For instance, still photography, although a category in itself, has some family resemblance to both film and painting; film, which certainly is an independent category, shares some critical features with television, books, and the performing arts.

Second, in spite of these overlaps, there are clear prototypical representatives of each category. Such prototypes may not exist in any concrete form, stored somewhere for inspection like the Golden Meter. Rather, these prototypes are hypothetical cases containing the essence of each medium's symbolic capabilities. Thus, when speaking of film, we would be referring to the symbol subsystem that film could potentially use, regardless of whether any actual film has realized the full potential. Still, we can judge specific examples of film as to how similar or dissimilar they are to the generic case.

The rationale sketched above may be compared with the one that underlies the research presently being carried out on the structure and comprehension of stories. Like symbol systems, stories and other constructions such as metaphors, journalistic accounts, and scientific treatises are modes of appearance. Stories have their unique grammars that distinguish them from other constructions (Bower, 1976; Thorndyke, 1977), and so do metaphors (Goodman, 1968; Winner, Rosenstiel, and Gardner, 1976). Unlike symbol systems, such modes of construction are relatively independent of media. To an extent, they are also independent of symbol systems.

The *conceptual* treatment of stories, however, resembles the one offered here. Stories constitute a category whose members bear family resemblances to each other. The critical or generic dimension of this category is the story-grammar. Some stories are more grammatical, and others are somewhat less grammatical and may constitute borderline cases. Most important, the category of stories can be represented by a hypothetical, context-free, prototypical grammar, resembling a set of computer rewrite rules (Bower, 1976). It is then claimed that every simple story fits the prototype to *some* extent. Obviously, the essential grammar of stories does not constitute everything a story entails, as symbol systems do not constitute everything that a medium-message entails. But the grammars capture the *essence* of stories, much as symbol systems do with respect to media.

Summary

Our discussion has led to two main propositions. The first is that the examination of media, when made from a cognitive-psychological and educational point of view, should not adopt a holistic approach but rather focus on specific, critical qualities of media. The second proposition is that the critical qualities of media to focus on are the symbol systems they employ that develop in interaction with their technologies. Although a medium is not to be equated with a technology or symbol system, the blend of symbol systems used by a medium best distinguishes it.

Other components of media, particularly their contents and the social situations in which they are used, are but correlates or outcomes of the symbol systems used and hence do not capture the essence of a medium.

Another major reason for focusing on symbol systems is that they may relate more directly than other aspects of media to cognition and learning. The acquisiton of knowledge from a coded message is mediated by skills of information reception and processing. We can entertain the possibility, to be explored in depth in the next chapters, that these skills are significantly affected by the specific nature of each symbol system into which the content of the message is coded. Thus, each medium, using symbol systems, may have its own specific effects on how the knowledge is extracted and on how meanings are arrived at. Indeed, this possibility is urged on us by Olson (1974) and Olson and Bruner (1974), who maintain that the contents of messages address themselves to the acquisition of knowledge, and their forms—their symbol systems—address themselves to the activation and cultivation of skills. It follows that media should be examined primarily as activators and possibly also as cultivators of information-processing skills that mediate the acquisition of knowledge. This is where a medium's specific import may be found. Whether these hypotheses can withstand logical and empirical tests is still an open question.

TWO

Characteristics
of Symbol Systems

❅ ❅ ❅ ❅ ❅ ❅ ❅

Any attempt to understand media and to relate them to cognition and learning through the symbol systems they employ would seem to require an explication of what symbol systems are. However, this is more easily said than done. Pictures differ qualitatively from prose, facial expressions differ from graphs, and film differs from chemical models; all this is obvious. But confusion arises when one attempts to introduce superordinate dimensions along which different symbol systems can be arrayed for the purpose of differentiating systematically among them and characterizing the media that employ them. Given the diversity of meanings ascribed to such terms as *symbol, sign, icon, symbol system, realism,* and *likeness,* we may find ourselves attempting to sort out, clarify, and define issues whose understanding is perhaps best served by intuition. To understand how symbol systems interact with cognition and learning *in principle* may perhaps require no more than an intuitive understanding of

28

how symbol systems function as modes of appearance—that is, how they express and represent communicable qualities in different ways. Going beyond our intuition, we run the risk, as Berkeley put it, of first raising the dust and then claiming that we cannot see. Yet, some analysis of the general issues concerning symbol systems seems necessary. This chapter begins with a logical analysis of symbol systems, following primarily the work of Nelson Goodman (1968). The reason for choosing Goodman's theory as the basis of my (rather sketchy) description of the nature of symbol systems is that his treatment is the logically most stringent, consistent, and clear. The logical description of symbol systems is then followed by a psychological treatment of some of Goodman's notions. Of particular interest is the question of resemblance, similarity, or *iconicity* in symbolic representation, an issue that figures prominently in the treatment of media in education. There are two reasons for choosing to begin with a logical analysis and to continue with a psychological one. First, not everything that follows from a logical analysis is psychologically consistent. Second, neither of the two approaches taken alone seems to suffice as a treatment of symbol systems.

The last section of the chapter is an attempt to apply the considerations of the logical and psycholgoical sections to the symbol systems of one medium, film, and it is based on Kjørup (1977), who follows Goodman in his attempt to describe film.

Symbols and Symbol Systems

Any object, movement, gesture, mark, or event can potentially serve in a symbolic capacity, provided it is taken to represent, denote, or express something beyond itself. Following Roupas (1977), I will limit the present discussion to symbols that can convey information—that is, symbols that allow the extraction of some semantic knowledge. In this sense, most objects, marks, events, models, or pictures that can serve as bearers of extractable knowledge are symbols.

Symbols serve as *characters or coding elements* (for instance, the alphabet) with rules or conventions of combining

and arranging them into *schemes.* The syntactic rules according
to which symbols are organized differ qualitatively from scheme
to scheme. The rules for putting words into a sentence that
denotes "Town *x* is to the north of river *y*" differ from the
rules that are used when combining cartographic elements to
denote a similar idea. The rules of combination differ also with
respect to their flexibility and formality. Some schemes have a
clear syntax that can be spelled out, as is the case in most languages. Whether a combination of symbols within such a scheme
is or is not acceptable can then be easily determined. Other
schemes do not have rule-governed syntaxes in the usual sense,
and many alternative combinations of symbols are legitimate, as
is the case with film. We may distinguish here between formal
rules of *prescription* and conventions of *coherence.* Rules of
prescription are more or less fixed and inflexible. They develop
out of social demands to assure unambiguous communication.
Conventions of coherence, typical of the arts, are much more
flexible and allow artistic experimentation. Adherence to such
conventions facilitates interpretable communication but cannot
prevent misunderstandings, as it entails many ambiguities and
open-ended meanings.

When a symbol scheme is in great social demand and
serves vital functions, conventions of coherence may not be
enough, as they are too fluid and open for interpretation. Conventions of coherence may then gradually become formalized.
The history of cartography is a fair example. Not until Napoleon's time were continental maps formalized (navigational
maps underwent this change much earlier, for obvious reasons).
The growing need to map new areas for large-scale military
operations dictated a rigid and agreed-upon symbol scheme, thus
replacing "poetic" cartography (McLuhan, 1965).

In most symbol schemes, the characters, or single (*atomic*)
elements, can be combined in particular lawful or conventional
ways to create compound elements. For instance, letters and
spaces can be combined into increasingly more compound symbols to form words and passages. Ordinary musical notations,
although more difficult to analyze than the alphabet, can also
be shown to entail atomic symbols (note-signs, clef-signs, and so

forth), which, when combined in lawful ways, constitute a compound, two-dimensional scheme. In pictorial schemes, any symbol can be regarded as atomic (a face, a line, a dot) and compound at the same time. In film, given its temporal dimension, single shots are sometimes regarded as atomic elements, and sequences of shots as compound elements (Worth, 1968). It should be noted that compounding of elementary coding elements can often take place on a number of levels. Letters are combined into words, words into sentences, and sentences into texts. In drawing, similarly, depictions of objects are combined into compositions, which in turn constitute a whole artistic work.

A symbol scheme becomes a symbol *system* when correlated with a field of reference. This field of reference can then be said to *comply with* the symbol scheme, or be *denoted* by it. Alternatively, the scheme can be said to apply to its field of reference, or to its compliance class, or to its denotata. Musical performance is the field of reference for musical notation; dance movements are the field of reference for labonotation; objects are the field of reference for photographs; sound events or pronounciations are the field of reference for the alphabetic notation. The field of reference of one symbol system may itself be a symbol system that has its own denotata. Musical performance, which is the denotatum for musical scores, is itself a symbol system of great expressive power. Similarly, in film, we may encounter a depiction of a particular person that itself is a symbol for an idea (the guy with the black hat denoting evil). The denotatum or field of reference for script is words, which are a symbol system with their own field of reference. There may be objects, relations, or other qualities in the field of reference that have no symbol, atomic or compound, in the scheme that complies with them. They then cannot be rendered, conveyed, or represented through that scheme of symbols. For instance, the conceptions of *we, nevertheless,* or *in spite of* can be communicated in language but not in photography; or, as Eisner (1978) points out, *suspense* (a temporal quality) through sculpture.

The correlation of a symbol scheme with a field of reference is not limited to a correlation between single symbols or coding elements and single objects or events. Also, the modes of *symbol combination* are correlated with the relationship among the denoted or depicted referents. Thus, the left-to-right succession of letter combinations in written English correlates with the temporal succession of sounds; the spatial arrangement of symbols in a map correlates with the distribution of selected objects in the described territory; and, as some would claim, the arrangement of objects in a perspective painting correlates with their arrangement in three-dimensional space. Münsterberg (1970 [1916]) argued that the arrangement of events in theater correlates with their order in life, but the arrangement of events in film correlates with the way we think. For instance, flashbacks in film comply with the associational mode of remembering.

The term *correlation*, used by Goodman to describe the relationship between a symbol system and its field of reference, is a pregnant one. The term may denote no visible similarity, one-to-one correspondence, or imitation. Is a picture depicting a scene correlated with that scene in the same way that a plotted distribution is correlated with the set of test scroes? The understanding of the correlation between symbol systems and their fields of reference is essential for the classification of symbol systems and for determining how a symbol system represents, describes, or expresses.

A single symbol element or character is often ambiguous and is sometimes even completely uninterpretable unless seen as part of a symbol system. Red lights represent one thing when part of a system of traffic lights, and something else on a boat at sea, and still something else in the window of an alley apartment. Numbers represent entirely different things when used as part of the numerical system and when used as symbols in a computer drawing. A tree in a painting expresses something different from a tree on a vegetation map.

In summary, a symbol system consists of two classes of components—the syntactic component (the atomic and compound symbols) and the rules or conventions of combining them, which together constitute the symbol scheme, and the semantic component (or the correlation of the symbol scheme with a field of reference), which makes the scheme into a system.

Notationality

An important issue in Goodman's theory is the analysis of the differences between symbol systems. Specifically, how and along what dimensions can symbol systems be differentiated? How do some symbol systems depict or represent, how do others describe or denote, and how is something expressed through a symbol system? Central to Goodman's theory is the concept of *notationality*, which entails specific criteria for characterizing symbol systems. The dimension of notationality provides a yardstick for classifying symbol systems. At one extreme of this dimension are symbol systems that fulfill the conditions of being notational systems, and at the other extreme are those symbol systems that fail to meet these conditions and hence are nonnotational systems. Or, "A notational system consists of a set of separate, discontinuous characters (for example, a musical score) correlated with a field of reference which is similarly segregated (sounded pitches) so that any character in the system isolates the object or objects it stands for, or, conversely, an object isolates the character that is correlated with it. Notationality contrasts with a continuous, unsegregated (for example, pictorial) system for which no alphabet or set of disjoint characters exists" (Gardner, Howard, and Perkins, 1974, p. 31).

For a system to be notational, *both* its elements and its referents need to be disjoint and segregated, such that there is a one-to-one correspondence between them. As language entails many ambiguities, it is only partly notational. A system that neither entails disjoint, unsegregated elements nor refers to a well-segregated field of reference is nonnotational. Pictures are in this sense nonnotational "inasmuch as their visual surfaces are not composed of readily identifaible inscriptions assignable to characters in a notational scheme" (Gardner, Howard, and Perkins, 1974, p. 32). Furthermore, no specific pictorial element can be said to represent one and only one referent. Thus, for example, lines in a painting could represent contours and folds and shades and depth in the same painting. Even when an identifiable object is depicted in a painting, it is rather difficult to know what exactly it stands for. Is the cat on the mat a painting of "my cat while digesting," of "mammals at rest," of "relaxation," or of "how animals can be domesticated"? Nonnotational systems do not permit unambiguous mapping to and from their fields of reference and thus can lead to multiple meanings. Some confusion arises also when pictures are used as elements in a notational system, or as pictographs. A drawing of a car that stands for, say, the production of one thousand cars is itself nonnotational but is an element in a notational system.

The difference between notational and nonnotational systems can be further illustrated by contrasting electric-wiring diagrams or decision-making flow charts with a map that represents elevations by means of shades that vary in saturation. An electric-wiring diagram, in spite of its pictorial appearance, is a notational system. The dots, lines, and other symbols are syntactically articulate, disjoint, semantically unambiguous, and differentiated. No two electrical elements are represented by the same symbol, and no symbol represents more than one differentiated element. Furthermore, the symbols, like their referents, are disjoint and discontinuous. Similarly, a decision-making flow chart is close to a notational system—a complex problem (the field of reference) is broken down into discrete units. Specific classes of these units, such as questions, answers, or directions, are then assigned to specific and equally differentiated symbols, such as squares, diamonds, and lines.

Contrast such modes of representation with a shaded map that represents elevations. In such a map between any two gradations of shade there can be other intermediate ones, and between each pair of those gradations, additional shades could be placed. Thus, the map constitutes a nonnotational, dense scheme. Now, suppose that each shade in the map stands for some object whose height in feet equals the value of saturation of that shade. Every shift in height, even the slightest one, would require a corresponding change in shading, and every change in shading would stand for a somewhat different height. This map is a nonnotational and dense *system*, since it "provides for an infinite number of characters with compliance-classes so ordered that between each two there is a third" (Goodman, 1968, p. 153).

We could, of course, make that map into a more notational one, in spite of the fact that we want to represent a continuous and dense quality such as heights of mountains. This
need not prevent our map from using a notational symbol
scheme. Many continuous and dense qualities can be segregated
into units to comply with a similarly differentiated symbol
system. The spectrum of colors and the way we label them is
such a case, and so are distances. So, we could add black dots to
the map to indicate vertical differences in elevation in intervals
of fifty feet. Still, as long as we read elevations off the map as
absolute heights above sea level, the dots serving only as aids for
approximate judgment, the symbol system would continue to
be dense. Only when both the scheme (shades, dots) and its
field of reference (elevation) are taken to consist of separate,
discontinuous characters and units, and when each symbol in
the system represents one and only one object (a specific height),
could the map become a notational system. Specifically, if we
read the dots indicating elevations as standing for mid-points of
height intervals, disregarding intermediate heights, and provided
that the elevations themselves were to be regarded as disjoint,
then we would have a notational system. The same notational
effect could be achieved by using shaded regions or color stripes
(like areas between coutour lines), with each stripe representing
another range of heights by means of a different shade.

The criterion of notationality to distinguish among symbol systems is, of course, only one of many possible criteria. It
does not account for all the differences among symbol systems.
In practice, however, some systems are made to approximate
notationality by creating increasingly finer differentiations (as
in measuring length). In other systems, where such fine differentiation is practically impossible, an arbitrary limit is imposed
on the minimal acceptable size. For instance, musical tradition
limits the minimum durational difference between sounded
pitches to 1/128 note. Without this limit, a pitch could belong
to an infinite number of note-inscriptions.

The requirements for notationality, as formulated by
Goodman, are stringent theoretical standards against which

symbol systems can be judged. Perhaps the only system that meets all these standards is musical notation. Languages deviate from these standards, because they do not meet some of the semantic conditions, and they are notational *schemes* but not notational *systems*. Other systems, such as maps, pictures, diagrams, and the like, deviate in varying degrees from notationality.

It is reasonable to expect that, as symbol systems vary with respect to their notationality, the way one reads them to extract information and the kinds of information one extracts from them vary accordingly. For example, in a nonnotational system, say paintings, every wiggle of line, every shade, hue, and shape counts (a quality Goodman calls *repleteness*). In comparison, the number of features that count in printed letters is relatively small. It stands to reason that one must read them differently, even employ different mental skills in dealing with these symbol systems. It is argued (for instance, Singer, in press) that, because of these differences, pictures need to be *recognized*, and words need to be *understood*.

Description, Depiction, and Expression

Goodman's conception of notationality also underlies his distinction between *description* and *depiction*. Traditionally, the difference between depiction (or representation) and description is attributed to the semantic relationship between a symbol and its referent. Thus emerged the concepts *icon* and *analog*. The more a symbol resembles, copies, or imitates its referent, the more it is a depiction of that object. On the other hand, a symbol that does not resemble its referent, is conventionally designed, or stands for an abstract idea is argued to be abstracted from its referent and is descriptive.

Thus, symbols have been ranked along a continuum, ranging from resemblance (to depicted object) to conventional, or from iconicity to abstractness. For instance, models are described as either replica models or symbolic models (Chapanis, 1961). Replica models are material or pictorial representations made with only a change in spatial or temporal scale. Symbolic models are usually tangible and use abstract verbal, numerical, or symbolic representations of conceptual systems.

Eisner (1970) has divided symbols into four classes. First, there are *conventional* symbols, which are arbitrary forms taken to stand for events or ideas in a particular culture (the Star of David or the Valentine's heart). Letters standing for sounds or names standing for objects would also qualify, according to this scheme, as conventional symbols. Second, there are *representational symbols*. These are "forms which are designed to represent, almost literally, the empirical aspects of reality," as is the case with so-called realistic depictions. Underlying this class of symbols is their imitative nature, or iconicity.

Third, *connotative* symbols result from morphological distortions of representational symbols in the service of emphasizing or highlighting a particular quality (the exaggerated shapes of Picasso's animals in *Guernica* or the elongated men of Giocometti). Finally, *qualitative* symbols are those in which an organization of qualities is designed to represent some idea or feeling that has neither objective referent nor arbitrary assigned meaning, as does the conventional symbol. Only the physionomic properties of the symbol, such as patches of color, lines, and shapes, evoke the intended qualities or feelings—for example, a color that evokes sadness or a line that evokes serenity.

Underlying Eisner's classification of symbols is the implicit dimension of *resemblance* between symbol and represented object or quality. Thus, representational symbols capture some crucial quality of their referents and depict them faithfully, but conventional symbols have nothing in common with their referents and are therefore arbitrary, even abstract. Connotative symbols deviate somewhat from faithfulness, as they introduce some distortions, as in caricatures; qualitative symbols, which express some quality through their physiognomy, entail what they express.

Indeed, the differences between depiction (or representation) and description (or denotation) were long held to be associated with the semantic relationship between symbol and referent. Thus, a *sign* is said to be *causally* linked to its referent (clouds signify approaching rain), and an *icon* is much like its referent (the painted landscape that resembles the real one). It then follows logically from such formulations that a symbol that *depicts* or *represents* somehow resembles its referent, and a symbol that *describes* has an arbitrary relationship to its referent. Thus, it would also follow that faithfulness of symbol to referent, or at least some measure of similarity between the two, is necessary for depiction or representation. Absence of such relationships of similarity or resemblance would then underlie description.

Such requirements are strongly argued against by Goodman on mainly logical grounds. His claim is that the mere postulation of an amorphous relationship of similarity between a symbol and its referent explains neither how certain objects get to become symbols nor in what respect they resemble their referents. Goodman argues that, first, one picture of, say, object A resembles another picture of a similar object, B, more than it resembles the depicted object. And yet, picture *a* is taken to represent object A rather than picture *b*. Thus, it is not the greater resemblance that determines representation. In other words, the depiction of a statesman as a lion may well represent him without resembling him. The picture may resemble a lion but does not represent that animal. Second, no depiction really imitates or copies its object. An object has many qualities. A man is a person, a swarm of atoms, a fiddler, a friend, a harsh person, a devoted father, and so on. If none of these qualities is the object *as it is*, there cannot be one way to resemble it. If one aspect is "copied," others are left out, as not all aspects can be rendered. The more one succeeds in rendering one aspect, the less would the result be a realistic picture. Goodman adds that no object can be depicted (drawn, painted, photographed, filmed) "as seen under aseptic conditons by the free and innocent eye," because there is no innocent eye. Thus, a picture "does not so much mirror as take and make." Susan Sontag (1978, p. 88) expresses a similar view about photography: "The photographer was thought to be an acute but noninterfering observer—a scribe, not a poet. But as people quickly discovered that nobody takes the same picture of the same thing, the supposition that cameras furnish an impersonal objective image yielded to the fact that photographs are evidence not only of what's there but of what an individual sees, not just a record but an evaluation of the world."

Thus, resemblance or similarity between symbol and referent is a logically indefensible dimension. Resemblance, as Goodman argues, while sometimes present, is neither a necessary nor sufficient condition for representation, because a picture can depict an object without really resembling it, as is the case with paintings of demons or unicorns, pictures of unfamiliar objects, or the depiction of Churchill as a lion.

What then distinguishes between depiction and description? The answer, according to Goodman, lies in the characteristics of notationality and its correlates. The essential difference is that, in a representational system (unlike one that describes), "smooth variation along some dimension or aspect of the symbol gives rise to a corresponding variation along some dimension or aspect of the object to which the symbol applies" (Roupas, 1977, p. 69). Consider the comparison provided by Goodman between a diagrammatic momentary ECG with a Hokusai drawing of Mt. Fujiyama. Assume also that the wiggly lines of both are exactly the same. What, then, differentiates between them? The answer does not lie in what is represented, as "mountains can be diagrammed and heartbeats pictured." Rather, "The only relevant features of the diagram are the ordinate and abscissa of each of the points the center of the line passes through. The thickness of the line, its color and intensity, and absolute size of the diagrams, etc., do not matter.... For the sketch, this is not true. Any thickening or thinning of the line, its color, its contrast with the background, its size, even the qualities of the paper—none of these is ruled out, none can be ignored (Goodman, 1968, p. 229)."

A nonnotational system such as a picture is *replete*. That is, the information it carries is embodied in a great many dimensions. Although the color, size, or type of print is not symbolically relevant for typical reading, such aspects are of central relevance in pictures. Thus, the number of dimensions, or symbolic aspects, from which meaning can be construed is indeed unlimited in pictures. Obviously, sketches are less replete than detailed paintings, but both are more replete than script or diagrams or even maps. No wonder, then, that pictures can simultaneously provide very exact information pertaining to some aspects (such as color or shape) of an object and yet be so ambiguous as to require prior familiarity with the object to recognize it (Gombrich, 1974). The essential difference, then, between a picture and a diagrammatic sketch is that the picture is nonnotational, dense, and includes more dimensions (hence is more replete) than the sketch. The dimensions in a sketch are "selected out" from those included in the real or hypothetical picture of the same object.

No symbol by itself is a depiction or description. The system to which it belongs determines its nature as depiction or description. "Status as representation," as Goodman puts it, is relative to the symbol system to which a symbol belongs. Thus, a picture of a man depicts a man when part of the pictorial system, but it is a command or description when part of the symbol system of traffic lights. In the latter case, but not in the former, it is a disjoint, unambiguous character in a notational system. What really counts, then, is the relationship of a symbol to the other symbols in the same system. Differently put, what makes a symbol depict or describe is its system. A system is representational only to the extent that it is dense, and a symbol represents (rather than describes) only if it belongs to a dense system.

Descriptions (most of which are verbal but need not be so) differ from depictions, not by virtue of being arbitrary, but rather through belonging to particular symbol schemes. Arbitrariness or abstractness are neither necessary nor sufficient conditions for description. The imprisoned lover who, in folklore, sent a letter to his sweetheart in which he replaced drawing for words still used a relatively notational system. He was describing his feelings and thoughts, not depicting them. Indeed, a system such as language can use onomatopoeic words (that is, nonarbitrary ones) in the service of description; Dali uses arbitrary symbols in his depictions.

But position on a notationality continuum is not the only condition for description or depiction. Roupas (1977) points out that depiction by pictures is also a function of the viewer's standard of interpretation, implying that the way one treats a symbolically coded message partakes in determining what that stimulus is. An architect's blueprint can be regarded as a description, if the objects depicted in it are taken as discrete, well-differentiated elements standing in a one-to-one correspondence to their ascribed referents. But the same blueprint can be considered as a nonnotational artistic picture when its replete and dense qualities are attended.

What, then, is expression? Both depiction and description are ways to denote. But expression, argues Goodman, is neither the feeling that a symbol denotes (I can say how angry I am in a rather mellow, unexpressive way) nor a feeling invoked in a listener or viewer (I show anger while you become amused). Expression is based on properties that a symbol *possesses*. Properties possessed by a picture (the red color of the sky in a painting) are not denoted by it; they are *in* the picture. As such, they *exemplify* something that can be denoted by a predicate ("redness"). Thus, a picture or a passage denotes what it depicts or describes, but it can only exemplify a quality it actually possesses, and *which is denoted by a predicate.*

However, expression is more than just possession of a particular quality. Not everything a picture possesses, even if it exemplifies a predicate, is taken as expressing anything. A painting may be heavy (in the concrete sense), but it need not express heaviness. Furthermore, the fact that a painting possesses the color red and exemplifies "redness" does not yet make it *express* anything. To express, a symbol must exemplify a quality *metaphorically*. The gray color in a painting is something the painting possesses, and it *literally* exemplifies the predicate "grayness." *However, it only metaphorically exemplifies "sadness."*

Metaphorical possession entails a tension between literal possession and borrowed or transferred meaning. The tension is created, because the transfer from one domain to another (for example, from that of color to that of mood) is contraindicative. Yet, in a metaphor, the transfer makes sense—that is, once the two domains are bridged, the relationship becomes understood as reasonable. Take, for instance, the many ways in which sexual relations have been metaphorically shown in films—the train rushing into the tunnel, the boiling kettle, the blurred picture. There is a tension beween what is literally shown and what is metaphorically meant, yet the relationship becomes apparent.

A painting that possesses the color gray and exemplifies "grayness" may come to express sadness only if what it literally possesses is taken to exemplify "sadness" metaphorically. A film may express the quality of gaeity to the extent that its pace literally exemplifies "fastness," which is taken to be a metaphor for "gaeity."

Not everything a symbol possesses is taken as exemplifying something; a film that possesses the property of weighing thirty pounds does not exemplify "heaviness." Nor is everything that is literally exemplified taken as a metaphoric exemplification, hence as expression. Public busses in Caracas, Venezuela, are colored in different ways and may exemplify "redness," "blueness," or "greenness." But these colors do not serve necessarily as metaphors; for most people, the colors on the busses express nothing. Expression is present only when, within a symbol system, certain properties are taken as metaphors. For this reason, colors and shapes are considered expressive in art but rarely in road signs. A curved line may be taken to express "smoothness" when in a painting, but as a description of population growth when in a graph. As with the distinction between representation and description, whether a symbol expresses some quality depends on the system to which it is ascribed and on one's purpose while encountering it.

Not all symbol systems are equally well suited to express, describe, and depict. Some systems, as Gardner (1978) notes, highlight denotational elements, as is the case with numerical notation, the table of chemical elements, or mathemetical graphs. Other systems are mainly expressive—improvised jazz has "only minimal denotational power but exhibits a wide range of expressive reference." There are systems with great versatility (language) that vary in terms of expression, depiction, and description; other systems are somewhat less versatile and, in spite of some descriptive power, lean more heavily on expression (painting) or vice versa ("realistic" drawings).

Psychological Considerations

Goodman's theory is logically very stringent, consistent, and compelling. The theory of notationality offers a dimension along which symbol systems can be examined and classified. However, it may be too powerful a theory, as it leaves little room for *psychological* considerations that are inconsistent with some of the theory's major elements. Of particular difficulty is the argument that resemblance to referent is neither a necessary nor a sufficient condition for representation or depiction, hence that this dimension is irrelevant for the examination of symbol systems, in spite of its observable presence.

Resemblance

Resemblance bewteen a symbolic depiction and a referent is often experienced and cannot be brushed away. Some pictures clearly appear to resemble their referents more than other pictures; other symbolic modes are clearly remote and detached from their referents. Because of the quality of resemblance, smaller children often erroneously perceive television shows as being exact copies of reality (Dorr, in press), and law enforcement agencies use pictures to identify suspects. In addition, one usually *knows* that a pictorial depiction is to be treated differently from a verbal description, and thus one applies to it specific standards of pictorial interpretation (Roupas, 1977). Barring a few exceptions, similarity to depicted objects is usually sought after or assumed to exist when *dense* symbol systems are encountered. No such assumptions are commonly made when notational systems are involved.

Indeed, as humans, we are born sensing similarities, and we keep searching for them. And, even though anything can resemble anything else in some way, as Goodman argues on philosophical grounds, we nevertheless search for *some* resemblances and not others. There are some indications that our nervous system treats a photograph, or "realistic" picture, as more like the real world (even if the subject depicted is totally imaginary) than a line of type or an abstract picture. For this reason, apparently, a symbol acquired on the basis of perceived similarity may be taken to stand for a referent without one's need to learn new connections between symbolic representation and referent (Huttenlocher and Higgins, in press). Our nervous system is apparently constructed to make us categorize perceived elements around conceptual prototypes (Rosch, 1975), in terms of natural classes such as *dog* or *lemon* (Putnam, 1975), or in terms of perceptual "good" examples (Anderson, 1978). Despite the fact that a particular person is a swarm of atoms, a stamp collector, and a thoughtful politician, we would probably reject depictions of the first two as failing to "capture a likeness." Depiction as a swarm of atoms or even as a stamp collector would fail to resemble the image or conception we have of that person.

Thus, although resemblance need not underlie depiction or representation when viewed philosophically, it is psychologically the case that we search for resemblance in nonnotational systems and consequently treat depictions as if they entail real or imaginary attributes of similarity.

Herein lies the crux of the problem. Goodman addresses himself to the relationship between symbols and their concrete, material referents (indeed, the depiction of Churchill as a lion does not resemble the man). But as Arnheim (1969) argues, concrete objects and events are hardly ever the intended referents. The depicted unicorn, which indeed has no material referent, denotes a *mental image*, "giving sensory shape, for example, to ideas of purity, chastity, and the soothing influence of love upon violence" (p. 9). The referents, very often, are internal images or conceptions which a depiction can be perceived to resemble to varying degrees.

Empirical findings suggest that *perceived* similarity is associated with representativeness. Tversky (1977) has defined *similarity* as a positive function of common attributes and a negative function of distinctive features. In one study, subjects were asked to rate the similarity between all sixty-six pairs of vehicles on scales ranging from 1 to 20. Another group was asked to list the characteristic features of each vehicle. The ratings of similarities and the list of common features (corrected for frequency of mention) correlated 0.84; the list of distinctive features and rated differences correlated -0.67. Thus, empirical evidence was found to support the claim that perceived commonality of features and rated similarity are interrelated.

More importantly, Tversky found that subjects systematically perceived similarities between drawings, concepts, countries, or geometric shapes as being asymmetric. Thus, A is perceived to be more similar to B than B to A (North Vietnam is more similar to Red China than Red China is to North Vietnam). Specifically, a variant is perceived to be more similar to a prototype than the prototype to the variant (13 is more similar to 10 than 10 is to 13). As there is one referent and many ways to represent or describe it, we may identify the variant with a symbolic rendering and the prototype with a referent. It follows, then, that the symbolic presentation would be taken to be more similar to the referent than the referent to the symbolic presentation. Tversky's findings bear this out. Also, daily observations would confirm these findings. A painting of Winston Churchill is taken to resemble him, more than Churchill is taken to resemble a painting. Hardly ever do we say that a king resembles his portrait or that Yosemite Park resembles a photo made of it. Rather, the portrait resembles or "captures a likeness" of the king, and a photograph captures Yosemite's beauty.

If A resembles B more than B resembles A, A is also more likely to be taken as *representing B*. Honore Duamier's sarcastic drawings of classrooms resemble the classrooms more than classrooms resemble the drawings, and we take the drawings to represent the classrooms rather than the other way around. Furthermore, a Daumier *drawing* of a classroom can be taken to resemble and therefore to represent classrooms, but a *real* classroom is taken to represent itself only. Daumier's drawings capture what we may consider to be the essence of classrooms better than real ones.

Resemblance and realism and their opposites are usuually looked at as *inherently* present in a stimulus or absent from it. However, whenever we examine these attributes psychologically, it is not the real presence of similarity that figures, but the *perceived* one. Tversky's studies (1977) showed that perceived common attributes of objects correlated with their ratings of similarity, their "reality" notwithstanding. Palmer (1975) asked subjects to draw the face of the building in which they worked. The subjects by and large drew inaccurate drawings, based on their stored conceptions of the building rather than on what they actually must have seen every day. Moreover, when shown drawings of the building and asked to select the most accurate (realistic) one, many of them selected the wrong drawing. That drawing was selected for its alleged accurateness or greater similarity to the real building. In fact, however, the drawing was selected for its similarity to the subject's stored knowledge (whether an image or not). This knowledge was shaded by the subject's concepts, experience, and expectations. Thus, realism was judged against one's knowledge, *not* against the real object.

Kahneman and Tversky (1973) show similarly that intuitive predictions (for example, the likelihood that a person is an engineer rather than a lawyer) are insensitive to the reliability of *available* evidence or to prior *known* probabilities of outcomes. What influences predictions is the perceived *representativeness* of the instances to be predicted from. Turning back to Palmer's findings, it is quite likely that, when his subjects judged the wrong drawing to be the accurate one, they compared it with their stored image, template, or conception of the building. They used their (somewhat inaccurate) conceptions as the most representative case while ignoring the building's real features.

Thus, realism or similarity could perhaps be judged against the real object when the latter is present and when it serves as the referent. But even then, the assessment of similarity is moderated by perceptual anticipatory schemata (Neisser, 1976), the task or context (Tversky, 1977), and previous knowledge (Gombrich, 1974). In the absence of the object, similarity is clearly judged against an internal representation of one kind or another.

Internal Representation

An important implication here is that the existence of an internal representation must *precede* the correct identification of a depiction. Neisser (1976) proposes that perception is guided by internal schemata of past experiences and knowledge that determine what stimuli will be picked up from a perceptual field. Anticipatory schemata, rather than the information entailed in a stimulus, determine how a presentation is to be perceived. Perception does not merely serve to differentiate information and to absorb it in existing schemata; it also provides the perceiver with new information. However—"although this is true, it is also true that without some preexisting structure, no information could be acquired at all" (Neisser, 1976, p. 43). This bears a great resemblance to Gombrich's argument (1960, p. 73): "The individual visual information . . . is entered, as it were, upon a preexisting blank or formulary. And, as so often happens with blanks, if they have no provision for certain kinds of information we consider essential, it is just too bad for the information."

If having common features with some preexisting image, scheme, or template underlies similarity, then one may ask why dense (analog) symbolic presentations are more often considered "realistic" than notational ones. It does of course happen that a notational symbolic presentation is wrongly treated as pictorial (for instance, electric wiring diagrams) and hence regarded as resembling its referent. But, by and large, similarity to the depicted is attributed to the dense systems. The answer pertains to the nature of our prevailing internal representations.

Shepard (1978a) reports evidence to show that internal images of objects and transformations applied to them are very similar to the real objects and transformations. This similarity he labels *analog*.

> By an analogical or analog process I mean just this: a process in which the intermediate internal states have a natural one-to-one correspondence to appropriate intermediate states in the external world. Thus, to imagine an object such as a complex molecule rotated into a different orientation is to perform an analog process, in that half way through the process, the internal state corresponds to the external object in an orientation half way between the initial and final orientations. And this correspondence has the very real meaning that, at this half-way point, the person carrying out the process will be especially fast in discriminatively responding to the external structure in exactly that spatial orientation. The intermediate states of a logical computation do not in general have this property [Shepard, 1978a, p. 135].

Analog images of objects and transformations are in large part "the same whether the transformation, or the object, is merely imagined or actually perceived" (Shepard, 1978, p. 135). Thus, the evidence suggests that the mental transformation is executed in an analogous way to the corresponding external object. Such analog images and operations seem to be particularly suitable for complex spatial and figural structures, a point that is supported also by Kosslyn and Pomerantz (1977) and others. Figural and spatial elements in our environment have a greater chance of being mentally represented by internal dense carriers (Huttenlocher, 1973). Consequently, a pictorial, dense, symbolic depiction, when encountered, has a good chance of being an analog of that internal representation.

In addition, it is often the case that the depicted "object" is a nonexisting entity, such as a unicorn. And still, one can judge how "realistic" the depiction is. The image or conception one holds of that "object" or event is in fact not a result of previous direct contact with it but a result of previous encounters with symbolic representations of it. "That a picture looks like nature often means only that is looks the way nature is usually painted" (Goodman, 1968, p. 39).

In other words, a previously encountered symbolic rendering of the "object" (regardless of symbol system) has given rise to an internal representation that now is perceived as the "real object." Another presentation is then compared for similarity to that stored image. Our conception of the *real* often follows art or scientific representations. For this reason, apparently, conceptions of "realism" vary across cultures.

To the extent that we use or can generate dense internal representations of some entities, externally provided dense presentations are likely to be perceived as realistic, lifelike, similar, or iconic. When, however, no dense internal representation can be generated, no external presentation, dense or notational, is likely to be regarded as realistic. For most of us, the Statue of Liberty is a realistic rendering of a woman but not of *freedom* or *liberty*.

Thus, not every pictorial presentation is necessarily perceived as similar to an object. Not many people would regard

Kurt Lewin's pictorial model of life-span typology as being "realistic." Nor is every notational presentation necessarily considered by everyone as nonsimilar to an object. Having no access to DNA, most of us would use the double-helix model as a pictorial representation of the "real thing." In my own work (Salomon, 1968), 56 percent of the seventh- and eighth-graders tested interpreted the circles that stood for cities in a map as representing "cities surrounded by round walls."

Symbol Systems and User Interaction

To conclude, symbol systems can be distinguished in terms of their logical syntactic and semantic characteristics. The dimensions of notationality that summarize these characteristics distinguish between notational digital symbol systems that describe their referents and nonnotational, dense, or analog systems that depict their referents. Expression, as we have seen, is a function of the qualities that a presentation metaphorically exemplifies, not of the qualities it denotes.

This argument, however, seems to leave out the qualities of realism, likeness, or iconicity as unnecessary and insufficient for distinguishing between symbol systems. Yet, one cannot ignore their psychological import, even if they are no more than correlates of density. But they seem to be more important than that. Similarity is correlated with representativeness. But similarity to what? I have argued that it is not necessarily similarity to object but to one's image or conception of the object. The fact that dense symbol systems are more likely to be assigned high similarity values may tell us more about how we represent the world to ourselves than about the symbol systems.

We can now distinguish between the notational qualities of a symbol system, which determines whether it depicts or describes, and its structural congruity with internal representations, which determines how "realistic" or iconic its messages are. Dense, nonnotational depictions are often taken to resemble their objects, *even if there is no real faithfulness, and even if there is no such real object,* by sharing some *structural* properties with internal representations (for example, density). Hence, they are often attributed the quality of iconicity. The analysis of symbol systems and their combinations entails, then, at least two interrelated dimensions—notationality and structural resemblance to internal representations. Notationality is an intrinsic quality of symbol systems, independent of who uses them and when and how they are used. Structural resemblance to internal representations depends to an extent on the user, his purposes, the content conveyed, and the context. Thus, notationality is an attribute of symbol systems, but resemblance, realism, iconicity, and remoteness are qualities that result from the interaction bewteen symbol system and user.

The utility of distinguishing between the notational nature of symbol systems and the way they are treated psychologically is manifold. First, it becomes possible to arrange symbol systems along a dimension that transcends sense modalities. (According to the latter, printed passages and paintings would be grouped together.) It also bypasses the logically tricky issue of "resemblance," which confounds depiction with resemblance, an association that is logically incorrect.

Second, having some logical "handles," such as repleteness and density, to attach to symbol systems allows us to study the extent to which children are capable of dealing with symbolic *qualities*, rather than with specific symbols. Carothers and Gardner (1978) recently found that children neither perceive nor exhibit repleteness (line variations) or exemplification (mood expressed in a drawing) in their drawings until about fourth-grade level. I find it very important to be able to deal with qualities that cut across symbol systems, because this allows the generation of more general explanatory propositions instead of descriptions of how one misinterprets a particular mode of presentation.

Third, once it is possible to order symbol systems along a common dimension such as notationality, it becomes fruitful to ask how cognitive and neuropsychological processes correspond to such an ordering. There are, for instance, indications that a brain hemispheric division of labor corresponds, although complexly, with the distinction between notational and nonnotational symbol systems of incoming messages (Gardner, 1974a). There are other indications that the development of symbolic mastery exhibits links among families of symbolic modes (for example, language being related to symbolic play, two-dimensional depiction with three-dimensional), corresponding to notational groupings (Gardner, 1978).

Fourth, and most important for the approach outlined in the following chapters, we can now ask what influence one's encounter with notational and nonnotational systems has on cognitive functions. This is where the distinction between the logical and the psychological attributes of symbol systems becomes most important. If, as we shall see later on, symbolic representations can vary as to their structural "distance" from one's internal modes of representation, then certain hypotheses pertaining to the amount and nature of translation activity (decoding) of external into internal representations follow logically. And if, as I will argue later on, symbolic components can become "tools of thought," then they would need to entail new ways of representing and handling information in thought. But if they are perceived to imitate reality, and thus to carry no novelty, then their utility in thought would be limited.

The Example of Film

I have thus far avoided comprehensive treatment of media to discuss some dimensions along which symbol systems could be analyzed. Nor will a thorough semiotic analysis of the different media be attempted here. Whatever medium we select, its symbol systems have either never been seriously examined along systematic lines, or, more commonly, their semiotic analysis is so wide, diverse, and disputed as to defy any comprehensive summary.

Rather, I will briefly apply some of the conceptions presented in the preceding sections to the medium of film. The choice of film is guided by two considerations. First, most of the research to be reported in later chapters pertains to film and television. Second, film is perhaps one of the most thoroughly analyzed technological media. Since the number of philosophical, semiotic, historical, and psychological analyses of film is very large, I have chosen to base the present account mainly on the work of Kjørup (1977),* who in turn was inspired by Goodman's work on symbol systems and by that of Christian Metz on the semiotics of film.

Film is not a symbol system, nor does it use one symbol system. It is a medium that utilizes many symbol systems simultaneously—photography, gesture, speech, dance, music, and, as we shall see, other, more film-specific systems as well. Film is therefore "a meeting place of multiple codes" that serves as "a means of communication in which stories are told" (Kjørup, 1977). As film is not just a collection of single, discrete utterances but a whole message-unit (whether a feature, documentary, or instructional film), it communicates through orchestration and compounding of messages within symbol systems and multiple-symbol-system episodes.

Compounding *within* any one symbol system is evident in the generation of sentences and dialogues using words or in the creation of increasingly longer photographic sequences using single shots. Compounding *across* symbol systems is evident in the establishment of single shots, each of which is already based on a number of symbolic modes (such as pictures, language, and music), and combining these into higher levels of articulation—sequences, *syntagms* (roughly parallel to paragraphs in text), and whole films. This kind of articulation or compounding is specific to film.

Following Goodman, we can examine film as a meeting place of multiple symbol *schemes* and as a meeting place of multiple symbol *systems*. As a *scheme*, film entails a number of levels of articulation—the shot, the sequence, the syntagm, the whole film. Each of these entails its own rules and conventions of articulation that pertain to the *transformation* and *composition* of events, objects, and relations over *time* and *space*. These modes of articulation—that is, syntaxes—need not be the same for all levels of articulation. The way a single shot is composed differs from the way a whole sequence of shots is composed.

---

*Other treatments of film can be found, for instance, in Arnheim (1957), Kracauer (1960), Worth (1968), Jacobs (1970), Münsterberg (1970), Mast (1977) and others.

Kjørup provides a sample of such compositional syntaxes. At the level of the single shot, one finds that the conventions of spatial composition determine, for instance, that an object seen from above is decreased in importance, and an object seen from below is increased in importance. Similarly, a person can be framed by a doorway or lost in a crowded background. The syntax of temporal composition pertains to such things as speed of movement, and a combined spatio-temporal syntax determines the speed and mode of movement in some space (the famous shot of a train, seen from below rushing toward the camera exemplifies spatio-temporal syntax).

Compositional conventions at the level of the sequence are more complex. Not only are there compositions within each shot, but there is composition in the way shots are put together in a sequence. A sequence of a person seen looking to the right, followed by a shot of a dish, followed by a shot of a clock, accompanied by rapid music, and followed by his wife seen standing nervously at a bus station communicates a different message from the same shots arranged in a different sequence. It is true that no formal prescriptive syntax is to be found here to parallel that of language, and that *any* arrangement of shots would communicate *something*. Still, as there are known conventions of coherence, only a small number of sequence compositions would succeed in communicating a *particular* message. (Disagreeing with this argument, and finding the conventions of film to be too complex and too flexible, the semiotician Umberto Eco abandoned the study of film's syntax and concentrated instead on the cultural symbolism depicted by film; see Mast, 1977).

Other, even more complex conventions govern the composition of sequences into syntagms and the syntagms into a whole film. Christian Metz (1974) has offered a scheme of eight types of larger units (*autonomous segments*) that can be identified in feature films. These segments constitute a whole *system*, based on six dichotomies. (For instance, sequences of single shots versus sequences of intercut shots; parallel sequences to show comparison or contrast; parenthetical sequences to show different aspects of the same situation, and so on.)

In addition to rules of composition, there are also conventions of transformation—a wide scene transforms into a
focused, enlarged scene by means of a close-up or a zoom-in;
time and space are transformed through gradual fades, cuts, or
overlaps; one reality (sleep) is transformed into another (dream)
by fades or blurring; an object is transformed by slow motion or
speeded-up motion, and so on. On higher levels of articulation,
transformations of time, space, causality, and movement are
achieved through interchanging whole sequences. For instance,
recall the way in which the movie *the Godfather* depicts the
simultaneous occurrence of baptising Michael's nephew and
settling the account with the rival families. A sequence of solemn
events in the church is interchanged with a rapid succession of
gruesome, warlike episodes while one continues to hear the
solemn passages of the ceremony. In general, then, film entails
numerous symbol schemes that are combined into increasingly
larger units according to syntaxes that parallel the size and complexity of the articulated units. There are syntaxes for montage
within a shot, and there are syntaxes for montage across shots.

As film is a meeting place of multiple symbol *systems*,
one may ask what fields of reference these systems comply with.
It has been argued that both the symbolic elements in film (the
objects, the people, the events) as well as their compositional
and transformational syntaxes comply with the "real world of
events and people." Charmonte (1970, p. 47), one of the pro-
ponents of this view, writes, "The one thing a film cannot do is
express complex ideas or meanings. . . . In the movies, there is
nothing but a void beyond the image. So, for example, an empty
street, which is supposed to indicate (who knows how or why)
the state of mind of a character—to say nothing of the ideas of
the director—is simply a static image. The picture of an empty
street can be superb as photography, but it is only the picture
of an empty street."

Others have claimed that film complies with dreams (for
instance, Tyler, 1970). Münsterberg (1970, p. 41) argues that
film complies with our mental functions: "We have [in film]
really an objectivation of our memory function. The case of the
cut-back is quite parallel to that of the close-up. In the one we

recognize the mental act of attending, in the other we must recognize the mental act of remembering." Hence, he claims the film (unlike theatre) obeys the laws of the mind rather than those of the real world.

Of course, film *can* be used simply as a technology for transmission, deliberately *avoiding* whatever unique symbolic renderings are available to it, to comply with the real world. But, as Kjørup shows, every film, even a documentary, is either totally staged or at least edited in such a way as to make it comply with no existing observable reality. Hence, even more than still photography (Sontag, 1978) or drawings (Shepard, 1978b), film complies with an internal "reality" which an artist externalizes.

The claim that neither film's symbol systems nor their combinations comply with real fields of reference does not rule out the possibility that film will be *perceived* as depicting real life. There are many reasons for such perceptions. First, the dominant symbol system in film is the nonnotational, relatively dense, replete system of photography. As pointed out earlier, whether rightly or wrongly, we tend to process such information *as if* it were lifelike. The actors, the scenes, and the events often bear great resemblance to the way we represent the world to ourselves. And, where deviations take place, we use the filmic depictions as a basis for our schemata. Indeed, Gerbner and others (1977) show how even adults base their erroneous perceptions of crime in the community on television stories rather than on experience or more accurate knowledge.

Second, film uses familiar symbol systems from outside the world of film—gestures, dress, modes of speech, facial expressions. Being familiar with such symbol systems and seeing them reflected in film strongly reinforce the impression of realism. Furthermore, such systems come close to being notational, since each of their elements more or less complies with a particular referent. In addition, film has its own unqiue symbol system of iconography, in which black and white hats represent the good and bad guys, a cut represents passage of time, and a dissolve represents change of space. Once learned, such an approximation to a notational system can easily be taken as a depiction of real events. Dorr (in press) reports the observation that smaller children assign real-life values to slow-motion or floating objects.

Third, a system such as language is composed of basic units that by themselves are meaningless. Only their articulation carries meaning. This, however, is not the case with some of film's symbol systems. The pictorial system in film may be said to be composed of shots, but these are not the most basic units. Every shot is a shot of something, which in turn can be further broken down to, say, a nose picture, an eye picture or an eyebrow picture. Thus, although the intended meaning of a film is to be found in *sequences* and *syntagms*, one can (and children often do—see, for instance, Collins, in press) extract meaning from the smaller units in film while disregarding larger compositions. By doing so, metaphorical meanings are replaced by literal ones, as the overall montage of a film, which complies with a nonrealistic chain of events, is overlooked for more realistic looking smaller units.

The photographic symbol system of film complies, of course, with the referent of light-reflecting objects. But, in juxtaposition with other symbol systems on the various levels of articulation, it complies with referents other than objects. Thus, by means of composing shots into specific sequences, ideas such as *at the same time, in spite of,* or *because* can be represented without recourse to a symbol system (language) through which such referents must be described or explained. Again, unlike other symbol systems, the photographic system in film allows literal, fragmented interpretations, hence giving the impression of realistic depiction. (Because of this quality of film, educational films often solve the problem of ambiguity by recourse to verbal explanation, thus greatly limiting the use of the medium's unique modes of presentation. By doing so, film as an educational device loses its potentially unique contribution to learning.)

How is all this related to questions of notationality? Film is a composition of many symbol systems, ranging from the more notational to the less notational. The conventions of composition and transformation, some of them uniquely filmic (split screen, slow motion, zoom, sequences of interchangeable shots), often approach notationality despite their pictorial nature. It can be argued that film, *as a unit*, can be segmented into well-differentiated components of the kind suggested by Metz (1974). (Such a segmentation divides film into single shots and syntagms. The latter are subdivided into those that entail or do not entail temporal relations. The ones that entail temporal relations divide into syntagms that represent simultaneous events and those that represent sequential ones, and so on.) Kjørup argues that, since such a classification bears a one-to-one correspondence to equally well-differentiated components in film, then film constitutes a near-notational system, like language.

Thus, one might conclude that film's symbol systems range from the notational to the nonnotational, from description to depiction, and that the *overall* nature of film is notational. But this is somewhat incorrect. Metz's system of segmentation is a partly notational system, but this relationship cannot be extended to film itself. (Similarly, a group picture of a family cannot be classified as notational simply because the symbol system that describes it, say, a family tree, is notational.)

The overall nature of film (and television) leans toward the nonnotational, dense end of the continuum. The *essence* of film is primarily pictorial, thus dense. Also, its various modes of articulation, although relatively distinguishable from each other, do not comply in unambiguous ways with any well-differentiated referent. The typical mode of alternating syntagms (episode A occurring in one place, then episode B in another place, then continuation of A, then B again, and so on) represents more than one kind of temporal, causal, or spatial relationship. Thus, interpretation is highly context-dependent, as is typical of pictures in general (Gombrich, 1960; 1974) but is less true of printed text (Olson, 1977a).

Given the limitations of a nonnotational system, the intention of film makers to go beyond depiction, and their desire to avoid depending on language as the major symbol system of film demands the use of many metaphors in film. The stone lions that leap into life in Eisenstein's *Potemkin* and the hut that seesaws over the cliff in Chaplin's *The Gold Rush* are metaphors. Unlike language, which need not make recourse to metaphors, film cannot avoid them. (The extensive use of metaphor explains the difficulty children face in comprehending feature films.) Being primarily pictorial, film uses realistic properties (dark hallway) to exemplify moods and feelings (danger). Thus, film is very expressive through exemplifications of experience from contexts outside the world of film. For this reason, film is the closest surrogate to experience, save experience itself (Mast, 1977).

If film draws upon many symbolic systems outside itself, then what is unique in film? As Kjørup suggests, "no code used by the film medium is specific to this medium . . . [but] its particularity lies in the combination of the nonspecific codes it uses" (Kjørup, 1977, p. 38). One could add that certain symbol systems, such as iconography, and certain conventions of composition (split screen) and transformation (fade out) are also unique to film. Whether film's conventions comply with our modes of thinking, as Münsterberg (1970) claims, or whether thinking gradually comes to comply with them is a question I will explore in the following chapters.

Summary

Our focus on media's symbol systems calls for some measure of clarity as to the nature of symbol systems. Every object, mark, or event can serve as a symbol, provided that knowledge pertaining to other entities can be extracted from it. Symbols become symbol *schemes* by means of specific rules of prescription (language) or conventions of coherence (art), according to which symbols can be combined, chained, arranged, and organized. A symbol scheme becomes a symbol *system* when correlated with a field of reference with which both the symbols and the rules of combining them comply.

Following Goodman (1968), symbol systems can be ranked according to their degree of notationality. Specific syntactic and semantic criteria allow us to classify a symbol system along a notational-nonnotational continuum. To be notational, a system must consist of separate and differentiated elements that correlate with (stand for) equally separate and differentiated referents in the symbol system's field of reference. The system of musical scores and its field of reference of pitches is a prime example of a notational system. It allows a faithful mapping back and forth to its field of reference (Gardner, 1978). Other systems are syntactically but not semantically notational, as they entail ambiguities (language) or do not meet any of the notational conditions (painting). The latter are relpete; that is, they entail a great many dimensions and elements, all of which convey meaning; they also are ambiguous in terms of the specific meanings of their messages. Nonnotational systems, such as pictures, do not allow unambiguous mapping back and forth between elements and referents, and their reading is more context-dependent.

Goodman explains the difference beween depiction and description in terms of notationality and repleteness rather than in terms of similarity or resemblance to referents. The latter he dismisses on logcial grounds as both unnecessary and insufficient for differentiating between description and depiction. Depiction is yielded by nonnotational, replete systems, and description by notational ones. Goodman also distinguishes between denotation by means of depiction or description and expression. Expression is based on a quality that a coded message has (gray color), which is denoted by a predicate (*grayness*) and is taken to metaphorically denote a feeling or mood (*sadness*). As nonnotational replete systems (dance) entail more attributes than nonnotational ones (wiring diagrams), they can better serve expression. Generally, then, the notational nature of symbol systems reflects the extent to which they are more denotative or expressive, and whether they are more or less versatile in terms of depiction, description, and expression.

One of the problems that results from Goodman's theory concerns the place of resemblance or similarity to referents as a criterion for examining and classifying symbol systems. Goodman excludes this aspect from his system, but it remains the case that people perceive similarities between representations and referents, and that similarity is associated with representativeness. However, there is evidence to suggest that, unlike commonly held views, it is not similarity between symbol and referent that counts but rather similarity with one's mental conception, image, or schema of the referent (many paintings depict non-existent referents and are still considered "realistic"). Thus, I argue that similarity or dissimilarity pertains to the mentally stored referent rather than to a "real" one. Whether a film about ancient Rome is or is not a realistic depiction in one's eyes depends on what one knows already about that topic, the historical or archeological faithfulness of the movie notwithstanding. Often, one's conceptions follow a presentation, which is the basis for later judgments of similarity, lending credence to the claim that "nature follows art."

It follows that, in addition to the notational quality of symbol systems, there is the quality of iconicity, or resemblance, which reflects the interaction between symbol systems and the cognitions of their users.

The last section of the chapter is devoted to an analysis of film. Echoing Kjørup (1977), I argue that film uses many symbol systems, which are combined on different levels of articulation—the shot, the sequence, the syntagm, the film. At each such level, there are syntactic conventions of composition and transformation. Film's fields of reference often appear to be real life. However, this is not the case. Everything is staged or at least edited in such a way that film creates its own field of reference. There are a number of reasons why film, which is mainly nonnotational and replete, is often mistaken for a depiction of reality. For one thing, some of its major symbol systems are taken from other media; for another, its intended messages are not to be found in its single shots or figures but in their juxtaposition.

The unique nature of film lies in the combinations of the symbol systems it uses, in the conventions of composition and transformation it employs, and in specific symbol systems that are particular to the medium.

THREE

Relationships of Symbol Systems to Cognition

✻ ✻ ✻ ✻ ✻ ✻ ✻

Media are modes of expression and communication, based on technologies, that give rise to new symbol systems or to new blends of symbol systems. By focusing on the symbol systems of media, we are able to ignore the common characteristics of different media and can consider only the most essential or prototypical characteristics of each medium—or, what "makes a difference." A single film may be likened to an utterance sampled from the universe of symbol systems that is available to the medium (Kjørup, 1977). This idea implies that each medium has its own universe of symbol systems. These universes, and particularly their unique elements, are the focus of the present discussion, rather than any specific sample drawn from a particular universe.

61

By focusing on media as combinations of symbol systems, an underlying assumption is that differences between symbol systems are correlated with differences of meaning and of information processing. In other words, symbol systems seem to play differential roles in cognition and learning. Although this assumption is not readily validated, it should not be lightly dismissed. If symbol systems do have differential effects on cognition that are ignored, then a psychologically and educationally important source of variance is overlooked. If, on the other hand, the assumption is uncritically accepted, then a distinction may be made that does not correlate with psychological differences.

A similar issue was raised by Brown (1958), with reference to onomatopoeic words—that is, words that are linguistically distinctive by their phonetic symbolism (for example, *buzz*). Only after evidence was marshalled to show that such words have universal psychological correlates (they communicate meaning even to a person who doesn't know the specific language) could the onomatopoeic class of words be accepted as "making a difference."

There is no common agreement to the assumption that differences among symbol systems play a significant role in cognition and learning. This assumption is taken for granted by philosophers (Langer, 1942; Goodman, 1968), aestheticians (Gombrich, 1974), historians of technology and science (Ferguson, 1977), and art educators (Eisner, 1970), but many cognitive psychologists either ignore it (Neisser, 1976) or reject it altogether (Norman and Rumelhart, 1975). Similarly, research done within the Piagetian tradition sidesteps the question of communication's symbol systems. As that line of research focuses on *universal* achievements, which are not related to any *specific* environmental situation and medium, other developments, which may be more specifically culture-, medium-, and technology-bound, are ignored (Feldman, in press). Piagetian research deals with the development of mainly one mode of cognition—logico-rational reasoning. The operations specified by Piaget are limited to the manipulations of real objects that lead to the internalization of the operations, yet manipulations of the cultural, symbolic environment are generally left out.

However, the observed differences of cognitive processes and learning outcomes that covary with differences of symbol systems of communicational and instructional messages cannot be ignored. Some recent research has identified structural characteristics of a medium (usually television) and investigated their relationships to cognition and learning. Atkin and Wood (1974) have studied the effects of "realistic" versus "fictional" television violence and found the former to be the key factor in facilitating the medium's effects on aggressive behavior through its disinhibiting function. Singer and others (1977), investigating the effects of pacing and change of scenes in television programs, found that children attend more to the fast pace of "Sesame Street" but learn more from "Mr. Rogers' Neighborhood." The authors concluded that the reason for the observed difference is that the pace of "Sesame Street" does not allow sufficient time for information processing. Tannenbaum and Zillman (1975) offered a similar hypothesis to explain how television's pace affects hyperactivity.

Research on other media also points to differences in comprehension and learning that can be attributed to the structural elements of media. Salomon (1968) found that seventh-grade lower-class Israeli children have little difficulty identifying single symbols in maps, but, when compared with middle-class children, they show greater difficulty in inferring directions and heights from symbol configurations in maps. Similar results were found by Feldman in the United States (Feldman, 1971). Most of the research done on pictures and words has shown that pictures are usually better recalled, and that their addition to prose reading enhances its comprehension (Pressley, 1977). Gardner (1972), who studied children's sensitivities to the denser aspects of symbol systems, found that preschoolers are too "subject matter" oriented to classify paintings by style. Only preadolescent children can learn to attend to the symbolically dense aspects of works of art.

Research of this kind, although often not explicitly studying media's symbol systems, encourages examination of the connections beweeen symbol systems, cognition, and learning. In what follows, I will develop four general propositions pertaining to these connections. I propose that symbol systems vary with respect to (1) the amount of mental translation required for the extraction and processing of knowledge, (2) the kinds of mental skills required for that purpose, (3) the meanings one can construe from their messages, and (4) the mental skills they cultivate. Each of these propositions is elaborated upon in Chapters Four through Eight.

Differences of Content and Ease of Processing

In a little-known short story (whose origin I have forgotten), a seeing person tries to explain to a blind person what *red* is. "Red is warm and soft," says the seeing person. "Oh, it is like velvet, isn't it? So why don't you call it 'velvet'?" replied the blind person. The attempt to explain the concept *red* turned into a frustrating experience. The quality of that color (or any color) could not be successfully rendered verbally. The linguistic symbol system is typically quite accurate in ruling out alternatives—"Give me the third object with the square cover, which is three inches to your right"—but it fails to render the critical qualities of a color.

It is evident that symbol systems address themselves, so to speak, to different aspects of the natural or symbolic world and present these aspects while excluding others. Some symbol systems emphasize mainly expression (ballet), some emphasize description (graphs) or depiction (pictures), and others are less restricted (languages). Many symbol systems are designed to capture a very narrow range of informational aspects (for example, the notation for dance movements), so that the extension of some symbol systems leads to misapplication and fuzzy communication. Cartographers in medieval times tried to use maps to describe not only the spatial aspects of the Holy Land but its historical flow of events as well. Thus, one finds in such maps more than one Jerusalem, and Moses reappears all over the map.

Heider and Olivier (1972) studied the codability of colors across languages and concluded that visual memory plays an important role in recognizing colors. They interpreted the results to mean that visual memory is more appropriate for the specific attributes of colors and is less affected by the distortions and biases imposed by language. Collins (in press) studied age-related aspects of children's comprehension and inference-making from televised plots. The observed differences among ages and program structures strongly supported the contention that television cannot present implicit causal relations, actors' motives, logical propositions, and the like, thus leaving their generation to the viewer.

Eisner (1978) describes such differences between symbol systems more generally—each symbol system has unique capacities. Each symbol system sets parameters upon what can be conceived and what can be expressed. Thus, through painting we are able to know *autumn* in ways that only the visual arts make possible. Through poetry we can know *autumn* in ways that only poems can provide. Through botany we are able to know *autumn* in ways that only botanists can share. How something is perceived and what we can know about it depend on the symbol systems we can use or can choose to use.

But the symbol systems used by media are not mutually exlcusive in terms of what they can render. Barring cases in which a symbol system is competely unequipped to represent some aspect of content (try to represent *suspicion* through sculpture), there are significant overlaps among symbol systems and media. Through film we sometimes try to capture the content of a novel; a verbal direction is given to a motorist in the absence of a map. A family history can be verbally described or presented via a family tree, and students in schools are asked to enact symbolically an event they have read about. Still, daily experience tells us that some symbol systems are *better suited* to carry particular content than others. The motorist, being unsatisfied with a verbal description, asks for another symbol system, a map, which he hopes will better serve the purpose of guiding his driving. A small child will misuse the medium of drawing when asked to represent a collision between two cars and will use the pencil and paper to symbolically reenact the process. Drawing, for him, is a relatively poor medium through which to express the quality of movement. Indeed, the intuitive experience that some media can better represent some content than others was the basis of the many intermedia research comparisons discussed earlier.

But what does it mean that one medium is "better able" to represent some aspects of content than another? If one medium has the means to represent a particular aspect while another does not, then the answer is self-evident. Gombrich (1974) points out that language allows a speaker to inform a listener of past, present, future, possible, or conditional states of affairs ("If it rains, I may possibly stay here"). Pictures cannot perform such functions, as they do not entail in their symbol system any logical connections equivalent to *if, nevertheless,* or *not.* Similarly, graphs are better capable of rendering mathematical relations between variables than, say, music, because music does not entail in its symbol system any code that handles such relations. There are, however, media that *have* the symbolic capability of rendering qualities that other media can also represent. But why do we get the feeling that all symbol systems, even when representing the same content, are not equally well suited to communicate that content?

One way to answer this question is by looking at the "resemblance" between the presented and the represented. One could argue that a symbol system that more closely "resembles" the referent, or copies it more accurately, can better convey it. However, as was argued in Chapter Two, *resemblance* is a philosophically ambiguous term. As there is no *one* way that the world really looks or is, there can be no question of resembling it in a better or poorer way. Rather, one can speak of *the correspondence between how an aspect of the world is presented and the images, conceptions, or, more generally, the schemata into which it is to be assimilated.* In other words, the factor that makes one mode of presentation better than another is the correspondence between the coded message and the mode in which it could best be *internally* represented and processed by a given person.

Recently, attempts have been made to show that all incoming information, regardless of format and symbol system, is processed in a unimodal fashion (for example, Pylyshyn,

1973; Palmer, 1975; Rosenberg and Simon, 1977). This proposed model for information processing is quite parsimonious, as it postulates that there is *one* mental representational system ("propositions"), which is well suited to the kinds of operations that are performed on it (Norman and Rumelhart, 1975). For instance, pictorial information is alleged to be processed sequentially and complexly and in a way that is modality-independent. Each stimulus needs to be decomposed into higher-level then lower-level propositions until reduced to primitive propositions about points, angles, and numerous other dimensions (Palmer, 1975).

The empirical evidence seems to weigh, however, more heavily in favor of a conception of a dual, even *multiple representational system* (for example, Kosslyn and Pomerantz, 1977; Anderson, 1978; Shepard, 1978a). Attempts to explain the differential effects of pictures and words on memory in terms of internal verbalization (Rohwer, 1970), thus postulating a unimodal system for internal representation, received less empirical support than dual-modality conceptions (Pressley, 1977). The conception of human cognition that emerges postulates the existence of a verbal representational system, an analog or parallel system, and possibly additional systems as well (Kintsch, 1977). The study of human intelligence (for example, Snow, 1978a) offers additional support to this conception, showing that different types of problems are served by different aptitudes.

Neuropsychological evidence, although somewhat ambiguous, supports the general contention that different symbolic modes of information are processed in different parts of the brain (Gardner, 1974a,b). With maturity, cross-modal associations in the brain allow increased combinations between incoming modalities. It is nevertheless the case that the left hemisphere seems to play a major part in the processing of linguistic, notational symbol systems, and the right hemisphere is more active in processing dense, figural ones (Gazzaniga, 1974; Gardner, 1977). In a recent study by Gardner (unpublished), sixty-one adults, including ten normals, fourteen unilaterally right brain-damaged patients, and thirty-seven aphasic patients were tested for their ability to identify different kinds of symbols. Patients with right-hemisphere damage showed much better performance with linguistic symbols and far poorer performance with pictured objects than did the aphasics (93 percent and 53 percent correct words in the former group versus 60 percent and 85 percent correct for the latter group). Traffic signs, word-picture matching, and trademarks did not discriminate between the groups. Right-hemisphere patients did less well with pictorial logos and better with letter-based ones (IBM), and the converse was true for aphasics.

It becomes reasonable to assume that different kinds of content are processed by different cognitive systems. In other words, different kinds of content are internally represented by means of different symbol systems. *Externally coded messages need then to be transformed, elaborated on, and translated into one's preferred (or task-required) internal symbol system.* For instance, Brooks (1967, 1968) asked subjects to "consider a set of several intersecting streets with which you are familiar." Then a series of specific spatial problems was presented to them. The subjects found it more difficult to check their answers off from a piece of paper than to report the answers aloud, indicating that to imagine looking at something makes it difficult to look at something else. In other words, checking answers from a piece of paper forced the subjects to deal with a symbol system that addressed itself to an internal representation already occupied with a similar kind of stimuli. Huttenlocher (1973) points out the consistency with which people report converting *verbally* presented spatial problems into *spatial* modes of internal representation.

These arguments lead to the proposition that there can be different degrees of correspondence between the incoming mode of a presentation and the mode in which the content is to be processed and stored. It follows that, *when there is a poor match between the modes of presented and internally represented information, additional translations, conversions, or elaborations are required.* When a medium-generated message is coded in relatively uncommon or novel symbolic elements, it deviates more from one's internal schemata and requires more elaborate translations into one's internal codes. Writes Kintsch

(1977, p. 315), "Novels or movies are easier when the natural order of events is maintained than when they are full of flashbacks and reversals, but since the latter invite deeper processing, they are more interesting to read or watch."

Evidence shows that the amount of mental elaboration has much to do with the correspondence or match between the communicational and internal representation. Rosch (1977) noted the consistency of people's rating of particular category membership (robins-birds) according to their "typicality." She argues that there is a *prototype* bird, and this is what people have in their minds when they use the word *bird*. In studies of verification times, it was found that the closer a word was to its stored prototype, the quicker it was verified.

Research on the comprehension of syntactically different sentences shows a similar pattern—transformations from surface to deep structure take time and mental effort (for example, Savin and Perchonock, 1965). The amount of mental elaboration required by a sentence depends, to a degree, on the distance between the presented surface structure of the sentence and its internal base structure (Olson and Filby, 1972). Jones (1966) has found that children have less difficulty complying with the instruction "Mark the numbers 3, 4, 7, and 8" than with the "Mark all the numbers except 1, 3, 5, 6." The reason apparently is that the negatively stated instructions require more mental transformation from surface to deep structure than the positive ones.

In studies on comprehension, Fillenbaum (1971, 1974) asked subjects to paraphrase sentences, some of which were perverse—"Don't print that or I won't sue you." Over 60 percent of the subjects paraphrased the perverse sentence as "If you print that, I'll sue you." It can be concluded that the subjects transformed the perverse information into a more straightforward internal representation.

From such studies, it appears that available options of a symbol system can put a heavier or lighter burden on the receiver of a message, depending on the correspondence between the presented symbol and the receiver's schemata. The closer the correspondence, the better (that is easier) the processing of the message. Hence, a hypothesis of compensation suggests that for learners with deficient skill-mastery, learning is enhanced when translation processes are circumvented or short-circuited for them. Cronbach and Snow (1977, p. 170) write, "Perhaps the learner with low verbal ability is poor at formulating in words what he observes. It would then be reasonable for the treatment to provide verbal statements for him. . . . The high-verbal learner who is weak in visualization might be supplied with extensive diagrams and left to generate his own verbal representations. Each treatment can be preprocessed by the needed aptitude to compensate for a particular weakness."

The comprehension of text is assumed to be aided by the generation of imagery-like meanings, and this generation requires mental elaborations. Thus, when children who are asked to learn prose are given *ready-made* pictures to accompany it, their learning improves. This is particularly the case with younger children or those who usually learn prose poorly (see, for example, Guttmann, Levin and Pressley, 1977). In a study by Pressley and Levin (1977), second- and sixth-graders learned a list of paired-associate words, which was presented at either a slow or fast rate. Some of the subjects were instructed to generate inter-active images, others not. Subjects were given a list of either high-imagery or low-imagery words. Second graders benefited from the imagery instruction when the pace of presentation was slow, or, under the rapid-pace condition, only with high-imagery pairs. Apparently, imagery instructions facilitated learning by leading younger children to translate the pairs from one mode to another. But, as this process takes time, such instructions can facilitate learning only when enough time is provided. Sixth-graders did not benefit from the instructions, apparently because they are sufficiently proficient with the verbal code.

If imagery is indeed required for prose learning, and if smaller children have difficulties generating the images, then providing them with ready-made images short-circuits or circum-vents that process and thus facilitates learning by saving the learner additional elaborations. The hypothesis follows that a medium such as television, whose principal symbol system is pictorial, may address itself to the viewer's nonlinguistic mental systems. And, as meaning frequently depends on the generation of images, a pictorially based medium can short-circuit the process of imagery-generation and be easier to understand than the same message in, say, print (see also Singer, in press).

As each symbol system has some underlying generic characteristics (for example, nonnotationality, density), we can generalize the case with the proposition that, *other things being equal, different symbol systems of the media address themselves to different parts of one's cognitive apparatus and require different amounts of mental translation.*

But the amount of mental translation to be performed is not determined *only* by the nature of the symbol system. Smaller children apparently need to transform verbal messages more often into nonverbal internal representations, but older children can process verbal messages more directly and need this transformation less. Similarly, older children process negative sentences nearly as fast as positive ones, but smaller children do not. It becomes evident that cognitive development plays an important role, aside from that played by the nature of the symbol system, in determining the amount of mental translation required for comprehension.

Another factor to determine the amount of needed mental elaboration is aptitude mastery or cognitive preference, reflected as individual differences within an age group (see, for example, Cronbach and Snow, 1977; Sternberg, 1977). Thus, for a learner who is more proficient with internal verbalization, a pictorial presentation may be more demanding than a verbal one, and vice versa. Consider what Einstein had to say about himself (Holton, 1968, p. 101):

> The words or the language, as they are written or spoken, do not seem to play any role in my mechanisms of thought. The psychical entities which seem to serve as elements in thought are certain signs and more or less clear images which can be "voluntarily" reproduced or combined. . . . But taken from a psychological viewpoint, this combinatory play seems to be the essential feature in productive thought—before there is any connection with logical construction in words or other

kinds of signs which can be communicated to others. The above-mentioned elements are, in my case, of visual and some of muscular type. Conventional words or other signs have to be sought for laboriously only in a secondary stage, when the mentioned associative play is sufficiently established and can be reproduced at will.

Shepard (1978b) quotes a large number of other scientists, such as Faraday and James Watson, who reported using imagery to generate some of their most elaborate formulations, suggesting that personal preference for internal representation often plays a crucial role.

A third factor that affects amount of elaboration is the task to be performed or the task one selects to perform. It is quite obvious that one's quick glance at a painting, aimed perhaps only at identifying the object depicted by it, requires less mental elaboration than studying its style and mode of depiction. Similarly, studying a list of paired associates in a rote manner requires less mental elaboration than attempting to generate sentences or images that interrelate the members of each pair. On the basis of a number of studies of problem solving, Olson and Bruner (1974, p. 127) argue that "information which was coded appropriately for purposes of recall was, as a consequence, coded inappropriately for purposes of solving a problem." Hence, they conclude that "knowledge is dependent on or is limited by the purposes for which it was acquired" (p. 127), which is congruent with the encoding-specificity hypothesis formulated by Tulving and Thomson (1973). According to the latter authors, no retrieval can help access to a particular memory unless the cue and that target memory were encoded together initially.

I can now modify my pervious proposition: *Relative to one's cognitive make-up (including cognitive growth and individual differences) and to the task to be performed, different symbol systems require different amounts of mental elaboration.* Why then does one symbol system appear to be better than another for the communication of some content? It should be evident by now that *better* means mentally *easier*. One symbol system communicates better than another not because of any resemblance between the presented symbol and its referent, but because *one symbol system, when compared with another, can present information in better correspondence to—or congruity with—the mode of internal representation that an individual with a given cognitive make-up and task can best utilize.* The closer the correspondence, or isomorphism, the easier it is for the learner.

To test this argument, I conducted a two-stage experiment with college students. Subjects (n = 86) in the first stage were asked to describe, depict, or represent, in whatever way they saw fit, the route they would take from one building of the campus to another. As expected, about one half provided a graphic depiction, and the other half provided a written description. A small minority provided a mixture of pictorial, graphical, and verbal description. In the second stage, a random half of the group was given a written description of an imaginary island, and the other half was given a map of it. Both the map and the description were accompanied by a series of true-false questions. Time to completion and correctness of response were measured. As predicted, two subgroups of subjects were the fastest—the graphcially inclined subjects who received the map and the verbally inclined who received the written description. The other two groups were significantly slower. There was no observable difference between the groups in correctness of responses, but we should bear in mind that two of the four grossly divided groups required less time to reach the same number of correct responses. The shorter response time required by the subjects in two of the four subgroups is a fair indication that they needed to employ less mental transformation than the others because of the hypothesized greater congruity between their preferred internal mode of representation and the message they encountered.

Pictures do not communicate "better" than verbal descriptions; as a *general rule* one medium does not communicate better than another medium. Nor do pictures communicate better (when they do) because they are more similar to the content. Rather, pictures can communicate better to the extent that the symbolic codes they use come closer to, or are more congruent with, the internal representation that the receiver ought to generate, given his cognitive make-up and the requirements of the task. The same is true for other media. To the extent that one needs verbal mediation to solve a problem, a ready-made verbal presentation would save him some mental elaborations and hence will be a better—that is, mentally easier— presentation. The less that person is capable of producing the needed internal verbalization, the more a verbal presentation facilitates his performance. Similarly, mathematical relations between variables are better communicated through graphs than through words, because a graph corresponds more closely to the internal representation of the relationships the learner should generate.

A number of new hypotheses can be derived from such considerations of the psychological differences between symbol systems. For instance, the popularity of home television viewing can be explained in terms of the relative ease of processing that its primary symbol system allows when the task requirements are freely defined by viewers. As some of its messages address directly the nonlinguistic internal systems, saving the viewer cross-modal elaborations, the messages may yield relatively satisfactory information *with little effort.*

Similarly, we could hypothesize that the use of a medium such as television could facilitate learning to the extent that its pictorial symbolic components are used to short-circuit critical mental elaborations that learners have difficulties carrying out on their own with respect to figural or spatial contents. However, television, or other media that use primarily nonnotational depictions, would not save much mental translation when logical propositions or negations are to be learned, unless the latter requires pictorial imagery for its acquisition.

Differences of Requisite Mental Skills

The propositions that different symbol systems render different contents, that they address themselves to different parts of our cognitive apparatus, and that they require varying degrees of mental elaboration do not exhaust the range of possible connections between symbol systems and cognition. One may ask whether two different symbol systems (attempting to convey the same content to the same person for identical purposes) would require the same sets of mental skills for the extraction and processing of the information. Thus, for example, holding content as constant as possible, does reading about some historical event require the same mental skills as seeing a film about it, seeing a series of pictures, or reading the events from a computer-generated flow chart?

The translation of information from its surface, communicational code into an internal one is a skillful process, often classified as decoding. (As nothing is being *de*coded, I will refer to this process as *recoding* a message from surface appearance to some internal form.) By calling the act of recoding from an external into an internal code a *skill*, we have only to assume that it is an operation that applies with some generalizability to a variety of contents that are coded in a similar way. We thus follow Olson (1976), according to whom invaraints in the environment across different actions constitute our *knowledge* of those objects and events; invariants in our actions across different objects and situations constitute *skills*. Thus, we come to *know* an event by applying different actions to it; we compare it, analyze it, integrate it with others, and so on. A *skill*, on the other hand, is an external or internal operation performed on a number of objects or events; we analyze a historical event, a mathematical formula, a concrete situation, or a speech.

Skill, as perceived here, is akin to Ryle's procedural knowledge of "know how" as distinguished from "know that" (1949, quoted by Olson, 1976). In effect, skill is identical to what is often called a *mental process* or *operation* (Snow, 1978b), or to what Neisser (1976) calls the "executing" function of our anticipatory schemata. Note that skills can be of varying degrees of generality, from a general ability such as Cattell's general verbal ability, through more specific ones such as spatial aptitudes, to highly specific ones such as digit span or visual memory.

Here I am concerned mainly with mental skills, their specificity not withstanding, that serve the function of recoding a message from its external code into an internal code. When differently coded information is dealt with by different parts of one's cognitive apparatus and is elaborated on in different ways until it is translated into the person's preferred modes, different mental operations, or skills, are utilized. A similar point is made by Perkins and Leondar (1977, p. 9), who state that "symbol systems are neither better nor worse but are simply different as the degree of notationality varies and as they differ in style of information processing they require of the maker or reader." Olson and Bruner (1974) argue likewise that the content of a message addresses itself to one's knowledge, while the symbolic carrier of the message addresses itself to one's skill. Cross-cultural research (Hudson, 1962, Deregowski, 1968) shows what role the acquisition of skill plays in interpreting line drawings and photos. Research on the comprehension of grammatically different sentences shows likewise that skill is required, and that different grammatical structures require different kinds of mental operations (Clark and Clark, 1977).

This contention would seem to apply to all coded messages, even those that appear to require less mental elaboration than others. Gombrich (1960, 1964) shows how skill is involved in processing pictures, even simple ones—we have to "read" the code of a black and white photograph without assuming that it is a rendering of a colorless world. The fact that we often fail to notice that different skills are involved in processing differently coded messages may indicate only that we are highly skilled in dealing with most messages, thus applying skills automatically.

Although most writers would agree that the processing of coded messages requires learned skills, the contention that code-*specific* skills are needed is often challenged. For instance, Wolf (1977) argues that reading a page, reading a map, and reading a picture constitute the same process. Kolers raises a similar argument based on empirical observations, claiming that "what makes the similarity [of mental skills involved] especially interesting is that text is linguistic and pictures are not, yet the mechanisms of reading the two share many characteristics" (1977, p. 163). But such claims are undermined by neuropsychological findings that show that some forms of brain damage debilitate recognition of nonnotational presentations, leaving intact reading ability, while other kinds of damage have the converse effect (Gardner, 1974a,b).

Whenever language-comprehension skills or reading skills are described (for example, Clark and Clark, 1977; LaBerge and Samuels, 1974), it becomes apparent that they are language- or script-specific. These skills are required by the very nature of language or script. It would be unreasonable to expect the *same processes* to play an *equal role* when pictures, movies, music, or maps are dealt with. If specific processes are required by the nature of language, then the nature of other symbol systems would require other types of processes. Consider, for example, the script of the Liberian tribe of the Vai, and the way it is used. Its effects on cognition were studied by Scribner and Cole (1978). As the Vai script does not entail a division into words or other language units, it requires "experimentation in pronounciation"—that is, saying strings of syllables aloud, while varying tone until they become meaningful. According to Scribner and Cole, such experimentation requires holding separate syllables in working memory until they can be integrated into words or phrases.

The specific structure of the Vai's script demands very particular skills for its use, many of which would not be demanded from a user of another script or under different conditions. If such a difference is reasonable when two kinds of *scripts* are compared, it would be even more likely to appear when two *symbol systems* are involved. Hence, Olson's contention (1970, 1976) that "intelligence is skill in a medium" leads to the proposition that, *due to their different natures, symbol systems vary as to the mental skills they require in the service of information extraction and processing.*

Furthermore, as argued earlier, one has to transform or recode a message from one code into another to construe meaning from it. But as each symbol system, and specific coding element within a system is differently structured, its transformation would require a somewhat different procedure. Therefore, mastery of reading skills is not related to mastery of skills needed for map reading (Salomon, 1968), nor are we all equally well equipped to read graphs, in spite of our proficiency to interpret pictures.

Differences of Construed Meaning

Other propositions and hypotheses derive from the proposition that different symbol systems call for different sets of mental skills. One such derivation pertains to the question of whether different symbol systems, *other things (such as content) being equal,* lead to the extraction of the same meanings. On the one hand, we could postulate that, as symbol systems convey different aspects of (even the "same") content, as they address themselves to different cognitive systems, and as they require different amounts and types of mental elaboration, the meanings one can construe from their message *must* be different. Hence, a tape recording of a speech will allow the extraction (or construction) of meanings that differ somewhat from those that can be extracted from a written transcript of the speech.

Although this conclusion seems to follow logically, it may be psychologically incorrect. The meanings of a coded message need to be construed, or extracted from it by the receiver, and thus one's anticipatory schemata, which contain past experiences and knowledge and determine what is to be perceived, are brought to bear on the message (Neisser, 1976). Symbol systems may diverge as to the skills they require but *converge as to the knowledge they specify* (Olson and Bruner, 1974). The reason, according to Olson and Bruner (p. 132), is that "knowledge is always mediated or specified through some form of human activity," and that knowledge acquired through any such activity has two facets—knowledge about the world and knowledge about the activity used in gaining the knowledge. Thus, from drawing an object, we acquire knowledge about the object and about the act of drawing. Whereas knowledge about the world reflects the content invariants in messages, knowledge about the activity—the skills involved—reflects the symbolic structure of the medium. Thus, Olson and Bruner conclude that the meanings arrived at may *ultimately* draw from the same knowledge base, although the skills utilized to arrive at meanings may differ as a function of the symbol system.

Kosslyn and Pomerantz (1977) argue that information, although dealt with in different internal modalities, results in the same outcomes regardless of the mode of mediation. Rosenberg and Simon (1977) have shown in their experiment that, when pictures are constructed from (identical) sentences by a set of rules *"designed to make alternative encodings unlikely,"* similar meanings are arrived at. Indeed, it makes good common sense to postulate that knowledge about, say, a zebra maps on a larger body of knowledge pertaining to zebras, and that it should not matter what symbol system is used to carry the new information about zebras (Olson, 1974).

But note that the assumption behind such a claim is that *there is a large knowledge base* into which the new information is assimilated. We can assume that the large body of stored knowledge pertaining to, say, zebras has reached a person through different symbol systems and has been elaborated on, processed, and transformed by the different cognitive systems. Knowledge, we know, does not necessarily stay in the system in which it was initially processed, nor does it stay unconnected to other, relatable knowledge. There is neuropsychological evidence to show that information can be processed cross-modally (Gardner, 1977), suggesting that, *as we have a wider knowledge base pertaining to some entity, the less modality- (or symbolically) specific it is likely to be.* To use Piagetian concepts, the more easily information is assimilated into one's schemata without requiring its accommodation, the less it matters how it is symbolically encoded.

But what if the incoming information entails much novelty realtive to one's schemata? Generally, it requires greater changes in the schemata, although *too much* novelty will lead to its rejection. Neisser (1976) points out that one's schemata determine what information is picked up; schemata perceive primarily the anticipated. However, *within limits,* these schemata "tune themselves to the information actually available"; they undergo changes, or accommodations, and by doing so allow the person to acquire new information. Greeno (1977, p. 6), summarizing relevant research, writes, "Learning that requires accommodation or restructuring involves the development of new knowledge structures, including new procedures that will permit the understanding of new kinds of information that was incomprehensive with the cognitive equipment that the student had earlier."

Unlike information that needs only to be assimilated, more novel information that calls for the development of new procedures can be expected to be more modality- or symbol-system specific. The newer the information, the more will its processing and storage be symbol-system specific. This characteristic explains, for example, the difficulties experienced by many students in introductory statistics courses when trying to internally represent the new basic concepts in ways that differ from the way they were taught. A person's ability to paraphrase a new idea, let alone translate it into a new symbol system, is closely related to one's more general knowledge pertaining to that idea.

There is evidence to show (cited by Cole and Scribner, 1974) that when culturally familiar objects are to be classified, the medium in which they are presented (real objects or pictures) does not matter. This is not the case with less-familiar objects—classifying them greatly depends on the medium. Such findings suggest that differently coded information maps on the same knowledge base, when the knowledge base is large enough to assimilate the information. However, differently coded information would be expected to yield different knowledge, or meanings, when it is relatively novel and requires much accommodation of schemata. Furthermore, more novel information requires more mental elaboration (Greeno, 1977). As more elaboration needs to take place, and as symbol-system-specific skills are involved, different meanings ought to be construed.

I can now summarize these points in the next proposition, that *the extent to which different symbol systems yield different meanings, other things being equal, is a function of the novelty of the conveyed information.* It follows, for instance, that it may not matter much through what symbol system a social scientist acquires information about, say, a new experimental design, but it may matter a lot whether be learns about space flights from a film or a lecture. His knowledge base pertaining to the former is relatively well elaborated, and therefore he will construe more or less the *same* meanings concerning the new experimental design, regardless of whether it is presented to him, say, graphically or verbally. However, his knowledge pertaining to the physics of space flights is probably more limited, and hence a film will lead him to construe somewhat different meanings than a learned lecture of the same content. Olson and Bruner (1974) acknowledge the possibility that each mode of presentation has a residual uniqueness of acquired knowledge. The question, it seems, is one of degree. *I propose that the more novel the information, the more unique to its symbolic carrier will the acquired meaning be.*

The argument presented thus far was based on the assumption that other things (content, person, and task) are held constant. However, more often than not, they are allowed to interact with each other. Of particular interest are the interactions between media and self-determined tasks. Rarely is a home television viewer guided by a particular task requirement. Rather, the viewer is free to choose how, and for what purpose, he views programs. The same applies in varying degrees to other media as well. For this reason, different media are found to serve different functions and to provide different kinds of gratifications (Blumler and Katz, 1974).

If, as I have hypothesized earlier, television allows easier processing, since it can address mainly the nonlinguistic mental system and save mental effort, then the meanings one would tend to secure from it would be less elaborate than those secured from reading (content held constant as much as possible). Reading, by its reliance on a symbol system whose referents are not directly linked to experiential and imagery cognitive systems (Greeno, 1977), requires apparently more mental elaboration than television (Singer, in press). Thus, the meanings secured from television are more likely to be segmented, concrete, and less inferential, and those secured from reading have a higher likelihood of being better tied to one's stored knowledge and thus are more likely to be inferential.

Meringoff (1978) has found that children who were asked to retell a story that was read to them exhibited greater facility in spontaneously associating the story with other realms of their experience than children who saw the same story on television. The former also showed a greater tendency to use other information in inference-making. Children who were exposed to the televised version showed better recall of actions and drew more inferences from the visual material. Children who listened to the story recalled more peripheral material. Most important, younger children were better able to reconstruct the order of story events when listening to the story. Older ones reconstructed better the televised story. Unlike Rosenberg and Simon's older subjects, Meringoff's subjects had a much poorer knowledge base available to them, hence the symbolic mode through which the information was conveyed to them led to the construction of significantly different meaning.

Differential Cultivation of Skills

The proposition that different symbol systems of media call for different mental skills leads to still another implication—skills that are called on and successfully utilized may also be cultivated. If a symbol system requires the utilization of specific mental skills, then these need to be developed.

To cultivate a skill, a symbol system must be sufficiently *demanding* to upgrade the skill beyond its previous level of mastery. Thus, *within limits, a mode of presentation can cultivate a skill to the extent that it reinforces its use on a higher level. And, as the skill requirements of symbol systems differ, so do the mental skills they can cultivate.* Elkind (1969) found that children who had no experience with pictorial representations for the first years of their lives showed poorer spatial and pictorial skills than children who had experience with the medium. However, as experience grew, the former group reached the mastery level of the latter.

This hypothesis appears to contradict the previously stated

proposition that some modes of presentation can save mental effort. If a flow chart of events summarizes for a learner a long and complex sequence of events, because it corresponds better to his internal representation and thus saves the learner some mental operations, then the "saved" skills cannot be cultivated on that occasion. Compensating for one's deficient skill-mastery by short-circuiting requisite mental operations would seem to prevent their development. Thus, Olson and Bruner (1974, p. 149) write, "The choice of a means of instruction, then, must not depend solely upon the effectiveness of the means for conveying and developing knowledge; it must depend as well upon its effects on the mental skills that are developed in the course of acquiring that knowledge."

Specifically, the employment of charts, graphs, or pictures could save mental effort and make the acquisition of knowledge more effective, but it will impede skill development. Samuels (1970) has shown in this respect that, due to the lesser effort required by pictures, early readers identify the pictured objects but do not read the words printed next to them. The communication was very effective indeed, as it saved mental effort by using the pictures, but this came at the expense of developing reading skills.

There is, however, still another issue involved here. To what extent are mental skills that can be developed by symbol systems generalizable beyond the requirements of the specific symbol system? Say that the nonnotational dense elements of television, or painting, develop specific skills, whose nature we do not know as yet. What would their utility be outside of television viewing or art appreciation? Write Olson and Bruner (1974, p. 149), "However, as to the skills they develop, each form of experience, including the various symbolic systems tied to the media, produces a unique pattern of skills for dealing with or thinking about the world. It is the skills in these systems that we call intelligence." However, for such generalizable effects to take place, more must be involved than just exercising skills required by the symbolic component of a medium. To become "intelligent," such skills need to become *tools of thought* applicable to entities outside the demands of a particular medium.

The proposition of Olson and Bruner assumes that one can learn to think in terms of the symbolic codes used by a medium. This, then, leads to an examination of language and thought beyond the boundaries of psycholinguistics, where it has been dealt with until now. Bruner writes (1964, p. 2), "Where representation of the environment is concerned it . . . depends upon techniques that are learned—and these are precisely the techniques that serve to amplify our motor acts, our perceptions, and our ratiocinative activities."

Assuming, as for instance Von Bertalanffy (1965) and others do, that we think in terms of symbolic representations, it is possible to postulate that *some of our symbolic-thought vehicles are adopted from communicational symbol systems,* perhaps like the alleged internalization of language (Vygotsky, 1962). This view ascribes a dual function to symbol systems—they both serve communication and serve as internal representations.

This possibility is reflected in the duality of *some* symbol systems, such as language, number, and spatial representation, which have measurable mental counterparts in the form of verbal, numerical, and spatial abilities. The fact that such internal symbolic counterparts are measurable reflects their importance in our society and their wide applicability. This, however, does not mean that other symbol systems—musical notation or graphs—cannot be used mentally as well. That their possible internalization has not been extensively studied may be a reflection of the print bias of schools rather than the cognitive potential of the media.

As this issue will be discussed in more depth in Chapters Five through Eight, I will not elaborate more on it here, aside from stating that *some coding elements of symbol systems can become internalized to serve as vehicles of thought.* Thus, a child who is heavily exposed to television would be expected to become better able to think in terms of, say, flashbacks and to represent events to himself in terms of quick juxtapositions. G. Lesser (1974) has hypothesized, along this same line, that an impulsively thinking child could be taught to represent internally information in slow motion and thus become a less-impulsive thinker.

To the extent that internal representations are developed by symbol systems (an issue to be explored in later chapters), they may afford new ways of perceiving and reorganizing experiences in new symbolic categories. For this reason, the cultivation of media-related skills can also serve *exploratory functions* (Olson, 1977b). Eisner (1976, p. 2), who is concerned with art and art education, reaches a similar conclusion: "We know most of what we know not in one way, but in a variety of ways. Each of our sensory modalities puts us in contact with the environment, and . . . each modality enables us to create a knowledge system that we use to know and express our conceptions of reality. Our conceptions of that reality are not only linguistic, they are visual, gustatory, kinesthetic, and even more." Thus, it appears that symbol systems may not only cultivate mental skills but also provide us with cognitive tools for dealing with the world.

Segall, Campbell and Herskovitz (1966) have suggested that "carpentered" environments, those that entail rectangles, straight lines, and right angles, make their inhabitants more susceptible to the Müller-Lyer illusion. The present proposition is somewhat analogous, inasmuch as it suggests that specific symbolic components of the media can be internalized to become tools of thought. To the extent that media of communication serve also to *externalize* internal representations (for example, Shepard, 1978b), we are faced with a bi-directional process: Internal representations are externalized and external symbols are internalized.

Two of the propositions presented in this chapter appear to be of greater importance than the others—that symbol systems vary as to the mental skills they *call upon* and *cultivate*. The other propositions seem to follow from these two. In spite of their central role in a theory of symbol systems, media, cognition, and instruction, these two key propositions have until recently received little direct empirical support. In the next chapter, I will examine the first proposition and provide some direct experimental data about it. In the following three chapters, I will do the same for the second proposition.

Summary

Artists often claim that, as styles in art differ, so do the experiences one has when encountering them. Theoreticians of media claim similarly that when a medium is "true to its nature," it can create a unique communicational experience. Historians sometimes claim that our perceptions of the world imitate, or follow, those suggested by art. All these, and other claims, seem to address themselves to the symbolic (or syntactic) qualities of modes of expression. In this chapter, I have tried to address this issue conceptually by asking whether the differences between symbol systems that are associated with media make any cognitive difference, and, if so, in what ways and for what reasons? To explore this issue, a number of propositions were formulated.

First, I argued that symbol systems address themselves to different aspects of the world, and that some systems render specific aspects better than others. This proposition led to the question of what *better* means. Does one mode of appearance convey an idea better than another because it is more similar to the referent? Rejecting this possibility, I proposed that symbol systems vary as to the cognitive systems they address, and that, given a particular content, person, and task, the information they carry requires different amounts of mental recoding and elaboration. Thus, the better the correspondence between the way information is presented and the way it can be mentally represented, the less recoding is needed and the easier is the communication. I proposed that better communication means easier processing. I was also led to consider the potential of symbol systems for saving mental effort by addressing themselves to cognitive systems in ways that better correspond to one's mode of internal representation.

But processing must always take place (there can never be absolute saving). This processing always requires skill. However, symbol systems call upon different sets of mental skills for the extraction and processing of the coded information. This is a central proposition, and if it is true, other propositions follow. One such derivation concerns the construction of meaning. The extent to which different symbolic renderings of the same content yield different meanings is a function of the content's subjective novelty. The less novel the content, the less it matters what symbol system is used. Conversely, it does matter with more novel contents.

Another proposition concerns the potentiality of symbol systems for cultivating the mastery of skills. Symbol systems vary as to the skills they require and cultivate, and skill-cultivation is negatively related to the saving of mental effort. Can such cultivated skills be transferred? As this question is extremely important from both an educational and psychological point of view, more elaborate consideration is left for later chapters. It does seem likely, however, that symbol systems cultivate skills that can be used as "tools of thought," thus allowing new ways of handling and exploring the world.

FOUR

Differential Uses of Mental Skills for Learning

ßß ßß ßß ßß ßß ßß ßß

In this chapter, empirical findings are presented pertaining to the propositions that symbol systems vary with respect to the amount of mental elaboration and the kinds of mental skills they require to extract knowledge from them. It is extremely difficult to test these propositions by contrasting symbol systems, because, as was seen in Chapter Three, symbol systems differ as to the kinds of content they represent. Hence, it would be virtually impossible to manipulate experimentally only symbol systems without at the same time also varying content. Indeed, whenever such experimental manipulations were attempted, covariatons of extracted meaning were either welcome (Meringoff, 1978) or equated (Rosenberg and Simon, 1977).

Testing of these propositions can be accomplished, however, if we manipulate coding elements within a system. We need only ensure that whatever applies to a symbolic element applies *in principle* to a whole symbol system, and vice versa.

As an example of research in this area, Snow, Tiffin, and Seibert (1965) found that students' prior experience with films in general predicted well how much they could learn from a series of physics films. The same would be true for any specific coding element of film (for instance, time reversals), prior familiarity with which would predict proper extractions of knowledge from it. Thus, it is possible to assume that the differential activation of mental skills by two symbol systems is analogous to that of two similarly distinct coding elements within a symbol system. However, the latter can be expected to call on less general skills. The extraction of knowledge from language calls for different skills than from, say, graphs, analogous to the different skills called on by two kinds of grammatical structures in language.

The experiment to be described here was based on the manipulation of coding elements that belong to the symbol systems of film and television. Results obtained from the experiment are then generalized to whole symbol systems.

Rationale

Two arguments were made in Chapter Three that may have appeared as incongruent: (1) Coding elements and whole symbol systems vary with respect to the amount of mental recoding (translation from external into internal representation) that they require relative to a person's abilities, content, and task. (2) All messages are coded in symbolic form, and even the most familiar ones require skill for their recoding.

In comparing these two statements, it would appear as if some codes require so little recoding or mental elaboration that hardly any skill needs to be applied to them at all. This, of course, is incorrect. When a coded message is easier for processing than another message, it means that the learner for whom that message is easier has a good mastery of the necessay skills and utilizes them automatically. Automaticity of skill-utilization is reflected in the absence of errors, in fast execution, in the generation of short-cuts that short-circuit intermediate steps of execution (LaBerge and Samuels, 1974), and in a reorganization of smaller-unit skills into larger compounds (Hayes-Roth, 1977).

Using Neisser's (1976) conception of anticipatory schemata (see Chapter Three), we might say that mastery of a skill means that one's relevant mental scheme carries out this executive function automatically. As the skill has become an integral part of the scheme, the scheme can be said to correspond to, or match, the code of the encountered message.

A coded message that corresponds less well to one's schemata, or internal representations, requires more mental effort for its recoding, as less well-mastered skills are to be applied to it. In other words, such a message requires more, and less well-mastered, mental elaborations. Greeno (1977, p. 12) points out that the difficulties many children experience with reading result, in part at least, from their deficient skills of translating graphic symbols into lexical entities: "Difficulty in decoding at the level of words and small phrases can cause a great deal of an individual's processing capacity to be used there, and when that occurs, there is less capacity left for the essential task of integrating the concepts of sentences into meaningful representations, and the propositions of a story into a meaningful structure." More proficient readers do not face such difficulties, as they have already mastered the necessary skills and carry them out automatically (LaBerge and Samuels, 1974).

It follows, then, that only coding elements that deviate from one's anticipatory schemata require skills of translation in which one is not proficient, thus leading to difficulties, errors, and variations among individuals. Writes Kintsch (1977, p. 315) with regard to the comprehension of stories, "Usually people tell a story in its natural order, and assuming they do so, the listener can disregard the cues indicating the order of events. However, when the story deviates from the natural order of events, the listener must use the linguistic structure to recover the natural order."

Anderson and others (1977, p. 377) make a similar point: "Distortions and intrusions will appear only where there is a lack of correspondence between the schemata embodied in the text and the schemata by which the reader assimilates the text." Bever (1970) has argued that in order to derive meaning from verbal messages, the listener uses mainly semantic strategies and performs syntactic analyses only when necessary. And such analyses are necessary when a discrepancy between external and internal modes is experienced. Thorndyke (1977) reports a study in which the effects of deleting the grammatical orderliness of a story were studied. When the theme line was deleted from the story, recall dropped from 80 percent to 58 percent. So did comprehension. Although no correlations between recall and skill-mastery were reported, one would expect them to be significantly higher under the deleted theme-line story condition.

To test whether alternative coding elements of a symbol system require different kinds of mental skills, one would need to use elements that deviate from the learners' internal schemata to a sufficient extent that variability among individuals can be observed. Only when such variability is present can a correlation with knowedge extraction be observed. And to test the proposition that alternative coding elements require different amounts of mental elaboration, one would need to choose elements that vary along the dimension of "deviation."

A range of deviations can be achieved in at least two ways. One way is to use a message that is as simple and straightforward as possible and does not entail unusual coding elements; its represented events would correspond to the way a young learner mentally conceives of such events. A second way is to use one coding element that deviates from learners' schemata and compare it with an alternative element that *overtly models, supplants, or simulates* some of the mental processes that the former element requires.

Consider a static picture of objects in space and a task requirement to show how these objects will look after a 270° rotation. Certain mental skills can be assumed to be *activated* under such conditions. Now, consider a film that actually shows how these objects rotate in space. Obviously, such a film would make the task relatively easy, as it overtly *supplants* the imagery processes that are required by the task. Whereas wide individual differences would be observed in the former case, a narrower range of variation would appear in the latter, as the film renders one's imagery skills relatively unnecessary.

This rationale leads to the following three hypotheses, which were tested experimentally.

1.   All other things being equal, messages that emphasize different coding elements call upon different kinds of mental skills in the service of knowledge extraction. Thus, the acquisition of knowledge from such messages depends on one's mastery of element-specific skills.

2.   All other things being equal, a message that emphasizes a coding element that supplants mental operations that another element calls upon saves mental elaboration and hence reduces the correlation between skill-mastery and knowledge extraction.

3.·   When a message is coded to use common coding elements that do not deviate greatly from learners' schemata, well-mastered skills are applied. Thus, only mastery of more general skills or abilities, but not element-specific ones, would correlate with knowledge acquisition from such a message.

The Television Experiment*

Subjects

The subjects were 220 fifth-graders, equally divided by sex, who were randomly assigned to view one of five film versions. There were 44 subjects in each group.

Materials

To test our hypotheses, some of the more salient coding elements of the symbol systems of film and television were chosen for manipulation. These represented three levels of

*A detailed description of the experiment can be found in Salomon and Cohen (1977).

symbolic articulation—the shot, the sequence, and the film. The coding elements of the close-up/long shot and the zoom-in/out were chosen from the level of the shot. Logical and spatial gaps (deletion of plot elements or of unifying spaces) were chosen to represent the level of the sequence. The level of film was represented by the nonnotational nature of pictorial depiction.

On the basis of these elements, five film versions of the same eight-minute television film were produced. The plot of all the versions was identical in all possible respects except the major coding element emphasized in each. The story line was about two youngsters who help in gardening to save money for their bicycles. One of them works hard, the other does not. The former finds a buried ancient jar and, upon handing it over to the house owner, receives a used pair of bicycles as a reward. These are stolen later by the other, less-industrious fellow.

One version of the television film was based on the *fragmentation of space* (FS version): Shots were taken from different points of view, conveying fragmented spaces that the viewer was expected to interrelate to acquire knowledge of the plot. The second version was based on *logical gaps* (LG version): Specific segments of four scenes were deleted, leaving brief gaps in the continuity of the plot. The third version was based on numerous *close-ups* interchanged with *long-shots* (the CU version). The fourth version was based on many zoom-ins and outs (the Z version). The latter two versions were produced so as to make the CU and Z versions completely identical, except for the fact that the shifts from long-shots to close-ups were accomplished by zoom-ins and outs in the Z version but were left out in the CU version. Thus, the Z version was expected to supplant the mental skills of connecting parts and wholes, which the CU version was expected to call upon. The fifth version emphasized *no unique coding elements in particular*. It was produced to be as simple and straightforward as possible (the O version).

Procedures

Each group of subjects was pretested on a battery of mental-skill tests one day preceding the viewing of the film. Prior to the viewing itself, subjects were told to pay close attention to the television monitors, as they would be asked questions about the film later. Posttests measuring knowledge acquisition were administered immediately following the film presentation.

Measures

The pretest battery included six tests that tap the mastery of specific mental skills corresponding to the manipulated coding elements. Two tests measured the ability to fill in missing gaps, which were mental skills that we expected to be required by the FS and the LG versions. The first, Closing Visual Gaps, required the subject to complete the sequence of a pictured story by choosing and inserting the correct pictured element (see Figure 1). The other test, Closing Verbal Gaps, required the subject to choose the sentence that correctly completed the sequence of a verbal story. A Space Construction test required subjects to rearrange positions of four separate and unordered components into an interrelated whole (see Figure 2). We expected performance on this test to correlate highly with knowledge acquisition in the FS version. Two tests required subjects to relate details to wholes. One test, Detail and Concept, measured the subject's ability to infer a missing detail from a picture, conceptualize its nature, and identify it in another picture (see Figure 3). In the second test, Detail and Whole, a detail of a drawing was presented alongside drawings of the whole object to measure ability to relate details to perceptual wholes (see Figure 4). We hypothesized that, although this skill is called upon in understanding all versions, it is particularly critical in the Close-up/Long-shot version. Finally, to construct cognitive relations in the LG and the CU versions, we anticipated that visual memory is required. We pretested subjects' ability to recall details after twenty-second exposure to a richly detailed drawing (see Figure 5).

The number of items within each test ranged from two items in the Visual Memory test to ten items in the Detail and Whole test. Cronbach alpha reliability coefficients ranged from 0.57 to 0.77. Although interrcorrelations between the six tests were moderate (0.02 to 0.50), a factor analysis of the test items yielded six factors with items of each test loading separately on

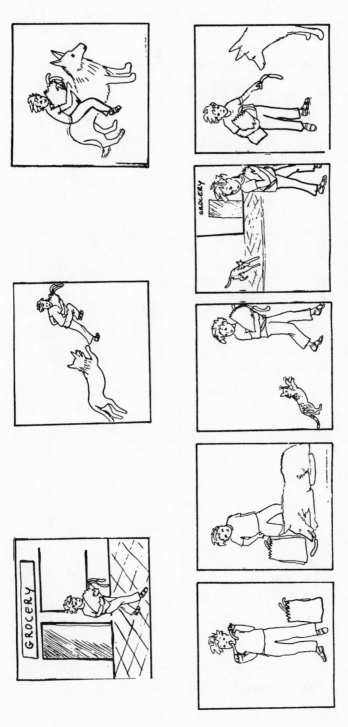

FIGURE 1. Sample Item from the Closing Visual Gaps Test.

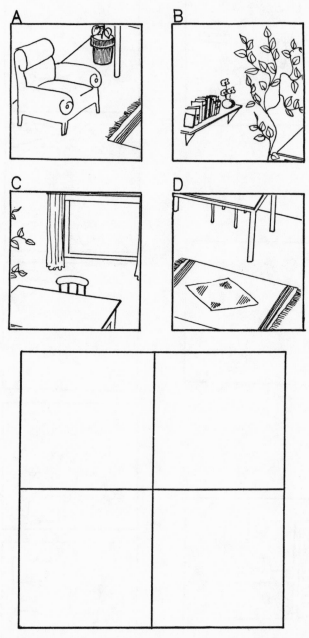

FIGURE 2. Sample Item from the Space Construction Test.

3

FIGURE 3. Sample Item from the Detail and Concept Test.

FIGURE 4. Sample Item from the Detail and Whole Test.

FIGURE 5. Sample Item from the Visual Memory Test.

one factor. We were able to assume, then, that the six tests measured six somewhat unique skills, and that the items within each test tapped the same skill.

Posttesting consisted of two knowledge-acquisition tests. A Specific Knowledge test consisted of twenty-four multiple-choice items directly related to the filmic content. A General Knowledge test consisted of three series of seven still pictures enlarged from the film, representing major events of the plot. Subjects had to reorder the random presentation in each series according to the plot.

Results

Table 1 summarizes the correlations between the six pretests and two posttests for viewers of each filmic version. The pattern of correlations across tests differs across versions of the film. Comparisons of the correlational patterns by Kendall's coefficient of concordance led to rejection of the null hypothesis of accordance among the correlational patterns for the Specific Knowledge Test ($p < 0.05$) and to a lesser extent for the General Knowledge test ($p < 0.10$). Since an analysis of variance on pretest scores indicated no significant difference among the five groups viewing the modified versions of the film, the different patterns of correlations do not reflect initial differences among subjects.

Specific knowledge acquisition in the Fragmented Space version required skill in relating details to conceptual whole ($r = 0.31$) and in closing visual gaps ($r = 0.42$); a similar pattern was required in the Logical Gaps version ($r = 0.39$ and $r = 0.35$, respectively). However, acquisition of specific knowledge in the logical gaps version also correlated with subjects' visual memory ($r = 0.32$), which was not the case with the Fragmented Space version ($r = -0.15$). Indeed, the Visual Memory test seems to have predicted performance only in the two versions in which the emphasized coding element disrupted continuity—that is, in the Logical Gaps version and in the Close-Up/Long-Shot version.

Specific knowledge acquisition in the Close-Up/Long-Shot version relied most heavily on the subjects' skills in relating details to conceptual wholes ($r = 0.67$) or perceptual wholes,

TABLE 1. Correlations Between Pretests and Posttests for Five Versions of the Film

	Pretests					
Film Version	Detail and Concept	Closing Visual Gaps	Closing Verbal Gaps	Detail and Whole	Visual Memory	Space Construction
Fragmented Space (FS)						
Specific Knowledge	0.31^a	0.42^b	0.23	0.10	-0.15	0.14
General Knowledge	0.07	0.33^a	0.12	0.19	0.16	0.42^b
Logical Gaps (LG)						
Specific Knowledge	0.39^b	0.35^a	0.18	0.17	0.32^a	0.26
General Knowledge	0.47^b	0.31^a	0.35^a	0.23	0.41^b	0.34^a
Close-Up/Long-Shots (CU)						
Specific Knowledge	0.67^b	0.18	0.16	0.32^a	0.33^a	0.33^a
General Knowledge	0.22	0.35^a	0.38^a	0.07	-0.11	0.40^a
Zooms (Z)						
Specific Knowledge	0.27	0.04	0.07	-0.03	0.03	0.07
General Knowledge	0.33^a	0.16	0.21	0.34^a	-0.02	0.37^a
Straightforward (O)						
Specific Knowledge	0.39^b	0.22	0.18	0.09	0.12	0.29
General Knowledge	0.10	0.14	0.27	0.16	0.18	0.21

[a] $p < 0.05$
[b] $p < 0.01$

(r = 0.32), visual memory (r = 0.33), and space construction (r = 0.33). This pattern is quite different from the one obtained in the Zoom version, in spite of their apparent similarity. This difference betwen the Close-Up/Long-Shot and Zoom correlational patterns strongly supports the expectation that element-specific skill-mastery is required for the acquisition of specific knowledge to the extent that the coding element deviates from the viewer's anticipatory schemata. Indeed, the Close-Up/Long-Shot version seems to call on specific skills, whereas the Zoom version overtly supplants them. Hence, initial mastery of the relevant skills is far less necessary for knowledge acquisition from the Zoom version.

Acquisition of specific knowledge from the straightforward (O) version correlated with only one measured skill—detail and concept. It is likely that specific knowledge acquisition correlates with other skills not measured here, skills of a more general kind, such as field-dependence (Koran, Snow, and McDonald, 1971) or spatial and abstract abilities (Cronbach and Snow, 1977). But general skills are expected to correlate with knowledge acquisition from all filmic versions, regardless of specific coding elements, since these skills pertain generally to the nonnotationality of film. In our study, the skill of relating details to conceptual wholes contributed to knowledge acquisition in nearly all versions and seems to be such a general skill pertaining to the more general nature of the studied symbol system.

For all groups, except the one viewing the Logical Gaps version, very low correlations between the two posttests (0.04 to 0.12) were observed, indicating that two quite independent aspects of knowledge acquisition were measured. However, in the Logical Gaps group, the two posttests correlated 0.48 (p < 0.01), suggesting that distortion of the total logic of the plot affected *both* aspects of knowledge acquisition. The low correlations between posttests in the other four groups also reflect the differential correlational patterns between pretests and posttests *within* each group. For example, in the Fragmented Space version, the Space Construction pretest correlated 0.14 with specific knowledge and 0.42 with general knowledge. Similar

TABLE 2. Means and Standard Deviations of the Two
Knowledge-Acquisition Tests for Each Group.

Posttest	FS	LG	_Group_ CU	Z	O
Specific Knowledge					
$\bar{X}$	11.22	11.88	9.84	12.60	13.30
S	5.70	5.10	5.58	6.06	6.12
General Knowledge					
$\bar{X}$	13.60	10.37	10.61	13.61	14.14
S	5.89	5.52	4.81	4.85	5.01

Note: N = 44 in each group.

differences across all groups indicate that the nature of the coding element interacts not only with the kinds of skills required
but also with the kinds of knowledge acquired. This suggests
that a three-way interaction exists when extracting information
from symbol systems—among coding elements, the requisite
skills, and the psychological demands of the task. I will return
to this point later.

Finally, we examined the mean knowledge-acquisition
scores of the five groups. These are presented in Table 2. As can
be seen in the table, groups differed significantly from each
other in terms of amount of specific knowledge and general
knowledge acquired (Overall $F(4,219) = 8.72$ and $7.41, p < 0.01$,
respectively).

A Newman-Keuls test performed on each posttest to
determine which groups significantly differ from which other
groups resulted in the following ordering of groups (groups that
are underlined by the same solid line do not have significantly
different means).

Specific Knowledge:

      O   Z   LG   FS   CU

General Knowledge:

      O   Z   FS   LG   CU

On both posttests, the O and Z groups had the highest means, and the CU group had the lowest. The high means of the O and Z versions support the expected effects of isomorphism (or absence of deviation from internal representation) and of supplantation. Achievement can be at its highest either when presentations are made to correspond to a learner's internal mode of presentation or when presentations overtly carry out necessary transformations for the learner. As the otherwise necessary mental skills are either automatic or overtly supplanted, achievement is not debilitated by subjects of poor skill-mastery. The lower means of the CU group can be understood along the same lines. If achievement correlates highly ($r = 0.67$) with skill-mastery, subjects with poor mastery necessarily depress the mean.

It is interesting to note also that the LG group performed poorly on the General Knowledge test. Only in the LG and the CU versions was some information deleted from the presentation, thus requiring subjects to supplement it from internal sources. Indeed, these were the groups in which visual memory was a needed ability for specific knowledge acquisition, and closing verbal gaps was needed for general knowledge acquisiton. Thus, it appears that these two versions employed the most mentally demanding coding elements, as they deviated more than the other versions from the subjects' internal schemata.

Discussion

The purpose of this study was to examine whether different coding elements within a symbol system are related to differences among requisite mental skills for knowledge acquisition when content is held constant. The rationale guiding the study was twofold. First, if coding elements differentially affect mental skills, the claim is empirically substantiated that "in mediated experience, or instruction, the content of the medium relates to the knowledge acquired while . . . the code in which the message is represented is related to the skills . . . that are called upon" (Olson, 1976, p. 21). The results indicated that different coding elements, typical of film and television, do call upon different kinds of mental skills. Thus, in spite of common content, knowledge acquisition is mediated by different kinds of skills, depending on the representational nature of the dominant coding element. This supports the major hypothesis of the study and the conceptual approach suggested here—that codes of media are critical attributes.

Secondly, this experiment has shown that differences of skill-mastery correlate with knowledge extraction as a function of the "distance" between external and internal codes. The straightforward version, which was the most common and least contrived one, hardly called upon any measured skills that the subjects have not well mastered already.

It is possible that knowledge acquisition from the O version could have correlated with other skills, whose mastery we have not measured. However, assuming that a relatively wide range of skills was measured by us, representing different domains of ability, this possibility is quite unlikely. The O version was apparently in better correspondence to the way our subjects process such information than the other versions. It deviated least from the perceived "natural order of events" (Kintsch, 1977), or the viewer's anticipatory schemata. Thus, it required more "automatic" skills than the other versions. Additional evidence to substantiate this claim can be found when the CU and Z versions are compared. The CU version called upon a number of skills—primarily the skill of relating details to conceptual wholes. Knowledge acquisition from this version highly depended on that skill's mastery, but not so in the Z version, in which the same skill was overtly simulated for the viewers. By overtly supplanting the skill, its utilization is circumvented, thus giving the learners of different levels of skill-mastery a more even start. Indeed, the mean learning-scores of the Z and the O versions were significantly higher than those of the other versions.

Another important finding of the study was the different pattern of correlations between skills and knowledge acquisition *within* each version. This finding, although not unexpected, focuses attention on the three-way interaction among the mental requirements of the symbolic elements, the subjects' mental repertoire, and the mental requirements of the knowledge-acquisition task. This offers some modification of Olson's contention, quoted previously. The content of a message does indeed relate to knowledge acquisition, but not independently of the skills that are called into play by the code. The acquisition of different kinds of knowledge (in this case, specific reconstruction of details and overall comprehension of logic), are served by different mental skills. This is much in agreement with Fodor's contention (1975, p. 165) that "the subject affects a rational correspondence between his performance and (what he takes to be) the demand characteristics of the experimental task."

Additional Considerations

Our experiment supports the proposition that coding elements vary with respect to the mental skills they require. In light of the other evidence cited in Chapter Three it is reasonable to apply this finding to symbol systems. But this proposition leads to two further considerations. The first concerns the range of stimuli, from whole environments to specific coding elements, as it relates to mental skills. The second concerns the role that learning tasks play in these relationships.

I have argued earlier that the skeleton hypothesis—symbol systems vary as to the skills they require—holds for whole symbol systems as well as for smaller coding elements. However, while the same general rule may apply whether music is compared with, say, poetry, or a zoom-in with a close-up in film, it would be unreasonable to claim that skills of the same *magnitude* are involved. More likely, the size of the symbol unit involved (for example, cartography in general versus contour lines) will be related to the generality of the skills called upon. When larger symbol units are involved, more general skills are called for, and when smaller units are involved, more specific skills are employed. This, then, implies two hierarchies—one for symbol systems, ranging from whole systems to specific coding elements, and one for abilities, ranging from general ability to highly specific aptitudes. It can be argued that these two hierarchies parallel each other, although I would hesitate to postulate a perfect match between the two.

This leads to the second point to be considered, namely,

the role that the task to be performed plays in this equation. By postulating that different symbol systems and specific coding elements require different mental skills, we seem to assume that the *same* required mental skills are *always* activated by symbol systems or specific elements. But mental processes, activated upon encountering a particular coding element, serve a purpose. The purpose is usually the extraction of knowledge from the coded message. However, there is never *one* and *only one* kind of knowledge to be extracted from a coded message, particularly when the message is nonnotational or dense. Nor are there necessarily *predetermined* levels or amounts of knowledge to be extracted. There are many ways to read a book or to watch a movie, and one can choose the depth of processing. The code, then, cannot be the only factor that determines for a specific person which mental processes are to be activated.

Wanner (1968) has shown in his study on the relationships between complexity of verbal statements and levels of recall that the kind of transformational processes activated in learners depended not only on sentence complexity but also on the instructions the learners were given. A similar pattern emerged in our experiment reported earlier. The different correlational patterns between skill-mastery and type of knowledge acquisition measured by the posttests suggest that the perception of the learning task to be performed participates in determining which mental skills are relevant.

Either an externally imposed or a personally chosen task can determine the kind of information one would select for acquisition and processing. Research on instruction bears this out (for instance, Pichert and Anderson, 1977). Thus, with specific anticipations in mind, the person is likely to deal more with some coding elements than with others. A motorist studying a map to find the next road intersection is not very likely to invest much mental effort in transforming coding elements whose messages pertain to elevation. In two studies by Salomon and Sieber (1970), subjects were asked either to generate hypotheses as to the plot of two short films or to report many factual details observed in them. Two versions of each film were produced—a straightforward, logically sequenced version and a randomly edited one. Results showed that, while the hypothesis-generation task led the subjects to handle mainly the overall structural codes of the films, instructions to notice factual details led them to notice other elements.

Olson (1970) theorized that each performatory act entails different choice points, and that selection between choice points requires different kinds of information. Hence, drawing an apple requires different information than catching one when thrown at you. It follows that, when given a coded message, different coding elements are regarded as justifying one's attention (and hence, application of relevant skills), depending on the task to be performed. *Task requirements, whether imposed or self-selected, determine what kinds of information are to be extracted, and this choice determines in turn what kinds of coding elements within the message are to be addressed.*

As suggested by Calfee and Drum (1978) with respect to reading, processing of coding elements seems to operate in two contrasting directions. One direction of processing starts from the coding element through a number of mental elaborations until meaning is construed. This is a "bottom-up" direction of processing, much like the one suggested by Gough and Cosky (1977) with respect to reading letters and words. However, it is reasonable to assume in light of our findings that that "bottom-up" processing is complemented or even guided by a "top-down" direction of processing. It is akin to the way McConkie and Rayner (1976, p. 154) describe reading a text. They assume that "reading is primarily an activity of generating hypotheses or guesses about the text yet to be encountered, and then using a small part of the visual details to check the accuracy of these hypotheses."

The perception of the task, as described earlier, determines what information is to be picked up and hence what coding elements are to be processed. This is a "top-down" process. However, the processing of the coding elements and the extracting of meaning from the messages coded by them is a "bottom-up" process. Following recent claims made about reading (for example, Goodman and Goodman, 1977), it is reasonable to expect that, during the time a learner acquires the skills needed to "read" the symbolic forms used in the media, the "bottom-up" direction dominates. With proficiency, however, as skills become automatically employed and organized into larger skill units, the "top-down" direction begins to dominate.

This contention is partly supported by Huston-Stein and Wright (1977), who studied the effects of television's formal (symbolic) formats on children's comprehension. Their findings are that younger children are more attentive to single, formal formats (such as special visual and auditory effects), and older ones attend more to content. For the latter, formal features become limited to "those which best serve as syntactic markers for the interpretation of the meaning of the content" (p. 11).

The contention that the task determines what information is to be picked up, and that this in turn determines what coding elements are to be skillfully dealt with, does not imply, however, that other, *task-irrelevant* skills are not also activated. In the Salomon and Sieber (1970) studies mentioned previously, it was found that subjects who were exposed to the randomly edited film and were asked to notice factual details performed quite poorly. The randomly edited film seemed to have aroused in them a state of uncertainty, consequently setting off a process of information search that was irrelevant—even dysfunctional—to the required task. Had only task-specific mental skills been activated in the subjects, there would have been no difference in performance between the logical and random film groups.

Thus, while a learner negotiates a message to extract task-determined information, he encounters many coding elements, but only some carry the expected information. These coding elements, to the extent that they significantly deviate from the learner's internal representation, need to be skillfully transformed. However, some of the skills that are applied to them can be irrelevant to the psychological demands of the task. When a learner is to compare two statements, each of which is grammatically so complex that it demands elaborate transformations, task-irrelevant mental skills are activated. Similarly, in the Salomon and Sieber studies, the randomly edited films activated mental processes that were dysfunctional for noticing

discrete facts but conducive to the task of hypothesis generation. The logically sequenced film, on the other hand, did not
facilitate hypothesis generation, since it did not arouse task-
relevant mental states of uncertainty.

We can, then, distinguish between the *cognitive effects* of
a symbol system and its instructional *effectiveness*. To elaborate
on an argument advanced elsewhere (Salomon, 1974a), the
effects of symbol systems or coding elements are the mental
skills they call upon in the service of information extraction, as
determined by the task. The *effectiveness* of communicating
through a particular symbol system depends on the match, or
the correspondence, between the mental skills that are thus activated and the skill requirements of the task. Whereas *effects*
reflect the interaction between a symbol system and one's
mastery of the needed mental skills, *effectiveness* reflects the
interaction between the activated mental skills and the skill-
requirements of the task.

The effectiveness of employing a symbol system for
instructional purposes depends on the extent to which the
specifically selected coding elements activate in the learners
mental skills that are sufficiently mastered by them and are relevant to the requirements of the learning task. One medium will
yield the same learning outcomes as another whenever *common
coding elements* are employed, leading in effect to the activa-
tin of the same (task-relevant or irrelevant) mental skills. *On the
other hand, when different coding elements are used, different
mental skills will be activated. To the extent that some of them
are more task-relevant than others, one medium will yield better
learning outcomes than another.*

Finally, since different symbol systems can activate
different sets of skills, they may be expected to differentially
serve learners of different abilities. Symbol systems can interact
with individual differences either by capitalizing on learners'
strengths or by compensating for learners' skill-deficiencies
(Salomon, 1971; Cronbach and Snow, 1977). Koran, Snow, and
McDonald (1971) found that subjects scoring high on a test of
field-dependency (have difficulties in separating an event from
its field) better acquired the teaching behavior of asking analytic

questions when shown a live model on videotape. More field-independent subjects learned better from a script presenting essentially the same information. These findings illustrate the interaction of symbol systems with learners' aptitudes.

Summary

This chapter examines more closely the proposition that symbol systems vary with respect to the mental skills they require. As it is difficult to experimentally compare symbol systems because of covariation of content, one needs to reduce the size of the symbolic units under investigation to coding elements within a system.

However, to see whether such elements indeed call upon different mental skills, one needs to compare sufficiently difficult elements—that is elements that deviate sufficiently from subjects' internal schemata and thus require skills less than perfectly mastered.

The hypotheses derived from this discussion were tested in a television experiment. Two hundred twenty fifth-graders were shown one of five versions of the same television film. The only difference between the versions was the coding element emphasized in each. The results have shown that the extraction of knowledge from each version depended on the mastery of different mental skills, thus supporting the major hypothesis. We also found that a common version, which did not emphasize any unusual coding element, corresponded well with the subjects' mental schemata. Thus, knowledge acquisition from it did not correlate with any of the specific skills we measured. In addition, a version in which a coding element overtly supplanted a needed skill made its mastery relatively unnecessary. Finally, we found that the activation of specific skills depended not only on the coding elements but also on the task that the subjects had to perform.

Two additional considerations were discussed. The first concerned the range of stimuli—from whole environments to specific coding elements—as it interacts with human abilities. I proposed the existence of two hierarchies—one ranging from whole symbol systems to specific coding elements, the other ranging from the more general to more specific human abilities and skills. These two hierarchies, I proposed, are generally parallel to each other. Thus, large stimulus units call upon more general abilities, and smaller coding elements call upon more specific skills.

But this proposal wrongly assumes that only the symbol system or specific coding element determines the kind and size of the skill that is called upon. The missing element is the *task* to be performed. Much depends on how a learner can, or wishes to, approach a message—that is, what "interpretive standard" (Roupas, 1977) one applies to the message. Even a dense picture can be read like a printed page. As Goodman (1968) points out, the mere presence or absence of letters or figures in maps, diagrams, or film does not make the difference. *What matters is how we are to read them.* Thus, I argued that the perception of the task to be performed determines the kind of information one wishes to extract from a coded message, thus entailing a "top-down" type of processing. In the service of extracting that information, codes are encountered and mental skills are brought to bear on them to transform then from external into internal representations, where meaning is assigned to them. This is a "bottom-up" process.

Learning can be facilitated to the extent that the activated skills are relevant to the demands of the learning task. Thus, when the task calls for some act of analytic comparison and the coded message activates imagery instead, the learning may be debilitated. For effective instructional communication, a match needs to be established between the cognitive demands of a learning task, the skills that are required by the codes of the message, and the learner's level of mastery of these skills. Thus, aptitude-treatment interactions between codes and learners can be expected.

FIVE

Cultivation of Mental Skills Through Symbolic Forms

In the preceding chapter, I discussed the proposition that since media utilize different symbol systems, they vary as to the mental operations they require. My next proposition is that media can cultivate the mastery of mental skills through the differential effects of the symbol systems they use. This, if supported, should be in keeping with Edward Sapir's claim that the product–thought–grows with the tools and media we use (Bruner, Olver, and Greenfield, 1966). In light of what has been said thus far, there should be little doubt that increased experience with coded messages improves one's skill in extracting information from such messages. However, one's experience with media's symbol systems may encompass more than the improved mastery of skills that serve better information extraction from the media. Eisner (1976, p. 6) expects from media and art more than the mere cultivation of "media literacy": "When in a culture certain expressive forms prevail, people are covertly encouraged to do *their thinking* in these modes of expression." Tikomirov (1974), analyzing the possible cognitive effects of computers, hypothesized that computers serve as a new tool for mental activity and "thereby transform thought." Although not yet emprically tested, such a hypothesis is of great interest, as it pertains to the cultivation of relatively general and widely transferable mental abilities.

These speculations raise two questions, which this chapter will attempt to answer. One question pertains to the ways in which media's symbol systems can affect the mastery of mental skills. To answer this question, we will need to look into the psychological mechanisms that may account for such effects. The second question is whether media's symbol systems can cultivate the mastery of mental skills that have utility *beyond* their application to the media that developed them. This question pertains to the transfer value of the mental skills that are cultivated by symbol sysems.

Cultivation Through Skill-Activation and Practice

Kolers (1976) asked subjects to practice reading inverted (upside-down) printed texts. Retesting them more than a year later, Kolers found the subjects to exhibit significantly improved mastery of the practiced skill. Such a finding demonstrates a known observation: Skills that are required for the extraction of knowledge become gradually better mastered. They become increasingly more automatic, less effortful, and less time-consuming, and they create less stress on one's mental capacity than so-called controlled processes (Shiffrin and Schneider, 1977).

According to Schneider and Shiffrin (1977), once processes become automatic, they are triggered by appropriate stimuli and operate independently of a subject's control. Thus, for instance, a skilled reader would be expected to process automatically surface structures of the texts (such as letters) but to employ controlled processes, which require attention and are capacity-limited, for the conceptual properties of a passage. With practice, more of the controlled processes become automatic, thus permitting the reader to process texts with greater ease. Shiffrin and Schneider write (1977, p. 170):

> For example, the child learning to read would first give control processing and then give automatic processing to various units of information. The sequence of automatically learned units might be foreground-background, features, shapes, letters, words, and meanings of phrases or sentences. The child would be utilizing controlled processing to lay down "stepping stones" of automatic processing as he moves on to more and more difficult levels of learning. The transition from controlled to automatic processing at each stage would result in reduced discrimination time, more attention to higher order features, and ignoring of irrelevant information.

As I have proposed in preceding chapters, one needs to translate, or recode, the information presented in a communicational code into an internal code. This operation results in the extraction of knowledge. To the extent that this extracted information is in accordance with what the person wished (or was required) to extract, the operations involved would be reinforced. With practice, their mastery would be improved and become automatic. As this procedure is well known and established, there is no need at present to further elaborate upon its details. Suffice it to say that media's symbol systems would be expected to cultivate the mastery of specific mental skills of code-transformation through the mechanism of *activation* to the extent that such skills are automatically utilized in the service of knowledge extraction.

Symbols as Tools of Thought

Cultural symbol systems, media's systems included, are claimed to cultivate skills in another, far more interesting way. Eisner mentions one's ability *to think in terms* of culture's expressive forms. Olson (1977b, p. 9) similarly postulates that "skill in the use of symbolic code constitutes a mode of thought" inasmuch as one is capable of "dissecting nature or creating artifacts in terms of whatever symbol system one considers relevant, useful, or interesting." Von Bertalanffy (1965) writes of our tremendous capabilities as symbol-creating and symbol-using creatures. The symbols we use in thinking, he maintains, are mainly cultural; their acquisition by the young—the distinctive character of human symbolism—develops their thought processes. Roger Brown (1965, p. 334), referring to language, writes, "Apparently an entity that can be efficiently transmitted from one member to another of the same linguistic community can be efficiently retained from one occasion to another by a single member of the community. When an effective message can be composed for others, an effective message can be composed for oneself. Encoding into the spoken language seems to be useful for information storage and retrieval." Indeed, when Blank and Solomon (1968) suggested verbal tutoring of disadvantaged children, their purpose was not to improve the children's language. Rather, they expected the verbal concepts to be used in *thought*.

All this assumes that symbols serve a dual function—as vehicles for communication and as vehicles for thought. This implies, in addition, some isomorphism between communicational and mental coding elements, an issue I have discussed in preceding chapters. Such isomorphism was assumed by Metzler and Shepard (1974), who stated that for the correct execution of specific spatial operations such as mental rotations, the internal representation or process has to correspond to the external object or its transformation. A similar argument is raised by Huttenlocher (1973).

This dual conception of symbol systems implies not only some isomorphism between external and internal coding but also *the adoption of the external for internal use*. As the developing child cannot be expected to reinvent culture's symbol systems, he uses some of their components in thinking and must somehow internalize them for covert use. Thus, for example, one seems to use language in thought (Bruner, Olver, and Greenfield, 1966), to visualize in terms of filmic slow motion (Lesser, 1974), or to mentally manipulate images adopted from television (Singer, in press).

A graduate student at Stanford University provided the following personal account:

> I am fascinated by how my daydreaming is influenced by movies. Processes and techniques of presenting events by this Hollywood symbol system are powerfully implanted within my cognitive system. I have observed third person narration, flashbacks, zooms, slow-motion emphasis of action, audience viewing, re-takes, "voice of conscience," multipersonality dialogue, background music, and many other movie means of expression in my head. I fear that there is very little original style to my daydreaming. It is all influenced by celluloid. . . . There are scenes where I am climbing steps to address a large audience, and television shots in slow motion symbolize the slow and hard road to this point in my career. There are zoom-ins to significant others and flashbacks to significant moments.

Even if we agree that external symbols are adopted for internal use in thought, we need to ask what functions such adopted symbols accomplish in thought. Huttenlocher and Higgins (in press) defined symbolic processes as entailing two kinds of mental elements—symbol (the mental representation) and a signification (the stored meaning, or referent). Based on this conception, the authors then argue that stored concepts of objects or events that represent or preserve information about those entities do not designate them (as words do). Thus, such concepts are not symbols that are linked to other mental elements but rather are basic mental entries of particular ideas. It follows, then, that concepts of objects or events, not being symbolic, cannot be adopted directly from external symbols.

Unlike concepts in long-term memory, Huttenlocher and Higgins argue, representations in active memory are symbolic, because they are linked to stored concepts in long-term memory. "The most obvious examples are those where mental processes involve elements which are isomorphic with external symbol tokens, like mathematical symbols, graphs, and so on. Such mental processes seem clearly symbolic" (Huttenlocher and Higgins, in press, p. 18).

It follows from Huttenlocher and Higgins' distinction between concepts in long-term memory (which are not symbolic) and representations in active memory (which are symbolic), that adaptation of external symbols for internal use is restricted to active memory. But this, it seems to me, is somewhat too restrictive. First, concepts stored in long-term memory serve in a representational capacity and thus are elements in a two-element structure, as the authors' definition requires. The stored concept of, say, *analysis* is designated for communicational purposes by a word, a gesture, a graph, and the like, and thus serves as the denotatum for such communicational symbols. But at the same time it also serves to internally represent—as a symbol— external events that really are, or are externally designated as, *analyses*. Second, a mental concept serves as a nodal point, a summary or anchor to a host of associations, stored memories, meanings, and experiences that are subsumed under it. Not always does the whole underlying structure need to be retrieved, yet it *can* be retrieved when needed. The concept serves as an internal representation of the structure subsumed under it and thus is the symbol for some denotata. It follows, then, that external symbols, depending on their compoundness and complexity, can become adapted for internal use for both long-term and active memory.

Language in Thought

We are faced with the question of whether components of a symbol system can be adapted for covert mental use. As language is our most elaborate symbol system, we ought to be able to learn from its extensive study something about the possible covert use of other symbol systems. The well-known Whorfian hypothesis comes readily to mind, as it directly addresses itself to the relationship between a cultural symbol system and thought. According to this hypothesis, "We dissect nature along lines laid down by our native language . . . the world is presented in a kaleidoscopic flux of impressions which has to be organized by our minds—and this means largely by the linguistic systems in our minds" (Whorf, 1956, p. 212).

Research on the Whorfian hypothesis developed along two lines—examination of a weak version of the hypothesis, that our perceptions are influenced by our language, and an examination of a strong version, that language determines our cognitions. Results, however, were generally confusing and ambiguous. Brown and Lennenberg (1954), in an often cited study, sought to find a relationship between the ease of naming, or coding, a color and the ease with which it is remembered. They reasoned that the more easily named colors are more frequently discriminated by the English-speaking community and therefore should have greater cognitive saliency (be better remembered). A low correlation between color codability and memory in a recognition task was found. Increasing task-difficulty resulted in a higher correlation. A replication of the study among the Zuni Indians upheld these findings (Lennenberg and Roberts, 1956), thus seemingly supporting the weak version of the Whorfian hypothesis.

In another series of studies, by Stefflre, Vales, and Morley (1966), in which communication accuracy replaced codability, substantial correlations were found with recognition scores. Such findings were replicated with native speakers of different languages, which vary as to their color differentiation. Thus, it would seem that ease of communication reflects ease of internal coding, and that language provides the tool for both internal and communicational coding.

However, other studies have failed to provide additional support to the hypothesis. When colors are similar to each other, it is the *less*-codable one that is better remembered (Lennenberg, 1961). Moreover, when the prototypical colors (the *focal* colors) are selected by native speakers of twenty languages, they are given shorter names *universally* and are better remembered by speakers of entirely different languages. This, then, may lead to the conclusion that underlying perceptual, cognitive factors influence the formation and reference of linguistic categories (Heider, 1972), not the other way around.

Studying the stronger version of the Whorfian hypothesis, Carroll and Casagrande (1958) found that the syntactic structure of language somewhat influences one's way of grouping objects, but that perceptual experience has a *similar* effect. Cole and others (1969) have found, contrary to predictions from Whorf's hypothesis, that the language structure of the Kpelle in Liberia has no influence on discrimination learning of Kpelle children. Some stimulus properties, they note, exert stronger control over behavior than language.

In their summary of the relevant research, Cole and Scribner (1974) conclude that, although Whorf's hypothesis has not received systematic support, it is difficult to reject totally at least the weak version of it. Most studies were carried out with a limited range of stimuli. The influence of language on cognition could be better tested with stimulus categories whose attributes are assigned by culture, not nature (for instance, social roles rather than colors). The observation of universally common perceptions does not rule out also culturally specific ones. But these would be found in areas in which differences among languages reflect more than just different lexicons, as pointed out previously.

Most importantly, we should note the noninteractional, univariate nature of Whorf's strong version of the hypothesis. Language is supposed to *shape* ideas and thought, to *guide* mental activity, even to *determine* it. Thus, research that attempted to test such strong claims had to imply, for instance, that if a certain language does not have names for specific colors, the colors would not be easily recognized. Similarly, if the verbs in a language are object-specific, the grouping of objects in that culture would differ from that of another culture in which verbs are object-independent.

In light of what is presently known in psycholinguistics and language development, such expectations appear to be somewhat naive. Could not language become a tool of thought without necessarily being its *cause* and without becoming the *only* vehicle for thought? Coming from a subtropical cultural zone, my familiarity with snow is very limited. My vocabulary includes fewer terms for snow than even that of a New Englander, let alone an Eskimo. But this does not mean that while attempting to balance myself on cross-country skis I do not detect the difference between kinds of snow. Some kinds I find to be easier for skiing than others. Some of these I can more easily code by means of available language codes than others ("icy snow" or "dull colored, soft, white snow"). Experience directs certain perceptions and distinctions, to which labels are then attached. In this context, Carroll (1974, pp. 162-163) may be correct in stating that, "Even if one restricts thought to those activities that can be carried on and formulated in linguistic symbols—and this is by no means all that there is to thought—one can be quite sure that thought is independent of language in the sense that its operations can occur independently of the particular language symbols and structures that are available in which to formulate it. Clothing thought in language is an operation that, as it were, takes place posteriorly to the act of thought."

Given such a claim, could it be that language not only does not determine thought, but that it follows thought altogether? And if this is the case with language, what grounds do we have to assume that other symbol systems operate differently?

Fodor (1975) strongly argued against the role of language in thought. Thinking, he claimed, goes on at a level deeper than the conscious use of words and in a different modality altogether—*mentalese*. Each word is a unit in the lexicon of mentalese. Most importantly, Fodor's argument is that a word in one's native language is understood by translating it into an item of the internal mentalese. Thus, each word in communicational language has its counterpart in mentalese.

But where does mentalese come from? If it is learned, then what is *it* related to in the *preceding* mentaleses? To avoid endless regress, Fodor postulates an internal language that is *innate*, a claim that he himself calls "horrendous" and "scandalous," yet inescapable. Schlesinger (1977a) strongly criticized Fodor's contentions on the grounds that Fodor assumes too much and predicts too little. Indeed, Fodor's nativism appears to be too high a price to pay, as it contradicts most of the research in language acquisition and cognitive development. Consider a few examples. Olson (1977b) reports a study by Ives in which children's ability to report another person's point of view in a three-mountain problem was enhanced by tutoring them in labeling the proper dimensions. Similar results are reported by Luria (1961) in support of his theory of the development of self-regulation through internalized speech. The well-known series of studies by the Kendlers (1962) on the development of reversal and nonreversal shifts in children clearly points to the mediational role played by linguistic concepts. As children become capable of using internal mediation, their ability to exhibit reversal shifts improves over that of performing nonreversal shifts.

The findings by the Kendlers could be interpreted as assigning language the determining role over cognition. However, one should note the importance of cognitive development in their studies. The ability to mediate through verbal concepts is a function not only of linguistic input but of cognitive maturation as well. Sinclair de Zwart (1967) tried to train nonconserving children to conserve. She taught them words that expressed the principles of conservation that were mastered and used by conservers. The experiment yielded mixed results. However, a similar experiment concerned with seriation yielded significant improvements. It appears that, as with the Kendlers, linguistic input has its effect on cognition, provided it is preceded by the necessary cognitive development.

Schlesinger (1977b) summarized the pertinent research and tried to bridge the gap betwen theories of cognitive determinism and hypotheses of linguistic input. Cognitive determinism (represented by Carroll, Fodor, or Piaget) would claim that concepts and relations that underlie language and constitute meaning are formed by cognitive development and are only expressed linguistically. The claim negates the notion that concepts or relations are formed as a result of a child's interaction with language, as claimed by environmentalists. The latter would claim that the child's linguistic experience accounts in part for the acquisition of concepts underlying language.

Schlesinger suggests that, when a child first encounters certain aspects of his surroundings, he may understand them only vaguely, but the manner in which his parents talk about them points to more specific distinctions, categorizations, and meanings. At the same time, however, cognitive development, independent of linguistic input, may facilitate the linguistic input. The knowledge gained from dealing with the environment sugsequently converges with that gained from the language that describes this environment. For instance, a child learns the categories of proper and common nouns through the interplay between his experience with such objects and the linguistic distinctions provided by the environment. The child becomes alerted to notice certain attributes in the environment through language, reinforcing already made, extralinguistic distinctions (see also Clark and Clark, 1977, and Rosch and Mervis, 1975, on the extralinguistic perception of natural categories).

Schlesinger (1977a) is led to distinguish between nonlinguistic thinking, which is associated with immediate, uncategorized experience, and linguistic thinking, which is mediated by semantic structures (corresponding roughly to the level of deep structure in generative grammar) and is subject to categorization and interpretations imposed by language. The preverbal child has only nonlinguistic thinking available, but linguistic thinking emerges from interaction with a language community. *Ultimately*, although not initially, a child "computes" thoughts in those structures, which serve in the production and comprehension of speech. Thus, the internal language which eventually emerges from learning the native language is firmly grounded on the latter.

Although language is not the source or cause of thought as Whorf claimed, it does play a vital role in thinking. "A modicum of cognitive development must precede any learning of language, because language remains meaningless unless referring to some already interpreted aspect of the environment. However, once some structuring of the environment has occurred and some primitive utterances can be understood in accordance with this structure, there is room for an influence of the form of these utterances on the child's cognitive development: they may direct him toward further interpreting events and states referred to"

(Schlesinger, 1977b, p. 21). Thus, linguistic input appears to prime cognitive operations, even to trigger them, but not before the ground is prepared by prior (extralinguistic and lower-level linguistic) developments.

Internalization of Language and Other Symbol Systems

Language that figures in thought comes from the outside world of communication. How then is it transformed from a communicational symbol system into an internal, mediational one? Vygotsky (1962) and later Luria (1976), working within a Marxian interactionist framework, suggest that language is interiorized, or internalized, by the child. Writes Luria, (1976, p. 9) "Children assimilate language—a readymade product or sociohistorical development—and use it to analyze, generalize, and encode experience." Not only words but also grammatical structures are interiorized; thus, "Humans have at their disposal a powerful objective tool that permits them not only to reflect individual objects or situations but to create objective logical codes" (p. 10). This, in turn, results in one's ability to deal with logical propositions that are far removed from daily experience as well as with abstract operations using "discursive thinking."

Vygotsky (1962) developed a theory according to which children's early thoughts and early language are independent of each other. Gradually, however, thought becomes verbally expressed, while language is internalized to become "inner speech," which is in effect "speech that turns into inward thought" (1962, p. 131). "Egocentric speech is a phenomenon of the transition from interpsychic to intrapsychic functioning, that is, from the social, collective activity of the child to his more individualized activity—a pattern of development common to all the higher psychological functions. Speech for oneself originates through differentiation from speech for others. Since the main course of the child's development is one of gradual individualization, this tendency is reflected in the function and structure of his speech" (p. 133).

Inspired by Vygotsky's research, Luria conducted a large-scale study in Central Asia, observing the cognitive changes that have taken place there following the introduction of collectivization and schooling of the villagers. Observations led him to conclude that as the sociohistorical manifestations of language were gradually internalized by the villagers, "graphic" thinking processes were transformed "into a scheme of semantic and logical operations in which words become the principal tool for abstraction and generalization" (1978, p. 52).

Vygotsky does not claim that thought is *created* by language, as Whorf would have it. The internalization of language results in a *reorganization* of thinking into higher order functional systems. Still, *internalization* serves as the key process. Even Fodor (1975, p. 83), the opponent of such views, finds it necessary to qualify his general argument by stating that, "though it might be admitted that the initial computations involved in first language learning cannot themselves be run in the language being learned, it could nevertheless still be claimed that a foothold in the language having once been gained, the child then proceeds by extrapolating his boot straps: The fragment of the language first internalized is itself somehow essentially employed to learn the part that's left. This process eventually leads to the construction of a representational system more elaborate than the one the child started with, and this richer system mediates the having of thoughts the child could not otherwise have entertained."

Olson (1970) rejects both the notion of internalization of language, as suggested by Vygotsky, and of actions, as suggested by Piaget. Rather, language, actions, or images, when used in a performatory task that creates choice points for its execution, provide the occasion for picking up the information needed for selection among the choices. Hence, specific information is acquired, but the actions or symbol systems are not. Such a conception, however, does not account for the use of symbols as internal representations allowing, as Olson claims elsewhere (1977b), manipulation and organization of new information. Thus, although the conception of internalized language may still be vague, we have no plausible alternatives to replace it with.

This chapter began by asking whether components of symbol systems used by the media can affect cognition by improving skill-mastery. I argued that codes require skills and thus cultivate them. I then turned to a more intriguing possibility—namely, that some communication codes can become mental tools—and examined studies on language and thought. The Whorfian hypothesis was too deterministic on both empirical and theoretical grounds and needed to be modified. Schlesinger's hypothesis, which takes into consideration the interplay between cognitive development and linguistic input, appeared to be the most promising alternative. This led to the question of how language is translated into thought, and Vygotsky's theory of internalized language appeared to be a good answer.

Vygotsky is very much in line with Bruner, Olver, and Greenfield's claim (1966, p. 56) that "Any implement system (that is, amplifiers of human motor, sensory, and ratiocinative capacities) to be effective must produce an appropriate internal counterpart." It is now possible to amend this claim by arguing that, to the extent that the analogy between media's symbol systems and language holds, such internal "counterparts" result from the internalization of the "implement systems." Let us examine this further.

Language is not the *only* symbol system that participates in thinking (see Chapters Three and Four). Miller, Shelton, and Flavell (1970) have tried to replicate one of Luria's studies concerning the use of externally provided verbal instructions for self-regulation by three- and four-year-olds. Although they failed to replicate Luria's findings, Flavell (1977) did not reject the internalization conception. Rather, he interpreted the failure as resulting from the assumption that only internalized *language* can serve for self-regulation. Other, nonlinguistic modes could serve equally well, or even better, for some children. Shepard (for example, 1978a) has shown how important nonlinguistic internal codes are in solving spatial problems. The work of Furth (1966) with deaf children shows that, even in the absence of a well-mastered language, thinking can be relatively well developed, suggesting that language is one of many ways whereby thought is carried out. Some of the aptitude-treatment-interaction studies reported by Cronbach and Snow (1977), a few of which were mentioned previously, clearly suggest that individuals differ with respect to their preferred internal mode of processing. Thus, language turns out to be but *one* (perhaps very effective) internal symbol system.

Could other, nonlinguistic symbol systems become part of our cognitive apparatus in a way that resembles that of language? Could a child learn to think in, say, *graphical codes* as he does with language? Hatano, Miyake, and Binks (1977) have shown that expert abacus users seem to have internalized the operations of the abacus. This is suggested by the observation that users at intermediate levels still need to use visible finger movements to accompany mental computations. When prevented from using their fingers, such users perform significantly less well. Experimental intervention of this kind has no appreciable effect on expert users. The finger movements of intermediate users of the abacus appear to be very much like egocentric speech, which, according to Vygotsky, is "overt thought preceding inner speech." Both are overt activities en route to becoming totally internalized and covert.

Although the Hatano, Miyake, and Binks study lends credibility to my proposition, it does not prove it. For one thing, it is a single study carried out on a small and selected group of people. For another, it leaves open the question whether abacus users internalize a tool and its techniques of use or a specific symbol system. As yet, there is little empirical evidence to support the proposition that nonlinguistic symbol systems, much like language, can be internalized to serve as transferable skills. This proposition has been submitted to a series of experiments and field studies to be reported in the following chapters. But, before turning to them, it is necessary to ask whether one could expect the internalization process of nonlinguistic symbol systems to be similar to that of language. A good analogy carried too far can be badly misleading.

Indeed, this pitfall could easily await the present issue. The acquisition of language is highly dependent on the *interaction* between a child and a language community. It is the *dialogue* that seems to account for the internalization of language. A child is an active member in a speech community, both encoding and decoding verbal messages.

This is precisely where the promising analogy between language and the symbol systems of most media has to end. Although all of us interact through language, only a very few of us (and children hardly at all) interact with others through media's symbol systems. Communication through media is by and large the domain of the few professionals. Even when children paint, the purpose is idiosyncratic rather than communicational. Thus, if interaction through a symbol system is a vital condition for its internalization, active interaction cannot be counted on to facilitate internalization of any symbol system, save perhaps language.

It would then appear that most of the nonlinguistic symbol systems could not be internalized by most people. It would also follow that, with the exception of language, hardly any other symbol system could be used in thought. Indeed, Olson (1973) argued that, as the acquisition of skills (by these he means mainly perceptual and motor acts) is based on active experience, media of communication cannot teach them. From watching television, Olson argues, "children will learn the skill of watching television (and to a small extent, the skill of producing it) but not the performatory acts portrayed there" (p. 33).

It would be helpful to distinguish here between *performatory skills*, such as writing, skiing, or riding a horse, and *mental skills*. The relations between the two classes are numerous and complex and need not bother us here. However, there is one difference between them of immediate relevance. Whereas performatory acts *are the acts themselves*, mental acts are *symbolic representations* of actions and operations carried out internally. It is one thing to physically rotate three-dimensional objects, and it is another thing to carry out such imaginary operations *mentally*. Although the latter, according to Piaget, may result from the internalization of the former, they are not to be equated.

Performatory acts require for their mastery active physical experience. In this respect, Olson (1973) is apparently correct in arguing that a medium such as television cannot teach a performatory act. However, symbolically represented operations can be acquired without actual physical experience. Much of Bandura's work on modeling, to which I will return shortly, attests to this. So do the studies in which children's problem-solving behavior has been enhanced through verbal guidance or tutoring.

Moreover, it can be argued that the children studied by Vygotsky did not internalize the *act of speaking* but rather the symbol system they were using (Vygotsky, 1978), and it is the internalized language, not the act of speaking, that figures in thought. For this reason, even deaf children ultimately internalize langauge, although they do not really speak it (Furth, 1966).

Internalization Through Observational Learning

If it is not the action itself that is being internalized but rather the symbol, then could not an action be internalized even without active interaction? The possibility of *learning by observation* comes readily to mind as a possible alternative to interaction (although interaction through language may entail observational learning). This alternative is particularly attractive in light of our assumption about the possible isomorphism between external and internal codes.

Observational learning of modeled behaviors is a learning procedure that "enables people to acquire large, integrated patterns of behavior without having to form them gradually by tedious trial and error" (Bandura, 1977, p. 12). However, modeling is not limited to overt physical acts. Observational learning also occurs with linguistic skills (for example, see Bloom, Hood, and Lightbown, 1974), conservation of liquids, attitudes, and emotional responses (Bandura, 1973, 1977). Underlying *all* these, according to Bandura, are common processes of attention, internal coding, rehearsal, and reinforcement by self or others.

Observational learning is not restricted to live models. Symbolically coded models (through film or verbal description) are learned as well. Bandura, Grusec, and Menlove (1966) have shown that televised models are very effective in capturing attention and the viewers learn much of what they see without special incentive or trials, hence the great interest in and concern about television's ability to model a very wide range of behaviors, expectations, attitudes, and concepts.

By and large, whenever "symbolic modeling" was studied (see Bandura, 1977, and Rosenthal and Zimmerman, 1978, for summaries), the symbolic mode served as the vehicle for a message. The observers had to infer the message and learn *it*; its symbolic code was only the communicational vehicle. Thus, for instance, children were expected to observe and learn particular responses to moral judgment but not the verbal or pictorial codes in which they were modeled. From this follows the importance that Bandura attributes to internal coding (particularly *verbal* coding) by the observer while learning from a model.

However, the teaching potential of modeling need not be limited to observational learning of behaviors of humans nor to the informative contents of "symbolic modeling." *One should be able to learn by observing the symbolic code itself as well.* Indeed, this is very much in line with Bandura's explanation of the role of observational learning in language acquisition.

Brown (1976) taught children passive sentences by means of modeling, with or without pictorial examples of their referents. Both kinds of treatments improved children's understanding of passive construction. The added pictorial examples helped those with poorer initial ability, and linguistic modeling without referential examples improved the comprehension of those with better initial understanding of such sentences. The important point to note here is that the *code* (passive constructions) was modeled and was learned. The fact that children with initially poorer understanding of passive constructions benefited from the pictorial examples clearly suggests that they also needed an image to mediate the transformation from passive to base structure. This was provided, ready-made, by the examples.

If observational learning, accompanied by repetition, internal rehearsal, and feedback, can lead to the generalized acquisition of linguistic syntactical structures, then why not nonlinguistic structures? Nothing in social-learning theory or in Piaget's accounts of imitation rules out such a possibility. Thus, it is possible to hypothesize that some symbolic modes of representation could be modeled, acquired, and internalized. When modeled in a large variety of instances, these codes could be internalized, schematized and transferred to new situations.

Thus, it appears that the internalization of language is aided by, among other things, interaction, but nonlinguistic codes can be internalized through observational learning.

The Mental Functions of Codes

Although observational learning is theoretically possible, there may be some drawbacks in practice. We are engulfed with a great many symbol systems and specific codes, and one could not expect all of them to be equally internalizable. Bandura's social-learning theory does not point out what behaviors are more or less learnable by observation. Nor does Vygotsky's theory point out what linguistic untis are more internalizable than others. Bandura's theory of social learning is an attempt to show the role that kind of learning plays in our lives; it is not a list of learnable and nonlearnable behaviors. Similarly, Vygotsky tried to show how we learn to use language in thought, not which specific nouns, verbs, or grammatical structures are internalizable.

However, lest we oversimplify the case by arguing that all symbol systems encountered in the media can be internalized and used as coding elements in thought, we must at least show *why* they are learned. The internalizability of codes must surely depend on their function. Once we have a plausible (if speculative) explanation, we should be able to generate specific hypotheses pertaining to the conditions in which specific coding elements are internalized.

A verbal construction or spatial depiction, to be learned and used in perception and thought, needs to accomplish some useful function for the learner. It must promise a solution for a perceived difficulty. As Cole and Scribner (1974) theorize with respect to cognition and cultural differences, a skill is evoked and potentially cultivated within the context of functional demands. Thus, for a coding element to become a tool of thought, it must accomplish some useful cognitive function. It needs to accmplish *for* the learner something that the learner cannot perform on his own yet needs to perform.

At this point, we should distinguish between two kinds of external and internal representational codes—those that represent stationary or static events or classes and those that represent relations, operations, and transformations. Representations of transformations change one stationary event into another. Formally, this relationship between stationary and transformational codes can be represented as:

$$S_1 \rightarrow T_r \rightarrow S_2$$

S_1 is a stationary code representing some event, T_r is the operation applied to it, and S_2 is the resultant stationary event. Less formally illustrated, we might say that, in film, a shot of scenery is S_1, a camera movement is T_r, and the resultant new scenery is S_2. In cartography, the globe is S_1, the process of projecting it on a two-dimensional surface is T_r, and the map is the resultant S_2. When carried out internally, transformations are akin to skills, the "size" of which depends on the generality of the transformation.

When a stationary code is given (for instance, a flow chart of historical events), and provided that it is a result of specific requisite transformations, it can be said to *short-circuit* the transformations that would lead to it, inasmuch as it *saves* the learner the necessary requisite mental operations. Providing a learner with a ready-made graphic representation saves him the mental effort of transforming information that is not graphically coded into a graphic code. Cronbach (1975, p. 119) states that "One way to reduce the effect of general ability is to bring in pictures or diagrams. . . . On the whole, the regression of outcome onto general ability tends to be relatively steep when the instruction requires the learner to actively transform information, and it tends to be shallow when the demands are less." This is what was meant when I argued in Chapter Three that some symbol systems can save mental effort and thus make learning easier.

A stationary code could be learned and used as a tool of thought only if it is in sufficient correspondence to or isomorphism with the internal code the learner *would have generated on his own.* To be learned and used as a transferable mental representation, the code needs to fit into an anticipatory scheme. More importantly, such a stationary code—to be internalized and *used as a mental tool*—requires the preexistence of the mental operations that lead to it. Sinclair de Zwart's (1967) subjects could not make use of the verbal principles to guide their conservation behavior, because they had not mastered the underlying processes. Deregowski's (1968) Zambian servants could not use graphic perspective in their thinking in the absence of the operations that transform two dimensions into three dimensions. Similarly, a child could learn to represent to himself historical events in terms of diagrams only when he has already mastered the requisite skills. Thus, short-circuiting requisite processes can save mental effort and facilitate learning when the requisite mental skills are not yet mastered. But short-circuiting cannot lead to the internalization of the code unless the requisite skills are already mastered.

The situation is somewhat different in the case of transformational codes. Such codes overtly perform a transformation, which the learner witnesses. To the extent that such overtly performed transformations are isomorphic to the ones that the learner should have employed covertly on his own, they seem to overtly supplant what should be taking place covertly. As supplanters of transformations or skills, such codes serve two functions—they save the learner mental effort by relieving him from carrying out some of the requisite internal operations, and they overtly *model* these operations.

The case of saving-by-supplantation has been demonstrated by the comparison between the close-up and zoom-in film versions in the experiment described in Chapter Four. Recall that the zoom version appeared to do for the learners what some of them could not carry out on their own, thus depressing the correlation between skill-mastery and knowledge acquisition from 0.67 to 0.27. In this sense, supplantation seems to function much like short-circuiting.

Consider now that such viewers repeatedly observe the code of zooming-in in a context that requires them to relate parts to wholes. One would expect them to gradually learn by observation and internalize the code so that they could use it as a mental transformation of relatively wide applicability. This, of course, would be the case if the modeling or supplanting code could overtly perform for the learners operations that they could not perform on their own but still needed or wanted to perform. When a code supplants mental operations that learners cannot yet perform well on their own, we might expect them to learn the code.

I have identified three possible functions of symbolic codes that could facilitate their acquisition for mental use. A code can *activate* a skill, it can *short-circuit* it, or it can overtly *supplant* it. Activation of skills can cultivate their mastery, but the prior existence of some reasonable mastery of the skill is required. Otherwise, there would be nothing to cultivate. Thus, a skill-activating code can benefit only learners with relatively moderate mastery of the relevant skill. Short-circuiting, although saving mental effort, cannot really cultivate the mastery of a skill, as it circumvents the need to apply the skill and assumes the prior mastery of it. Finally, overt supplantation can allow the learner to internalize the code itself, as it simulates a needed operation the learner has not yet mastered. Supplantation would benefit mainly those with initial poor mastery of the skill.

The hypotheses I have advanced here are skeleton hypotheses of the kind described in Chapter One. They do not enumerate the codes that function in one way or another, as a code's function depends very much on the learner's cognitive make-up and the demand characteristics of the task that he encounters. One could argue, as I will do later, that some symbol systems, like those in film, have the *potential* of supplanting specific (usually figurative) mental skills and therefore can be made to have skill-cultivating effects. But one cannot attribute a fixed psychological function to each code and assume that it accomplishes the function for all learners under all conditions.

The three functions I have attributed to codes can be arranged in a continuum, with activation at one end, supplantation at the other, and short-circuiting in between. It is possible to take any given code that belongs to a symbol system and place it on this continuum with respect to a particular person and task. (Thus, a code could accomplish different functions along the continuum for different people.) To the extent that a repeatedly used code is critical—that is, needs to be transformed in the service in information extraction—it can be expected to cultivate skill-mastery by activating the skill. Similarly, to the extent that a transformational code overtly supplants a skill that is needed but not mastered by a learner, it can be expected to cultivate it.

One might question some of the implications that follow from the present rationale. The logic presented thus far suggests that skill-cultivation by supplantation should precede cultivation by activation. The former offers a model for an operation, but the latter assumes its existence. However, as Olson and Bruner (1974) contend, learning from a model requires skill. In addition, for a learner to incorporate a modeled or supplanted skill into his anticipatory schemata requires prior preparation. It may well be the case that a modicum of specific skill-mastery needs to precede learning of a supplanting code. The question of what kind of learning precedes and what kind follows will have to remain unanswered at this point. I will return to this question in Chapter Nine after reviewing the empirical data pertaining to it.

Transfer of Cultivated Skills

Consider the possibility that media's symbol systems, particularly some unique coding elements within these systems, are empirically found to cultivate the mastery of skills. Would these skills be extremely specific, limited to the extraction of knowledge from the media, and thus of no transfer value?

Scribner and Cole (1978), who studied the effects of literacy without schooling on cognitive skills in the Liberian tribe of the Vai (see Chapter Three), found these effects to be task-specific. Literacy affected some communciaton skills (such as the ability to memorize and integrate syllables into meaningful units) and even transferred to related tasks. However, such effects were highly specific rather than exhibiting any generalized competencies, such as abstraction or verbal reasoning, which are traditionally ascribed to literacy. Such findings support Cole and Scribner's position (1974) that cognitive skills are cultivated as a response to one's cultural demands and are organized accordingly. Thus, for instance, the extent of mastery of discrimination skills exhibits itself by a cultural group where and when discrimination is required, not as a generalized ability.

Herein lies the answer to the transfer question. The more complex the demands and the better practiced the skills, the farther the transfer of skill mastery. We should note the relationship between a hypothetical single coding element, symbol systems, and media. Codes, as described in Chapter Two, can be of varying sizes. Some coding elements, regardless of symbol systems, are minute, but others are much larger units that entail some of the most pervasive characters of a symbol system (the spatial point of view of maps, for instance). Yet, the hypothetical functions that can be attributed to coding elements are independent of their sizes. Symbolic units of increasingly larger size call upon increasingly more general abilities, as I have argued in Chapter Four, and can also cultivate increasingly more general abilities.

The skill of upside-down reading, whose cultivation was observed by Kolers (1976), is of course highly specific. But then, there is little opportunity to practice such a skill outside the realm of Kolers' experimental tasks. A very specific (and artificial) demand is invented, and, as one would expect, only an accordingly specific skill is developed. But many of the demands and models provided by the symbol system of media are encountered quite often and may be useful for many tasks (recall the description of the student's dreams, quoted earlier in this chapter). Indeed, as skills become increasingly more automatic and less capacity-limited, their transfer value often increases as well, provided they are suitable to new domains and tasks. Scribner and Cole (1978, p. 24) write, "As practice in any activity continues, we would expect the range of materials which engage it to be extended and skills to become increasingly free from the particular conditions of the original practice. Skills, then, will be more available for what has been called "far transfer," including tasks and situations that do not involve the written modality. When skill systems involved in literacy are many, varied, and complex, and have wide applicability, the functional and general ability approaches will converge in their predictions of intellectual outcomes." This statement justifies the hypothesis that media's symbol systems affect, or can be made to affect, the mastery of mental skills with potentially great transfer value.

In the next three chapters, I will report findings from a number of experiments, field studies, and a cross-cultural study in which the rationale and hypotheses discussed in this chapter were tested.

Summary

If symbol systems of the media can cultivate mental skill-mastery, what psychological mechanisms could account for such possible cultivation, and how transferable would the cultivated skills be?

Coding elements (or larger units thereof) could affect cognition in three ways—activation of skills that transform external codes into internal ones, short-circuiting skills by overtly providing the end result of mental transformations that a learner should have employed, and overt supplantation, or modeling, of processes by means of transformational codes. Skill cultivation by activation is a typical procedure of evoking mental processes and reinforcing them, but short-circuiting and supplantation could turn a communicational code into a tool of thought.

The notion of an internal tool is inspired by theories that attribute an important role in thought to language. This idea also borrows the conception of internalized language from those theories. However, the analogy with language is limited, as internal speech is acquired through interaction with a language community, whereas no interaction with media's symbol systems is viable. Alternatively, I suggested that observational learning can account for the internalization of some of media's coding elements.

Two types of coding elements are available to observational learning—stationary codes and transformational codes.

Stationary codes usually short-circuit prerequisite transformations. They can save the learner mental effort when they provide the results of transformations and are sufficiently isomorphic with the internal representation the learner has generated
on his own. But such codes (for example, a diagram of historical
events), to be internalized as mental tools, must be matched by
the learner's ability to generate the transformations that would
lead up to them. Thus, they cannot really cultivate skill in learners who have not already mastered them.

Transformational codes can overtly supplant or model a
skill. To the extent that they fill a need, they can be learned by
observation and be internalized. They should, then, benefit
mainly the poor skill-masterer. However, this hypothesis leads
to new difficulties. Would not a prior mastery of a supplanted
skill be needed to allow the internalization of a skill-supplanting
code? Thus, could a child internalize, say, slow motion without
being able to transform it into internal representations? This
question is left unanswered but will be addressed in Chapter
Nine.

The question of transfer of skills was dealt with in general
terms. Larger-unit environments and symbolic elements can
cultivate more general skills; smaller-unit codes cultivate more
specific skills. A number of sociocultural, cross-cultural, and
instructional studies support this claim. Additionally, specific
skills, cultivated by specific coding elements, can be transferred,
provided they are well practiced and are applicable to an array
of new instances.

SIX

Impact of Films Designed to Cultivate Mental Skills

✂ ✂ ✂ ✂ ✂ ✂ ✂

In Chapter Five, we identified three skill-cultivating functions of symbolic elements—skill activation, skill short-circuiting, and skill modeling. These functions can affect the mastery of specific mental skills in interaction with learners' initial levels of skill-mastery. This chapter is devoted to reporting four experiments that were designed to test the skill-cultivating functions of some filmic coding elements. Before going into the details of the experiments, it is necessary to point to a basic distinction, one that differentiates between the experiments reported here and those reported in Chapters Seven and Eight.

By saying that media's symbol systems affect cognition, we can mean two things. The claim can mean that media's symbol systems affect cognition "naturally," the way environments

139

in general affect mental growth. Experimentation would then aim at capturing the phenomenon and examining it under controlled conditions. But the claim can also mean that media's symbol systems *can be made* to affect cognition under specific favorable conditions, although they need not have such effects under more natural ones.

The distinction between what *is* and what *can be made to be* differentiates between attempts at recording an existing phenomenon and attempts at realizing a potential. A typical study of the first kind is, for example, the one in which the interaction between mother and child is closely observed, and some of its components are experimentally manipulated. Singling out interaction components for experimentation is done with an eye on external validity, without which no findings can be generalized. A typical study of the second kind is, for instance, the one in which mothers are encouraged to watch "Sesame Street" with their children (Ball and Bogatz, 1970). As Cook and others (1975) point out, the only mothers who received such encouragement were the ones who participated in the Ball and Bogatz evaluation study. Thus, the effects of mothers' encouragement, as found by these researchers, indicated only what effects encouragement can be made to have, not what effects it usually has.

By realizing the skill-cultivating effects of media's symbol systems, one can show what could possibly be expected if certain conditions are met. But this would not prove that such effects of media's symbol systems occur outside the confines of the experimental setting, when exposure to the media takes place under less favorable conditions. Still, showing that media's coding elements can be made to affect cognition may be a necessary prerequisite to studying their more natural effects, because, if we cannot produce such effects under favorable conditions, how can we hope to detect the effects under less favorable conditions?

Aside from being a prerequisite for the study of natural events, studying how symbolic elements can be made to affect cognition is important in itself. As argued in Chapter One, media have been used primarily as conveyors of information-to-be-learned, and thus as alternative educational means to old ends. As a consequence, little attention has been given to the symbolic nature of media, and its potential effect on cognition has not been realized. Discovering, therefore, that media's symbol systems have little effect on cognition under natural conditions would prove only what is already known—a generally unrealized potential yields no results.

For these reasons, we have focused first on how media's coding elements can be made to affect cognition. Only later did we examine the extent to which our experimentally derived effects are replicated by media outside the experimental setting. Thus, whereas the "potential-extracting" experiments (reported in this chapter) have mainly educational ramifications, the "recording-of-natural-phenomena" studies (reported in later chapters) have primarily psychological and communicational implications. With these distinctions in mind, I turn to the description of the experiments.

The Experiments: General Considerations

Four experiments were designed to test the following two hypotheses: (1) Filmic coding elements can be made to facilitate the mastery of specific mental skills. (2) Coding elements that activate skills facilitate skill-mastery in already skillful learners; coding elements that short-circuit skills have little cultivating effects; and coding elements that overtly model skills facilitate skill-mastery in initially unskilled learners. Two of the experiments were also designed to examine the role that verbal ability and verbal mediation play in this context. (A more detailed account of the first three experiments can be found in Salomon, 1974b.)

Three transformational coding elements typical of filmic symbol systems were chosen as stimuli for the experiments—the zoom, the "laying out" of solid objects, and the rotation of objects. The zoom was assumed to overtly model the process of singling out details from a visually rich display. It could be contrasted with either a succession of long-shots and close-ups, which was assumed to short-circuit the same process, or with a static long-shot that can be made to call upon the process of singling out details. The same applies to the other two elements, each of which was assumed to model a mental skill and could be contrasted with short-circuiting or skill-activating elements.

Experiment I: Zooming and Cue-Attendance

Subjects

Eighty eighth-graders, all from one school, were random-ly assigned to four groups (n = 20). An equal number of boys and girls were in each group.

Stimuli and Procedures

There were four experimental conditions in the study—modeling, short-circuiting, activation, and control (no treat-ment). The *modeling* condition consisted of three films, each depicting a Breughel painting. The camera zoomed-in on details and zoomed-out to the entire picture eighty times within each film.

The *short-circuiting* condition consisted of three series of slides of the same Breughel paintings. Within each series, the entire picture, then a detail, then the picture, then another detail, and so on were repeated eighty times. The details singled out were identical to those in the modeling condition. The *activation* condition consisted of the three slides of the paint-ings. The control group saw neither film nor slides but was pre-tested and posttested.

Subjects in each of the three treatment conditions were directed to write eighty details they had noticed in each of the three films or slides, or 240 details altogether. Time for each condition varied. Subjects in the modeling and short-circuiting groups worked according to the speed of the presentations. Subjects in the activation group were allowed to work as long as necessary while the slide remained projected until the last sub-ject had finished.

Measures

Subjects were pretested and posttested with two tests of cue-attendance, whose properties and relations to other abilities were tested in previous studies (Salomon and Sieber-Suppes, 1972). The two tests, group-administered, were similar but not identical. Subjects were shown a slide depicting a very rich and complex montage of objects and were asked to report in writing the maximum number of items they had noticed. There was a time limit of seven minutes for the test. The purpose of the cue-attendance pretest was to serve as a baseline measure upon which posttest scores could be regressed.

Results and Discussion

     Pretest cue-attendance scores were similar for all groups. One-way analyses of variance of posttest scores and subsequent Newman-Keuls tests showed that all three treatment groups obtained significantly higher posttest scores than the control group, and that both the activation and modeling groups obtained significantly higher scores than the short-circuiting group. Thus, the results clearly showed that the coding elements used together with the task requirement could be made to affect the mastery of the cue-attendance skill. On the average, activation and modeling had the same positive effects.

     Regressing posttest scores on pretest scores separately for each group yielded a strong and significant aptitude-treatment interaction (ATI) between initial cue-attendance scores and the conditions of activation and modeling, as shown in Figure 6. Low initial scorers benefited little from activation but profited far more from the modeling condition. As hypothesized, activation called upon mediators not available to low-aptitude scorers, whereas modeling provided a highly explicit symbolic code that could be imitated and internalized. Initially high scorers performed *less* well following modeling and far better following activation. The explicit modeling films seemed to interfere with the mediational capability of the high scorers, but the condition that evoked partly mastered skills led to their improvement. Short-circuiting, which did not lead to as large improvements as did the other two treatments, favored mainly the initially more skillful subjects.

     These results lend tentative support to the hypotheses. However, they leave a number of questions unanswered. Did the

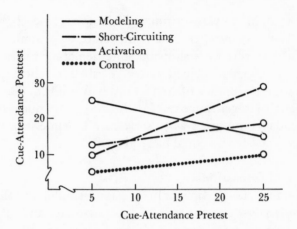

FIGURE 6. Cue attendance posttest scores regressed on pretest scores for each gruop.

modeling stimulus *supplant* the skill that the initially low scorers should have but could not employ? What indications are there to show that something was learned by observation and internalized? Was the learning purely visual, or did verbal mediation partake in this process? If verbal mediation plays an important role in this process, then the modeling-supplantation-internalization hypothesis could be questioned. And why did modeling inhibit learning of the initially high scorers?

A second experiment was designed to answer some of these questions. This time we added induced overt labeling of the items singled out by the camera in the modeling condition or by the subject in the activation condition. We expected that, if verbalization plays a mediating role in learning, then induced labeling should improve posttraining performance. Subjects low in verbal ability were expected to gain more from labeling than subjects high in verbal ability, since the latter are more likely to employ this strategy on their own anyway.

Experiment II: The Role of Verbal Mediation

Subjects

Fifty-six eighth-graders were randomly assigned to four groups (n = 14). Within each group, the fourteen subjects were subdivided randomly to form two groups of seven subjects. Experimentation and testing took place in those subgroups.

Stimuli, Procedures, and Tasks

A factorial design was created using two stimulus conditions—modeling and activation—and two verbalization conditions—overt verbalization and nonverbalization. This design, then, yielded four treatment groups. The *modeling-verbalization* group saw the three modeling films of Experiment I. While groups of seven subjects viewed a film, one subject was randomly called upon in each trial to label aloud the detail being zoomed-in on. Since the subjects never knew which of them would be called next to provide the label, it was assumed that all subjects were covertly labeling all details. Each group aimed toward a criterion of labeling forty-two details for each of the three films. The *modeling-nonverbalization* group was run in the same fashion but without overt labeling. Subjects were asked to "notice what exactly the camera does and to note to themselves the details they observe." In the *activation-verbalization* condition, the materials used were the slides of Experiment I, but the labeling procedure was as in the first group. Finally, the *activation-nonverbalization* group watched the slides in silence; subjects were told to note to themselves the details observed, as in the modeling-nonverbalization group.

Measures

A battery of pretests was given the day before the experiment—the Cue-Attendance test and an Israeli Standardized Verbal Ability Test (MILTA). On the day after the experiment, subjects were given a Cue-Attendance posttest, which required writing down details from a complex and rich visual display. An additional measure was taken from subjects' listings—an Organization measure of the spatial ordering of the listed details. We included this measure to test the hypothesis that, in addition to learning the act of zooming-in on details, the random order of details focused upon might also be learned.

Results and Discussion

Factorial analyses of variance on Cue-Attendance pretest and posttest scores failed to produce statistically significant main effects (modeling versus activation, verbalization versus nonverbalization) or interactions. Although the ages of the subjects in the first two experiments were similar (eighth-graders) and the stimuli were identical, the results differed. However, there was a major difference in level of training criterion between the two experiments. In the first experiment, subjects were required to write eighty details noticed in each of three films or slides. In the second experiment, each subject was required to report verbally only six details for each of three films or slides. We postulated, after the nonsignificant results in the second experiment, that the assumption that all subjects in the verbalization groups engaged in spontaneous labeling while expecting to be called upon appears to be questionable. More likely, the students with low verbal ability labeled details only *after* being called upon. Hence, the criterion of eighteen labels per subject in the training situations was far too low to affect a change in mediational behavior.

However, since our major hypotheses centered on aptitude-treatment interactions, we regressed posttest scores on aptitude scores for each treatment group. This procedure uncovered several important interactions between the subjects' initial aptitudes and the treatment conditions. When the two nonverbalization conditions were compared, the results of Experiment I were replicated. Thus, initially poor cue-attenders performed best when exposed to the modeling condition, but the initially good cue-attenders performed best when exposed to the activation condition (Figure 7). The difference between the two regression lines is significant. However, no such clear interaction emerged when the two verbalization conditions were compared. Examination of regression lines reveals a simple pattern—requiring overt verbalization does *not* affect the performance of the initially poor cue-attenders, but it does affect the performance of the already skillful subjects.

Regressing cue-attendance posttest scores on verbal-ability (MILTA) pretest scores yielded essentially the same results. As MILTA and Cue-Attendance pretest scores correlated 0.47 with each other, there is nothing surprising in this finding.

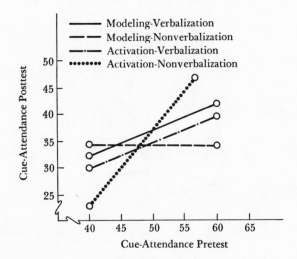

FIGURE 7. Cue-attendance posttest scores regressed on pretest scores for each group.

The modeling condition also displayed a random order of zooming-in on the paintings' details. Although unintended, one could ask whether modeling such random scanning of a visual field has an effect on the subjects' way of scanning the details in the posttest. The organization score, obtained from the posttest, was designed to measure this effect. The regression of organization scores on MILTA scores for each group yielded, as before, a significant ATI (Figure 8).

Low MILTA scorers received significantly lower organization scores after exposure to the modeling stimuli than similar subjects who were exposed to the activation stimuli. Thus, it seems that they have learned not only the zooming-in operation but also the random order in which this operation was modeled for them. High MILTA scorers received particularly *high* organization scores after exposure to modeling, suggesting that they used their relatively high verbal abilities to compensate for the randomness in scanning they encountered. The induced verbal mediation through overt labeling had only a small effect on organization scores, but it accentuated somewhat the differences

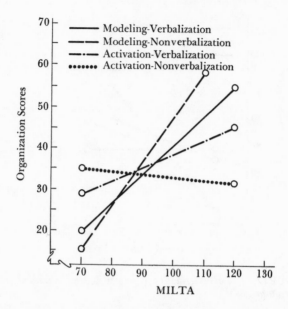

FIGURE 8. Organization scores regressed on MILTA pretest scores for each group. (MILTA is an Israeli Standardized Verbal Ability test.)

between low verbal scorers in the two modeling conditions—low scorers who were required to label items overtly in the modeling condition showed even poorer organization than their counterparts who did not overtly label.

To summarize, verbal mediation appears to be utilized by subjects with high verbal ability. Faced with a compelling visual model, they use their verbal skills to overcome the model and compensate for its influence. Subjects with low verbal ability seem to operate differently. They perform best when shown a visual model. Inducing verbal mediation in them impedes rather than facilitates their performance. Their learning appears to be visual rather than verbal.

To the extent that learning filmic coding elements takes place, more verbally inclined subjects appear to learn through verbal mediation, whereas less verbally inclined subjects learn through visual observation and possibly by internalization of the visual coding element. It stand to reason that activation of a skill allows more freedom to the learner in applying mental processes. Acivation of a skill thus favors those who can either apply the required skill or apply verbal mediation. Modeling, possibly functioning as supplanter of a skill, is much more compelling. Verbally inclined subjects try to impose their verbal logic on the model, but this may be a wasted effort, as not all modeled operations yield to verbal logic. To test this possibility, we conducted a third experiment.

Experiment III: Filmic Laying Out and Its Effects on Visualization Skills

The third experiment was designed to test the hypothesis that verbally able subjects (assumed to rely mainly on internal verbalization) would benefit from visual modeling as much as those less verbally able; the former group would be expected to learn through verbal mediation, and the latter group would be expected to learn through internal visualization.

To test this hypothesis, a filmic operation was needed that could be modeled overtly and that could also be carried out through internal verbalization. Thus, the operation of laying out solid objects (gradually transforming visualized objects into "floor plans") was chosen. Mastery of such an operation is measurable by means of Thurstone and Guilford's tests of Paper Folding, Surface Development, and Form Board (French, Ekstrom, and Price, 1963).

Subjects

Forty-two ninth-grade students from an all-male vocational school were randomly assigned to three groups (n = 14).

Stimuli and Procedures

Three conditions were studied—modeling, short-circuiting, and control (no treatment). *Modeling* consisted of a fifteen-minute film that showed five solid objects, each of which was gradually laid out, side after side, to produce a two-dimensional plan. Once laid out in the form of a two-dimensional plan, the object was gradually folded up again to become a three-dimensional object. In the *short-circuiting* conditions, each object was shown on two slides, one depicting the three-dimensional solid object and the other its laid-out two-dimensional plan.

Subjects in the modeling and short-circuiting groups viewed either the films or slides once each day for three consecutive days. No responses were required; rather, the subjects were merely asked to watch the film or slides carefully. The control group received no treatment.

Measures

Three pretest measures were taken—a Paper Folding test measuring visualization ability, a language test, and a mathematics test. The posttest consisted of Thurstone's Surface Development test, which measures visualization ability.

Results and Discussion

Analysis of covariance, followed by Scheffe's post hoc comparisons, showed that the visualization posttest scores of the modeling group were significantly higher than those of the short-circuiting group, and that both were higher than the scores of the control group. Thus, additional support was obtained for the claim that coding elements can affect the mastery of skills.

Correlational analyses yielded a significant ATI between students' language scores and the treatment conditions (Figure 9). In the control group, high language scorers performed far better on the visualization posttest than low language scorers. This indicates that, in the absence of intervention, language or verbal ability contributes significantly to visualization test performance.

In the modeling group, the relationship between language and posttest visualization scores was negative. Thus, low language scorers learned the most from visual modeling, and high scorers learned the least. The slope in the short-circuiting condition was not significantly different from zero.

The positive correlation between language and visualization scores in the control group (r = 0.63) suggests that, as

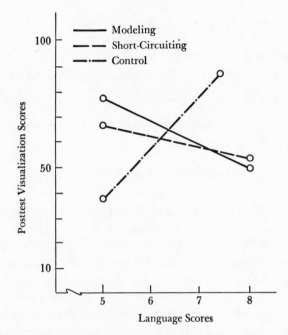

FIGURE 9. Visualization posttest scores regressed on language grades for each group.

assumed, visualization problems of the kind employed in the study can be dealt with by means of verbal mediation. Would not verbal mediation also occur in learning from the modeling film? As the results show, this is not the case. If verbally inclined subjects would successfully impose verbal logic on the material, then their posttest scores should not have been this low, nor should they have learned less than the low language scorers.

One possibility is that the operation of laying out defies treatment by means of verbal logic. But this possibility is ruled out by the results obtained from the control group. A second possibility is that modeling of the kind studied in these experiments indeed accomplishes a supplanting function and thus leads to the internalization of the model. However, such internalization *interferes* with the already established verbal habits of verbally inclined subjects or with the way in which already skilled subjects visualize laying out of objects. (As visualization pretest scores and language scores correlated 0.54, we may be referring here to more or less the same subjects.)

In more general terms, visual modeling does not just provide a stimulus to be processed through verbal mediation; it is a model to be internalized *as is*. Verbal mediation seems to interfere with this process. It is, however, conducive to skill-improvement through activation.

Experiment IV: Changing Points of View

The fourth experiment was essentially a replication of Experiment I, with only a difference in the stimulus materials. The purpose of this experiment was to test the hypothesis that the same skill-improvements observed in the other experiments with the coding elements of the zoom and laying out can be replicated with another coding element. The element chosen for study was the change in points of view that occurs by the movements of a camera around an object or by the rotation of an object in front of the camera.

The materials were based on Piaget's Three Mountain problem, in which a child is asked to describe what another person sees when seated across from the child and watches the same display of three mountains that is in front of the child. As Urberg and Docherty (1976) point out, it is important to consider the difference between structural and content components in perspective or role-taking tasks. The structural components are the cognitive processes involved, such as changing a point of view or a number of dimensions to be considered by the child. Content components, associated with a child's familiarity with the actual objects or roles, are the concepts to which the operations are applied. Indeed, when Borke (1975) changed the three mountains into a "Sesame Street" character (a change of content), three- and four-year-olds performed far better than expected.

The purpose of the study was then to test whether activating, short-circuiting, or modeling the *process* of changing point of view of objects, whose structural complexity is gradually increased, improves the capacity of seven-year-olds to take alternative perspectives. The age-group of seven-year-olds was chosen, because children at that age are already capable of decentering on successive aspects of stimuli but still face difficulties with simultaneous decentering (Selman and Byrne, 1974).

Subjects

Seventy-two second-graders, equally divided between boys and girls, were randomly assigned to four groups (n = 18).

Stimuli and Procedures

There were four experimental conditions, replicating those of Experiment I. The *modeling* condition consisted of a film in which an object (or a number of objects) was seen on a table facing the viewer. A "smily" face was seen behind the object(s). Then the camera slowly moved around the table to where the "smily" was and showed the way the object looked from "smily's" point of view. This was repeated with symmetrical, then asymmetrical objects, with one, then two, then three objects; and with 180° and 90° rotations. All objects were familiar, such as a cup, shoe, or orange.

The *short-circuiting* condition was essentially the same, expect for one difference. Instead of the camera's gradual movement, subjects saw a slide of the initial position and a second slide of the final position of each rotation. The *activation* condition consisted of only the first slide of each pair, depicting the initial position only. The *control* condition consisted of pretesting and posttesting with no treatment.

Subjects in the three treatments were first given a number of perspective-taking examples and then were asked to "guess how smily sees the object(s) on the table." No verbal reponses were required.

Measures

Pretesting and posttesting consisted of individually administered tests that measure a child's ability to change points of view in a spatial-figural situation. The tests, like the treatment, included increasingly more complex items. Although produced by us, the test items were designed in accordance with the tests used by Fishbein, Lewis, and Keiffer (1972) and by Huttenlocher and Presson (1973). Each child was shown a scene and asked to select a picture that depicted somebody else's way of seeing that scene.

Results and Discussion

The mean pretest scores of the four groups were in the midrange of possible test scores, thus leaving room for posttraining improvements. Analyses of variance followed by Newman-Keuls tests performed on the posttest replicated the findings of Experiment I—the activation and modeling groups did significantly better than the short-circuiting group, which in turn did better than the control group.

Correlational analyses yielded the already familiar pattern —an ATI between pretest scores and treatment. Activation catered to the already relatively skillful subjects, whereas modeling benefited mainly the initially less skillful ones. Short-circuiting catered to the more skillful subjects but had only a small effect on their skill-mastery.

The four most difficult posttest items were singled out for comparison among the treatment groups. About a third of the modeling subjects answered these items correctly, as compared with only two subjects of the activation group. However, all the subjects that succeeded on these items were already high scorers on the pretest. This finding should not surprise us, as more advanced children would be expected to progress beyond the others as a result of training.

The important thing to note, however, is that the modeling treatment had a stronger effect than the activation treatment. This suggests, although it does not prove, that a proper way to use coding elements to cultivate skills is first by modeling or supplanting the code overtly and only later cultivating it by activation. This issue will be discussed further in Chapter Nine.

Summary

The experiments reported in this chapter were designed to test whether the coding elements of a medium's symbol systems can be made to affect the mastery of cognitive skills. These studies attempt to realize a potential without generalizing results to nonexperimental settings; other studies, which record and analyze "natural" events under controlled experimental conditions, will be discussed in the next chapter. Not claiming that our experiments capture a natural event, the danger of poor external validity is of little concern to us at present. The experimental results can show only what *can be done* with filmic coding elements.

Taken together, the four experiments reported here suggest that at least three kinds of covert skills—singling out details, visualization, and changing points of view—can be affected by filmic coding elements. Two other studies, one by Rovet (1974) and one by Salomon and others (unpublished), replicated these findings with respect to two additional skills—visualization of rotations in space and the identification of embedded figures. In the study by Rovet, subjects either saw a film that overtly supplanted the process of rotating cubes in space, saw stationary slides and had to execute the rotations in their imaginations, or manually rotated actual solid cubes. In the study by Salomon and others, subjects either saw a film that supplanted the process of separating a complex visual field into puzzle-like components to reveal an embedded figure or had to execute such a process covertly on their own. The results of both studies were virtually the same and replicated the cultivation effects and ATIs observed in the other studies.

The results have shown that two types of coding elements can be made to affect skill-mastery—those that activate a skill by providing the initial state of a transformation (S_1), and those that model the whole transformation ($S_1 \rightarrow T_r \rightarrow S_2$). As expected, activation of a skill benefits the learner with some initially fair mastery of it, who can carry on the process from its initial state, whereas modeling benefits the less skillful learner who cannot. There were also indications that the modeling procedure leads, as speculated, to the internalization of the transformational coding element. As the modeled operation supplants its mental counterpart it interferes with the smooth mental application of the modeled skill by already skillful subjects. Thus, modeling depresses their scores.

No claims can be made on the basis of these findings that the observed cultivating effects are stable over time, nor can it be claimed that the improved skill-mastery has great transfer value. These were not the objectives of the experiments. Whether an improved skill-mastery is retained over time depends on how often it is called upon or modeled. And whether the improved skill is more or less transferable depends on its utility in other situations. Cue-attendance may be of greater daily utility in many tasks than, say, one's ability to visualize laying out of objects. Indeed, a measure of subjective uncertainty was added to the posttest in Experiment I. Previous research (Sieber and Lanzetta, 1966; Salomon and Sieber-Suppes, 1972) has shown that cue-attendance is positively related to experienced uncertainty. As expected, those subjects in Experiment I who became better cue-attenders also received significantly higher uncertainty scores, as measured by an entirely different task. Such a finding does not settle the transfer question, but it suggests that some skills learned from a medium's symbol system can be transferable. Although visualizing laying out of objects may be of little utility to most learners, it is of much greater use to the vocational school students who participated in Experiment III.

Finally, the experimental results do not suggest that using a medium's symbol system is necessarily the best educational method to cultivate a skill. There are numerous other methods of possibly greater impact. The claim is made, however, that in contradistinction to the instructional roles usually assigned to the medium of film, its symbol system can be made to affect cognition, and thus film offers new ends for its educational utilization.

SEVEN

Effects
of "Sesame Street"
on Television-Naive
Children

❃ ❃ ❃ ❃ ❃ ❃ ❃

Even if specific filmic coding elements can be made to affect
the mastery of mental skills, we are left with the question of
whether the same effects occur naturally under less controlled
conditions. Do the symbol systems of film or television, as
commonly employed, affect children's mental skills, as children
commonly watch movies and television programs? What do children need to bring with them to the viewing situation to be so
affected? Restricting such questions to film and television reflects, of course, personal interests more than anything else.
Scribner and Cole (1978) had other preferences and asked more

or less the same kinds of questions about the effects of literacy. The opportunity to study the cognitive effects of a medium's symbol systems under nonexperimental, natural conditions came when "Sesame Street" was brought to Israel in the fall and winter of 1971-1972. It turned out to be a rather unique research opportunity for two reasons. First, although one would like to reach conclusions pertaining to a *medium*, preferably even media in general, studying the effects of a *program* allows far better controls. A program's broadcast starts on a particular day, and no child can possibly have had exposure to it prior to that date. A program is shown a specific number of times and entails specific messages. It is relatively easy to obtain unconfounded measures of real amounts of exposure for each child without having to make any questionable assumptions. Thus, a program is a definite input whose particular effects one can study.

Second, and of greater importance, is the novelty factor of "Sesame Street" when introduced to a television-naive population, as was Israel in 1971. Instructional television was introduced in Israel in 1966, and general television in mid 1968. There was only one black-and-white station, broadcasting for about four hours every night. Of these four hours, thirty minutes were children's programs; the rest were Arabic and adult programs.

"Sesame Street" was originally designed for American preschoolers, capitalizing on their television-viewing habits, information-processing skills, and preferred attention span. The latter, it was assumed, is relatively short, possibly a result of much prior exposure to the formats of television commercials (Lesser, 1974). Television-viewing habits of mothers, who often switch channels, were considered as well. The program was not originally intended for countries whose children were only slightly familiar with television and completely unfamiliar with the kaleidoscopic style of "Sesame Street" or anything less continuous and smooth than "Lassie" or "Flipper."

However, not everything in the program was novel to everybody. Since most Israeli children attend preschools from age three, and virtually all of them are enrolled in preschools at age four, most of the program's *contents* were of little novelty to them. The novelty of the program was entailed primarily in the *way* it presented its contents—that is, in the way television's symbol systems were utilized. Consider a few examples—kaleidoscopic structure, absence of plot, rapid cuts, frequent camera movements, and fragmented spaces.

Thus, studying the effects of the program on Israeli children appeared highly desirable, as there was a definite novel input in precisely the area we wanted to study—the medium's symbol system. This feature of the program allowed us to study the program's effects on the mastery of specific mental skills, not just on the acquisition of the knowledge it conveyed.

Although the study of "Sesame Street" reported in this chapter was aimed at studying "what is" rather than "what can be made to be," it would be difficult to claim that its findings can be generalized to television at large. The same reasons that made the introduction of the program into Israel so attractive for research purposes also limit the generalizability of the findings. Being such a unqiue case, the results can apply only to similar cases, and these are few indeed. Nevertheless, such findings are important, as they can show what cognitive effects a program may have under special, yet not artificial, conditions.

Unlike our experiments, in which we had nearly total control over all the inputs, "Sesame Street" was aired as a package consisting of many components. Some of its coding elements surely modeled mental skills, while others activated or short-circuited them. But it was impossible to verify this empirically. It was possible to *hypothesize* that *certain* skills may be called on or modeled a sufficient number of times, thus allowing us to expect their cultivation.

Thus, we asked, (1) Does exposure to the program enhance the development of the specific skills that we hypothesized to be related to its coding elements? (2) How are age and prior mastery levels related to the skill-cultivating effects of the program? (3) How is skill-cultivation by the program related to the acquisition of knowledge from it? (4) What are the effects of encouraging mothers to coobserve the program with their children?

Our investigation* of "Sesame Street" consisted of three studies: a longitudinal study (n = 317), in which we studied the program's effects over time; a field experiment, whose subjects were part of the longitudinal study (n = 93), in which we studied the effects of encouragement of mothers; and another experiment (n = 114) to study some additional effects of the program.

The Longitudinal Study

Subjects

Ninety-three five-year-old preschoolers, 106 second-graders, and 118 third-graders took part in the study. Of those, 132 children were from schools of low socio-economic status (50 preschoolers, 40 second-graders, and 42 third-graders). The other 185 children were from middle-class schools (43, 66, and 76, respectively). The number of boys and girls in the sample was about equal. Both low- and middle-class schools were selected by means of stratified randomization from the Jerusalem school district.

Method

Since the program was broadcast nationally, it became impossible to assign subjects to a nonviewing group. Therefore, all subjects in the sample were allowed to watch the program (aired twice per week for six months) as they pleased. Subjects were pretested on a mental-skill battery prior to the program's onset. Also, demographic and other data were collected then. Once broadcasting started, amounts of viewing, comprehension, and enjoyment of each subject were measured on six unannounced occasions during the broadcasting season. At the end of the season, all subjects were posttested on the original test battery (independent probing determined that the six-months period between pretesting and posttesting was enough to minimize carryover from pretest to posttest).

*The studies were carried out by the author in collaboration with Lewis Bernstein, Sol Eagelstein, Debora Malve, Allen Mintzberg, and Leorah Welner. A detailed report of part of the studies can be found in a summary report in Salomon (1976).

The amount of accumulated exposure to the program, being the major independent variable of the|study, yielded scores covering the whole range of possible scores in a near-normal distribution. Using multiple-regression techniques with forced orders of variables' entry, it became possible to partial out (that is, to statistically control) the contributions of background variables and of pretest scores to posttest variances. This allowed us to examine the residual, net contribution of exposure to posttest variance and to compute predicted posttest scores for different levels of exposure within and across ages and socioeconomic levels.

Measures

The Test Battery. The test battery used for pretesting and posttesting consisted of two kinds of tests—(1) tests that were originally designed by Ball and Bogatz (1970) for their evaluation of the program, which measured acquired knowledge explicitly taught by the program, and (2) tests designed by Ball and Bogatz, by others, or by us to measure mastery of specific mental skills, not directly taught by the program's content.

The knowledge part of the battery consisted of the following tests—Letter Matching, Number Matching and Picture-Number Matching (the subject selects the correct letter or number that matches a given letter, number, or picture), Relational Concepts (the subject points to a picture depicting a given relation such as *above*), Classification (the subject has to choose one pictured item that fits with the others), and Parts of the Whole (the subject has to select the picture of the correct object when shown a stimulus picture of its components). Cronbach alpha reliabilities ranged from 0.65 to 0.85.

The skill part of the battery consisted of tests that did not measure anything directly taught by the program. They were expected to measure skills that we hypothesized to be affected by the program's coding elements. These were Field-Dependence (Witkin's Children's Embedded Figure Test (CEFT), adopted from Karp and Konstadt, 1971), Picture Ordering (the subject reorders a series of pictures and tells its story), Changing Points of View (the subject selects a picture showing

how somebody else sees an object), Figure and Ground (the
subject identifies single and compound items in a montage picture), and Close-Up (the subject identifies the correct long-shot
picture of an object shown enlarged). Cronbach alpha reliabilities
ranged from 0.53 to 0.78. (Sample items of the Picture Ordering and the Points of View tests are shown in Figures 10 and 11,
respectively).

The preschool test battery consisted of all the knowledge
tests and two of the skill tests (CEFT and Picture Ordering) and
was administered individually by trained testers in the preschools.
The battery for second- and third-graders consisted of only two
of the knowledge tests (Classification and Parts of the Whole)
and all the skill tests. This battery was group-administered in
the classrooms.

Measurement of Exposure. As previously stated, the children's exposure to the program was measured on six unannounced occasions at three-week intervals. The measures were
taken on a day following the broadcasting of a show.

Three factors defined exposure to the program—the
instrumental factor (the actual amount of viewing), the *affective* factor (enjoyment of the program), and the *cognitive* factor
(comprehension and recall of the content). Exposure was thus
measured by viewing, enjoyment, and comprehension. In addition, a fourth measure was taken, consisting of a twelve-item
multiple-choice test administered at the end of the season
together with the posttests. This was the Sesame Street test,
pertaining to the after-the-season recall of salient contents of
the program.

Measurement in the preschools was done by personal
interview, in which each child was asked about the amount of
viewing of the program he did the previous day and how much
he enjoyed what was shown. The children gave their answers by
pointing to one of four circles—the first nearly empty, the
second half filled, the third three-fourths filled, and the fourth
completely full ("I watched a little," "I watched half the time,"
"I watched most of the time," "I watched all the time"). In
answer to the question of enjoyment of the program, the child
pointed to one of three faces—a happy, indifferent, or sad face.

Instructions to child: "Here are a few pictures which tell a story. But they are in a confused order. What should the proper order be?"

FIGURE 10. Sample Item from the Test of Ordering of Pictures.

Imagine that you are the girl sitting on the window sill. How would you see the painter?

FIGURE 11. Sample Item from the Test of Changing Points of View.

Measurement of comprehension was done by four-to-six specific multiple-choice content questions. Questions on the end-of-the-season Sesame Street test were selected from the comprehension items. The measures of exposure in the second and third grades were group-administered.

In a special questionnaire given to the parents (n = 121) similar to the one given to the children, the parents were asked about the amount of program viewing their children did the previous day. The correlation between the parents' and the children's answers was 0.72.

Background Data.   Data on the following variables were collected for all children participating in the study—age, father's and mother's country of origin, father's occupation, father's and mother's level of education, parents' knowledge of English, number of children in the family, and the child's general exposure to movies, newscasts on television, and instructional television broadcasts. Most of the information was collected through questionnaires sent to the parents by the teachers. Some data were taken from each child's file in school or preschool.

Viewing the Program

Before reviewing the results pertaining to the program's effects, let us briefly look at the data describing the subjects' exposure to the program. These data may explain some of the observed effects of the program.

In spite of the fact that the program was broadcast in English with a Hebrew voice-over, it had a great appeal to the subjects. On the average, about 91 percent claimed to watch parts of the program, and about 49 percent claimed to watch the entire program all the time. However, there was a gradual decline in the amount of viewing over time, from 56 percent who claimed to be watching the program all the time at the beginning of the season to 37 percent at the end. The decline was sharpest among middle-class second- and third-graders, who initially were the heaviest viewers. Lower-class preschoolers, who started as light viewers, devoted increasingly more time to watching the program. At the end of the season, they watched more of the program than middle-class school-age children.

Enjoyment of the program followed a parallel trend. Subjects enjoyed the program more at the beginning of the season than toward the end. Middle-class grade-school subjects lost more interest in the program than younger lower-class subjects. Among lower-class preschoolers, the trend was reversed, as was the case with amount of viewing. Indeed, the overall correlation between the two measures was 0.66.

Comprehension of the program lagged behind both viewing and enjoyment. Usually, only about half the subjects who claimed to be heavy viewers could answer all the content questions. At the beginning, younger and less-advantaged children showed the least comprehension of the program, but, with increased exposure, their comprehension improved and reached the level of the middle-class grade-school subjects.

Examination of the interrelations among the three measures of exposure (viewing, enjoyment, and comprehension) reveals a number of interesting points. First, correlations among the measures became increasingly stronger as time passed. For instance, viewing and comprehension correlated 0.49 at the beginning of the season, but they correlated 0.77 toward its end. This suggests that whereas the program's formats may have had great initial appeal, its content was not immediately comprehended. Second, correlations of enjoyment with comprehension were systematically higher for lower-class subjects than for middle-class subjects (0.52 versus 0.28 in preschool, 0.29 versus 0.04 in schools) and for younger subjects than for older subjects (0.47 versus 0.30). This suggests that enjoyment of an educational program is more conducive to learning for lower-class children than to middle-class children. Third, correlations of age and any one of the three exposure measures were stronger in the lower-class group. For instance, age and comprehension correlated 0.66 in the lower-class group and 0.41 in the middle-class group, $p < 0.05$, suggesting that the program was more demanding for the former group.

Most interesting is the finding that fathers' occupational levels correlated positively with the program's average comprehension in the preschool sample ($r = 0.45$, $p < 0.01$), but it correlated negatively with comprehension in the third-grade sample ($r = -0.24, p < 0.05$). Closer examination reveals that the correlation between fathers' occupational level and comprehension was moderate in all age groups at the beginning of the season (from 0.23, $p < 0.05$, to 0.34, $p < 0.01$), but it became stronger in the preschool group and weaker in the grade-school group.

These descriptive data lead to a number of conclusions. First, although the program generally appealed to children, its comprehension did not come easily, particularly to the younger and lower-class children. Their comprehension of the program was apparently more contingent upon their sustained enjoyment of it than the comprehension of older and more-advantaged children. The latter adjusted to the program much faster.

Second, it appears that, as the latter subjects adjusted to the relatively novel coding elements of the program, its contents ceased to interest them. They seem to have discovered that the instructional content was not sufficiently novel for them. (This should come as no surprise, since the program's contents were designed for inner-city three-to-six-year-olds, not middle-class third-graders.)

Generally, the program appears to have been quite novel and mentally demanding, possibly due to its novel modes of presenting material rather than to the material itself.

Results

Preschoolers' knowledge and skill. To examine the effects that exposure to the program had on posttest scores, all preschool children were first divided into four viewing quartiles. The effects of background and initial (pretest) achievement were partialled out, and, for each of the two extreme quartiles (heavy and light viewers) *predicted means* (the means expected on the basis of the regression equation) of posttest scores were computed. This analysis revealed that heavy viewers of the program received significantly higher predicted scores when compared with light viewers on the Letter Matching and the Number Matching tests and on the test of Parts of the Whole and Classification.

As the program was designed directly to instruct in these areas, learning gains by heavy viewers should not surprise us. Exposure, however, did not seem to affect mastery of the skills that were not dealt with explicitly by the program but were related to its coding elements (CEFT and Picture Ordering).

The comparison between viewing quartiles, revealing as it may be, excludes in effect half the subjects. Analysis of the contribution of exposure to the program to posttest performance when *all* preschoolers are considered is presented in Table 3, separately for lower-class (LC, n = 50) and middle-class (MC, n = 43) subjects. This multiple-regression table presents the posttest variance accounted for by background and pretest scores (first two columns) as well as their total contribution when added up (third column). After the contribution of these factors had been partialled out, the combined exposure score was entered, and its *additional* contribution to the posttest variance was tested for significance.

The overall analysis, based on all preschool subjects, yields a picture similar to that provided by the comparison of weighted means. But the present analysis provides more detail. As we have found in the previous analysis, exposure to the program did not contribute to the variances of the two skill tests (CEFT and Picture Ordering) in either the lower-class or middle-class groups. However, the more detailed analysis showed that exposure did contribute to performance on all the knowledge tests in at least one of the socioeconomic groups.

Comparing the contributions of exposure to posttest performance of the middle-class and lower-class groups, we find that, on the three tests of matching and on the test of Relational Concepts, exposure to the program accounted for significantly more of the posttest variance in the lower-class group. The opposite is the case with the tests of Parts of the Whole and Classification, where exposure to the program accounted for a larger portion of the variance in the middle-class group. This finding is somewhat surprising, since it is rarely the case that, other factors held constant, lower-class children benefit more than middle-class ones (Cook and others, 1975).

Examination of the mean scores and the respective

TABLE 3. Percentages of Posttest Variance Accounted for by Background, Initial Achievement, and Exposure for Each Socioeconomic Group at Preschool Age

Test	Source of Variance	All Background Variables ΣR^2	All Pretests $+R^2$	Total ΣR^2	Contribution of Exposure $+R^2$	F
Letter Matching	MC [b]	14.8	36.0	50.8	4.3	1.96
	LC [c]	26.7	21.1	47.8	16.3	5.40[a]
Number Matching	MC	38.2	16.6	54.8	11.0	4.50[a]
	LC	25.2	31.3	56.5	17.8	7.30[a]
Picture-Number	MC	14.1	46.8	60.9	10.1	4.76[a]
Matching	LC	16.8	45.2	62.0	14.0	5.20[a]
Parts of the	MC	19.0	17.8	36.8	18.3	6.90[a]
Whole	LC	20.9	27.6	48.5	6.6	3.60
Relational	MC	16.1	39.1	55.2	4.2	2.10
Concepts	LC	16.9	26.4	43.3	17.7	8.10[a]
Classification	MC	30.1	24.3	54.4	14.3	6.90[a]
	LC	8.2	52.3	60.5	9.2	4.80[a]
Picture	MC	29.1	28.9	58.0	7.4	3.40
Ordering	LC	14.0	27.3	41.3	5.3	2.10
CEFT	MC	3.7	28.4	32.1	9.6	3.75
	LC	15.3	28.5	44.8	5.1	2.20

[a] $p < 0.05$ [b] N = 43   [c] N = 50

standard deviations makes the possibility of a ceiling effect in the middle-class group quite unlikely. Thus, for example, the mean posttest score of the middle-class group was 5.27 (SD = 2.20) on the test of Letter Matching, out of a possible score of 8; their mean Number Matching score was 8.04 (SD = 1.98) out of a possible score of 11; and their mean score was 6.37 (SD = 1.04) on the test of Relational Concepts out of a possible score of 8.

Might there be a profound difference between the goal areas in which each group was more affected? A closer examination of the tests suggests that the different tests of Matching and the Relational Concepts test require an *analytic* approach, calling for differentiation and (partly, at least) visual discrimination. On the other hand, the Parts of the Whole and Classification tests appear to require an approach of *synthesis*—that is, combining elements and abstracting a new entity on the basis of the new combination.

If indeed these are the factors differentiating between the two types of tests, then, on the basis of a taxonomic–hierarchical view of skills, we could hypothesize that improvements in synthesis need to be contingent upon *prior* achievements in analysis. It follows that children who have reached an initial fair mastery of analytic skills should be able to improve in synthesis. On the other hand, children with initially poor mastery of analytic skills should improve first in analysis. Thus, we would expect early achievements on tests that require analysis to predict later achievements on tests of synthesis, but early achievements in synthesis should not predict later preformance on analytic tests.

The hypothesis can be tested by means of the crossed-lagged correlation panel. Pretest and posttest acheivements on both types of tests are intercorrelated, and the magnitude of these correlations is then examined. The tests of Classification and Parts of the Whole were considered to represent the area of synthesis; the other tests were considered as tests of analytic and discrimination ability.

Examination of the correlations made it evident that prediction from early mastery of analytic skills to later mastery of synthesis is far better than prediction in the opposite direction. For instance, pretest scores on the Number Matching test (assumed to be a test of visual analysis) correlated 0.41 with Classification posttest scores. However, pretest Classification scores correlated only -0.02 with Number Matching posttest scores (difference significant at $p < 0.05$). Similarly, pretest scores on the Picture-Number Matching test correlated 0.22 with posttest scores on the Parts of the Whole test, but pretest scores of the latter correlated -0.24 (difference significant at $p < 0.05$) with posttest scores on the matching test. (Path analyses conducted at a later date confirmed these findings.) Thus, there seems to be evidence to support the claims that (a) the tests pertain to two classes of abilities, analysis and synthesis, and that mastery in synthesis is contingent upon *prior* mastery in the area of analysis.

In light of this finding, one can better understand why lower-class preschoolers, whose initial mastery was relatively low on all tests, benefited more in one area, while middle-class children benefited more in another. Since middle-class children started with a relatively high level of analytic mastery, their synthesis ability could be affected by the program. Lower-class children, on the other hand, needed to improve their analytic abilities before exposure to the program could improve their abilities of synthesis. It is reasonable to conclude that exposure to "Sesame Street" had differential effects. Each child gained from the program wherever the individual deficiency (relatively poor mastery) was more basic, hence the stronger effect on lower-class children in areas measured by the tests of matching and the Relational Concepts test and the stronger effect on middle-class children in areas measured by the Classification and Parts of the Whole tests.

The absence of any evidence to show that exposure to the program accounted for variance on the two *skill* tests suggests one of two things. It is possible that the two tests measured irrelevant skills. But this possibility can be ruled out because of the strong positive effects that exposure had in precisely these skill areas in the grade-school sample (see below).

The other and more likely possibility is that our preschool subjects attempted to extract knowledge from the program that did not require them to mentally handle any of the coding elements that could have either called upon or modeled the measured skills. In other words, given their overall level of cognitive development and the generally fragmented way in which children of that age extract knowledge from a television show (Collins, in press), they did not face any difficulty with the novel coding elements—they simply ignored them.

Knowledge and Skill of Second- and Third-Graders. The test battery for the grade-school subjects included only two of the knowledge tests adiministered to the preschoolers (Parts of the Whole and Classification) and five instead of two skill tests. Two of the skill tests (CEFT and Picture Ordering) were similar to the ones used with the preschool sample. Statistical analyses carried out on the grade-school data were identical to those done with the preschool data.

As with the preschool sample, heavy viewers (upper quartile) were compared on the posttest scores with light viewers (lower quartile), after all other measured sources of variance had been partialled out. There were significant differences between heavy and light viewers on *all* posttests. Exposure to the program accounted for the largest portions of variance on the Classification, Close-Up, and Parts of the Whole tests. It accounted for smaller amounts of posttest variance on the remaining tests.

Multiple-regression analysis based on the *whole* school sample (n = 224) is presented in Table 4 separately for middle-class (MC) and lower-class (LC) subjects.

The first point to note relates to the contribution of exposure to the variance of the tests, irrespective of socioeconomic group. After partialling out the contributions of the background variables and initial achievements, it becomes evident that exposure contributed substantially to the variance of two tests—Parts of the Whole (17-26 percent) and Classification (13-30 percent). Exposure accounted somewhat less for the variance of the tests of Close-Up (12-21 percent) and Figure and Ground (4-14 percent), and it accounted for even smaller portions of the variance on the remaining tests. In general, the program contributed more to the variance of the tests in the intended goal areas of the program (Classification and Parts of the Whole) and somewhat less in the unintended skill areas.

The second point to note pertains to the differential contribution of exposure to posttest variances in the two socioeconomic groups. Exposure appears to contribute more to the posttest variance in the middle-class group than in the lower-class group. For example, exposure accounted for 21.3 percent of the Close-Up test in the middle-class group, but it accounted for only 12.2 percent of the variance in the lower-class group. This difference cannot be explained by different distributions of scores in the two groups, as the standard deviations were surprisingly similar.

TABLE 4. Percentage of Posttest Variance Accounted for by Background Initial Achievement and Exposure for Each Socioeconomic Group.

Test \ Source of Variance		Background and Pretests ΣR^2	Contribution of Exposure $+R^2$	F
Parts of the Whole	MC[d]	10.3	26.5	52.61[c]
	LC [e]	25.6	17.1	19.06[b]
Classification	MC	13.4	30.6	66.76[c]
	LC	30.1	12.9	14.67[b]
CEFT	MC	33.8	6.7	13.78[b]
	LC	24.5	9.7	9.39[b]
Picture Ordering	MC	23.4	9.8	18.45[b]
	LC	34.4	4.8	5.02[a]
Points of View	MC	14.8	12.0	21.27[c]
	LC	20.9	8.7	7.98[b]
Figure and Ground	MC	29.9	14.5	34.27[c]
	LC	27.7	3.7	3.33
Close-Up	MC	19.0	21.3	45.22[c]
	LC	28.8	12.2	12.65[b]

[a] $p < 0.05$ [b] $p < 0.01$ [c] $p < 0.001$
[d] N = 142
[e] N = 82

The only exception is the CEFT, where exposure accounts for more variance in the lower-class group than in the middle-class group. This brings back the hypothesis that lower-class subjects gain more in analysis (particularly visual analysis), and middle-class subjects benefit more in synthesis and abstraction.

To examine whether this hypothesis is also supported in the school sample, a crossed-lagged correlation panel analysis was performed. It was expected that, since analysis precedes synthesis, early achievements in analysis should predict later achievements in synthesis, but not vice versa. CEFT, known to be an analytic test, was intercorrelated with scores on the tests of Classification and Parts of the Whole (assumed to pertain to synthesis) at two different times. The analyses upheld the hypothesis. CEFT pretest scores correlated 0.24 with Classification and 0.20 with Parts of the Whole posttest scores. But Classification and Parts of the Whole pretests correlated only 0.01 and –0.03 with CEFT posttest scores.

It is worth comparing the amount of posttest variance attributable to exposure in the school sample with that in the preschool sample for Classification and Parts of the Whole. Although exposure accounted for only 8.4 percent of the Classification variance in preschools, it accounted for 21.6 percent in the schools. The respective figures for the Parts of the Whole test are 13.3 percent and 21.8 percent. Does this mean that the program taught the school children more than the preschoolers?

It should be noted that the total amount of variance of these tests accounted for by background and pretests in the preschools is far larger than in the schools (53.7 percent versus 16.8 percent for Classification and 20.3 percent versus 9.2 percent for Parts of the Whole). This suggests that posttest performance of preschool children is much more contingent upon their background and prior achievements, but these relationships are far weaker in the schools. Thus, the posttest performance of the school children, being less accounted for by home environment and prior knowledge, appears to be more responsive to external stimulation.

A similar pattern can be found in the school sample with respect to the amounts of posttest variances accounted for by background and pretests in the two socioeconomic groups. We systematically find that more of the variance is accounted for by these variables in the lower-class group than in the middle-class group. The only exception is the CEFT, where there is a stronger relationship between background and posttest in the middle-class group. This is also the only test on which lower-class subjects benefited from exposure to "Sesame Street" more than middle-class subjects.

It becomes evident that, as the contribution of background variables to posttest scores decreases, the contribution of exposure to those scores tends to increase. This is, on first sight, only a statistical artifact. However, it may suggest a rather important and profound difference. First, no such difference between the two socioeconomic groups was found in the preschool data, although there were differences in the amounts of posttest variances accounted for by exposure. Second, there is no evidence to suggest that, as the amount of variance accounted for by one source decreases, another source becomes *necessarily* a more significant predictor. Nor is it the case that the lower-class group is either more heterogeneous or more homogeneous from the outset than the middle-class group. Thus, we cannot avoid the conclusion that background variables predict posttest scores of preschool children better than for school children, and that, among the latter, posttest scores of lower-class children are more contingent upon their background than those of middle-class children.

A similar finding was reported by McCandless, Roberts, and Starnes (1972). Their study was conducted on 443 seventh-graders in the United States. Initial skill measures were found to be highly correlated with later achievements in their LC sample ($r = 0.74$), but no such correlation was found in their MC group ($r = 0.20$). It appears as a general case that older and more well-to-do children are more susceptible to educational stimulation than younger and less well-to-do children. The latter's achievements are more strongly bound by their background and prior achievements (White, 1976).

Relations of Skill and Knowledge. The results of our study indicate that skill-mastery was affected to a lesser extent than the achievements in the program's original goal areas. For example, exposure to the program accounted for 30 percent of the knowledge acquisition test of Classification in MC school children, but for only 10 percent of the skill test of Picture Ordering in the same group. This pattern of more knowledge acquisition than skill-mastery improvement is consistent across ages and socioeconomic groups. Since gains from the program's content (knowledge gains) were hypothesized to be contingent upon improvements of relevant skill-mastery, we examined the relations between them as they changed over time. It was reasonable to hypothesize that, although it was not essential for the two areas to be interrelated *before* the broadcasting of the program, they should become increasingly associated toward the *end* of the season. Such a change should occur in the group of heavy viewers but not in the group of light viewers. Moreover, if skill-mastery in knowledge extraction improves, then early skill-mastery should predict later knowledge acquisition, but not vice versa.

By and large, the correlations between the two sets of variables, knowledge and skill-mastery, before broadcasting of the program began were quite low. The pattern changed significantly after the broadcasting season. There was an increase in the size of the correlations in both viewing quartiles. However, the increase in the light-viewing group was far less salient than in the heavy-viewing group (median correlation of all skill tests with the knowledge tests was 0.29 in the former group and 0.56 in the latter group). It thus appears, as expected, that much exposure to the program made learning of the program's content closely related to skill-mastery.

The results of crossed-lagged panel correlation analyses confirmed the hypothesis about the order of effects. Scores on the CEFT, Picture Ordering, and Close-Up tests predicted later achievements on the Classification and Parts of the Whole tests to a moderate extent (0.20 to 0.44); the converse was not the case. In other words, early knowledge scores did not predict later skill-mastery scores, suggesting that skill-mastery improved in the service of knowledge acquisition.

An Experiment: Encouraging Mothers to Coobserve the Program*

This experiment was part of the longitudinal study. Its purpose was to examine the extent to which both knowledge acquisition from the program and skill-cultivation by this mode of presentation could be enhanced when mothers coobserve the program with their five-year-olds. Ball and Bogatz (1970) found

*A more detailed description of the study can be found in Salomon (1977).

that encouraging mothers to encourage their children to watch "Sesame Street" resulted in better learning. Although Cook and others (1975) questioned this finding, other studies show that mothers' involvement improves children's learning (for instance, Karnes and others, 1970).

Specifically, the experiment was designed to answer the following questions. Assuming that skills can be cultivated by exposure to the program's modes of presentation, does the coobservation of mothers make any difference beyond the effects of sheer exposure? If mothers' coobservation has an effect on knowledge acquisition and skill-cultivation by the program, what may account for it?

Method

The mothers of half the preschool sample (n = 50) that took part in the longitudinal study were asked on two occasions to coobserve the program with their five-year-olds. They were not told what to do with their children or anything else, except to be with their children each time the program was shown. The mothers of the other children (n = 43) were not contacted at all and thus may or may not have coobserved with their children.

About half the subjects in the encouraged group were of low-socioeconomic status and the other half were from middle-class homes. The composition of the not-encouraged group was similarly divided between the two socioeconomic classes.

No measures of compliance by the encouraged mothers were taken, but there were clear indications (through the complaints of mothers of time taken from daily household chores) that mothers did as they were asked. As this study was embedded in the larger study, the data gathered for the larger study were used for analysis of this study.

Results

Middle-class subjects received significantly higher pretest scores than lower-class subjects in both the encouraged and the not-encouraged groups. However, these differences persisted on the posttests of the not-encouraged group, but they became strikingly smaller in the encouraged group. It became evident that encouragement of mothers to coobserve the program with their children had a positive effect on the learning gains of lower-class subjects.

However, this effect was indirect. When *all* other variables were held constant, encouragement did not contribute significantly to any posttest variance in either one of the two socioeconomic groups. The only exception was the CEFT variance, to which encouragement contributed 13.0 percent ($F = 5.17$, $p < 0.05$) in the middle-class group. Examination of the contributions of encouragement to exposure revealed, however, that it accounted for 23.6 percent ($F = 25.2, p < 0.01$) of the *enjoyment* variance and 6.1 percent ($F = 6.28, p < 0.05$) of the *comprehension* variance in the low-status group. It did not account significantly to any of the exposure measures of the middle-class group. Thus, encouragement seems to have affected learning of the low-status subjects indirectly through its effects on enjoyment and comprehension of the program.

The effects of encouragement were best seen when the amounts of variance accounted for by socioeconomic differences were examined in the encouraged and the not-encouraged groups. As one would expect, socioeconomic differences accounted for large portions of the exposure and posttest measures in the not-encouraged group. These accounted-for variances range from 0.1 percent on the Parts of the Whole test to 44 percent on the Picture Ordering test. Socioeconomic differences accounted for dramatically less variance in the encouraged group. *Generally, the amount of variance accounted for by socioeconomic status was reduced to half or even less by the encouragement of mothers to coobserve.* Thus, encouragement made lower-class subjects benefit from the program nearly as much as middle-class subjects. Only on the CEFT did encouragement *facilitate* the learning of middle-class subjects but not that of lower-class subjects.

Discussion

The coobservation of mothers had a positive indirect effect on the learning of lower-class subjects, but this effect was restricted to the instructional goal areas of the program.

Encouragment had also a direct significant effect on the achievements of middle-class subjects in one of the two skill areas expected to be affected by the program's modes of presentation (CEFT).

The school-age subjects in the longitudinal study were affected in this area (lower-class subjects somewhat more than middle-class subjects) *without* any planned participation of mothers. In the preschool group, only mothers' coobservation could produce such an effect, and it was restricted to the middle-class group. That group started out with already higher CEFT scores than the lower-class group ($\overline{X}$ = 5.03, SD = 1.75 and $\overline{X}$ = 3.35, SD = 1.77 respectively; t = 4.26, $p<0.01$).

Could it be that mothers' coobservation affects learning more strongly in those subjects who have a better head start? This possibility must be ruled out in light of the stronger encouragement effects in most other measured areas for the lower-class group. That group started out with generally poorer scores than the middle-class group.

Note that mothers' coobservation affected lower-class subjects indirectly. Its effects on middle-class subjects, although restricted to the CEFT, were direct. Possibly, no one mechanism accounts for both effects. Recall that enjoyment was found to predict comprehension better for lower-class subjects than for middle-class subjects. The finding that mothers' coobservation affected the learning of lower-class subjects primarily through the mediation of *enjoyment* of the program suggests that the mother may have served as a situational energizer, or source of general arousal to the child (Zajonc, 1968; Epps and others, 1971). This may have led to more "time on task," or to the children's attempts to process the presented information at deeper levels. This does not imply, however, that the children attempted to extract information beyond the limits of their existing capabilities by trying to handle the program's relatively novel modes of presentation. They may have processed the information more deeply, thus gaining more from the program's instruction, by applying mental skills that they had already mastered.

The direct effect of mothers' coobservation in the middle-class subjects is somewhat different. First, for these subjects, mothers' coobservation is a less outstanding event (there are significantly fewer siblings in these families), thus having less of a *general* energizing effect. Second, their overall initial levels of knowledge and skill were higher than those of the lower-class subjects, thus making them more likely to attempt to handle some of the novel coding elements of the program. The coobserving mother may have served for them as a more specific tutor who exerts control over specific input stimuli (Levenstein, 1970; Gray, 1971).

Why, then, did the coobservation of mothers affect only CEFT scores in the middle-class group? For, if coobserving mothers serve these subjects as specific tutors, why does their tutorship fail to affect other areas of knowledge and skill? I can only suggest a speculative answer at this point, as there is little in the data obtained in the study that pertains to the question.

Two lines of research are relevant here. One line suggests that lower-class American children derive significantly fewer messages from a televised episode than middle-class children (Columbia Broadcasting System, 1974). The implication of this finding may be that the coobserving mother of the lower-class child, by functioning as a general energizer, helps him to extract more message-units from a program. As information-extraction efforts become spread over a relatively wide span of messages, lower-class children gain more knowledge in a variety of areas, as indeed was the case. The middle-class child, however, extracts more messages on his own and thus can be tutored or encouraged to focus more on details to be selected out from the program.

The second line of research shows that children's field-independence is cultivated in home environments where specific comforting practices are used by mothers (Dyk and Witkin, 1965) and where mothers use more specific teaching-helping procedures (Johnston, 1974). It seems plausible to argue that our coobserving middle-class mothers may have provided direct tutoring in the selection of specific items from the program, thus affecting their children's field-independence.

These are but speculations, based on somewhat questionable generalizations. The reader should be cautious in accepting them as empirically verified conclusions.

A Replication: "Sesame Street" Versus Adventure Films

To compensate for some of the obvious methodological deficiencies of the longitudinal study, notably the absence of a control group, an experiment was designed. One hundred fourteen second-graders from a Jerusalem school, representing different socioeconomic levels, were randomly assigned to watch either eight hours of "Sesame Street" on a wide screen or to watch an equal number of hours of adventure and nature films. It was assumed that the modes of presentation in the adventure films were well known to the subjects, but those of "Sesame Street" were not. The subjects were shown the films or "Sesame Street" one hour per day for eight days. Viewing was done in groups of 57 subjects.

The measures employed were the same skill tests used in the longitudinal study. A Perseverance test was added. Subjects were given a booklet filled with random numbers and asked to cross out specific digits. They were told to cross these digits out as fast as they could and to keep on doing this as long as they could, for "the more they crossed out, the better it is." Such a task we assumed to simulate nonrewarding tasks required, for instance, as part of school homework and to measure children's willingness to persevere. Similar measures were used by Hamilton and Gordon (1978) in their study of preschoolers' behaviors. Comparison between the groups on data obtained from school files indicated that the groups were comparable.

Results

The findings of the longitudinal study pertaining to the second-grade age-group were essentially replicated in this study. The "Sesame Street" group performed significantly better than the adventure-film control group on CEFT, Points of View, Figure and Ground, and Close-Up tests. The difference between the groups approached significance on the Picture Ordering test.

The results pertaining to the Perseverance test were surprising. The control group performed significantly better than the "Sesame Street" group on that test. The difference in treatments accounted for 26 percent of the Perseverance variance, $F(1,112) = 12.4, p < 0.01$.

Discussion

The findings of this study generally replicated those of the longitudinal sutdy, although the measured effects were substantially smaller in this study. Exposure to "Sesame Street" in the experiment accounted for between 3.0 percent and 12 percent of the test variances, compared with 3.7 percent to 21.3 percent accounted for on the skill tests in the longitudinal study. This should come as no surprise, since the treatment here consisted of only eight hours of viewing, whereas heavy viewers in the longitudinal study could observe up to forty-eight hours of the program. The fact that the same effects, although weaker, were found at all was a pleasant outcome.

The relatively poor perseverance by the "Sesame Street" group in comparison with the control group can be interpreted in two ways. It is possible that "Sesame Street" had no effect on the subjects, and that they had a lesser tendency to persevere from the very beginning. But this interpretation must be ruled out by the randomized assignment of subjects to groups and the initial similarity of the groups, as determined by comparing their grades, parents' education, and ages.

The second interpretation is that the program indeed had an effect on the subjects' *tendencies,* rather than their skills, for dealing with an unrewarding task. Obviously, the *ability* to persevere was not affected; rather, it must have been the subjects' willingness to persevere that was affected by their exposure to the fast-paced, kaleidoscopic structure of the program.

Summary and General Discussion

The findings from our three "Sesame Street" studies can be summarized as follows:

1. The symbolic coding elements of a television program can affect the mastery of specific mental skills, not only under controlled experimental conditions but also under normal viewing conditions.
2. The levels of knowledge and skill that children bring with them to the viewing situation determine in what areas of knowledge and skill they benefit more or less.

3. Preschoolers are far less affected by a program's coding elements than second- and third-graders.
4. Coobserving mothers affect learning from a program, apparently by serving as general energizers for some children and as specific tutors for others.
5. A program's coding elements affect not only skill-mastery but preferences or tendencies for information processing as well.

The longitudinal study showed that children's mastery of specific mental skills was affected by exposure to "Sesame Street." Since there was no explicit tutoring of these skills by the program, it is reasonable to conclude that exposure to the coding elements, rather than to the content, affected skill-mastery..

Exposure to the program accounted for the largest portion of variance on the Close-Up test (up to 21.3 percent in the middle-class group). This test bears much resemblance to the Detail and Concept test (scores on the two tests correlate 0.64 in a sample of forty second-graders), which measured a skill called for by nearly all coding elements that we have manipulated (see Chapter Four). This resemblance suggests that coding elements, not content, affected the mastery of skills.

But the magnitude of the variances accounted for by exposure on some of the knowledge and skill tests may raise suspicion. Could exposure to a program, even if extended over a six-month period, account for up to 26 percent of the variance on a test like Parts of the Whole and up to 21 percent on the Close-Up test? Such magnitudes of variance appear somewhat questionable.

Since the findings of the longitudinal study were replicated in the second experiment, it becomes clear that, even if the magnitude of the effect is somehow inflated, the existence of a genuine effect cannot be denied. It seems that the combination of two factors may have accounted for what is indeed a spuriously large effect. First, there is the statistical factor. If more relevant background variables would have been measured, thus accounting for more posttest variance, less variance would have been accounted for by exposure. Second, there is the genuine effect of the program's novelty. It is doubtful whether this program could have affected less television-naive children to the same extent. Indeed, when only eight hours of the program were shown in the second experiment, to subjects who by then already had two months of exposure to the program, the observed effects were much weaker.

Thus, it appears that the program's coding elements did have skill-cultivating effects, but their observed magnitude was influenced by both the temporary novelty of the program and the statistical methods used.

The finding that lower-class children learn more in analysis and middle-class children learn more in synthesis is quite revealing but not new. It proves again that a medium's effects depend not only on its messages but also on what children bring with them to the viewing situation. However, this dictum—by now already classical—can be extended into additional areas.

Comparing the preschool with the grade-school results, we observed that only the skills of the latter were affected by the program's coding elements. Grade-school children apparently brought with them to the viewing situation something that the preschoolers did not. Generally, preschoolers obtain only fragmented bits of information from a television program, but school-age children attempt to interrelate them (Collins, in press). This is in agreement with the finding that preschoolers use the medium of drawing to create their own language to express what they desire, while school-age children are more oriented to reality, obsessed with accuracy, and concerned with reaching closure (Gardner and Wolf, 1978).

For reasons of cognitive development, the preschooler evidently aims at extracting that kind of information from a television program which does not require him mentally to transform or imitate novel coding elements. This means that the preschooler has a smaller chance of being affected by novel coding elements, as he ignores them altogether or transforms them mentally by applying skills that are already mastered but often inappropriate.

One of the conclusions in Chapter Four was that the kind of information a learner is required to extract from a message ("top-down" process) determines what coding elements are dealt with and hence also what mental skill is applied ("bottom-up" process). It is possible now to extend this conclusion by suggesting that not only the task but also a child's cognitive development determines the "top-down" process, which in turn determines what coding elements are dealt with. However, while a learning task determines what information (and what coding elements) one *should* address, one's cognitive development determines what one *can* address.

Mothers' coobservation, as we have seen, can have some effects in this respect, but these are limited by the kinds of information a child can extract. Coobservation does not seem to lead the child to extract knowledge beyond his capacity. Coobservation can, however, make the child invest more effort, extract quantitatively more information, and therefore gain more knowledge. Perhaps only when the child is capable of extracting relatively much information anyway can mothers' coobservation (coupled apparently with specific tutoring) lead him to cope with novel codes and consquently to be affected by them.

Finally, the second experiment, which partly replicated the longitudinal findings, showed that exposure to "Sesame Street" leads to a decline in perseverance. There are two issues related to this finding. First, was it the ability or the tendency to persevere that was affected? Second, was it the program's kaleidoscopic nature (that is, its symbolic way of structuring information) or simply the short duration of each episode that might have affected perseverance?

Perseverance is often conceptualized as a motivational factor. But as Hamilton and Gordon (1978) have shown, children's perseverance at an unrewarding task is strongly affected by situational factors, such as reinforcement and helpful suggestions. Thus, it would be unreasonable to claim that perseverance, as measured by us, taps more than one's situationally contingent tendency to persist at a task.

This leads to the second question—namely, what were these situational factors in the treatment that caused the large decline in perseverance? One could argue that the short duration of each episode, which did not call for the accumulation of information, affected the children's perseverance, rather than any specific coding elements. However, such an attribute is very much a part of a medium's mode of appearance or symbol system. One of the characteristics of a symbol system, discussed in Chapter Two, is its rules of creating increasingly more complex units of characters or coding elements (syntagms in film, paragraphs and chapters in texts). Creating a kaleidoscope or montage of such units is one mode of appearance (not necessarily unique to television). The continuity that characterized the adventure films in the experiment is another mode of appearance. Thus, the short duration of unrelated episodes, which indeed may have affected perseverence tendencies, *is* a part of the program's symbolic nature.

In summary, an extremely novel television program can affect the mastery of specific mental skills thorugh the coding elements it employs. Such changes in skill-mastery serve the purposes of information extraction. Since children of different ages and levels of skill-mastery are capable of extracting different kinds and amounts of information, the observed effects are not uniform. Much depends on what children are already capable of extracting.

The "Sesame Street" studies were carried out under normal conditions, but the program itself was far from typical. Its high degree of novelty when introduced into Israel in 1971 is typical neither of the television programs and films to which children are exposed nor of other media, such as books or comic strips. What, then, are the effects of a medium's symbol systems as *commonly* used? This question is dealt with in the next chapter.

EIGHT

Cross-Cultural Cognitive Effects of Television Exposure

⚉ ⚉ ⚉ ⚉ ⚉ ⚉ ⚉

In the preceding chapters, I presented the rationale for the general hypothesis that media's symbol systems can cultivate mental skills. I also provided empirical evidence to suggest that some coding elements can be made to have such effects, and that they also have some effects under common conditions of exposure, when the coding elements are sufficiently novel.

As I argued at the end of Chapter Seven, it is still unclear whether regular daily exposure to common messages cultivates mental skills as well. Although the general rationale may apply also to the latter case, in practice, children may not be sufficiently motivated to handle many of a medium's symbolic components. Similarly, there may be no need for them to extract the kind of knowledge from coded messages that requires them

187

to activate relatively poorly mastered skills or to imitate supplanting coding elements. Deregowski (1968) found that Zambian domestic servants did not show greater facility in dealing with three-dimensional perspective in drawings than mine workers, in spite of their greater exposure to European drawings. Thus, although three-dimensional facility can be taught, daily passive exposure to drawings does not have such an effect.

Studying the cognitive effects of a medium's symbol systems requires, first, a pervasive medium to which children of equal education are exposed to varying degrees over an extended period of time. The medium of television serves in this capacity better than other media. Studying the effects of television on the cultivation of mental skills clearly calls for a wide variation of exposure to the medium. Such a variation can be found within any given culture, but a cross-cultural comparison allows for even larger variation. Such variation would be highly desirable in our study, as it would allow the comparison of heavy versus light televiewers.

Samples taken from different cultures may be said to represent individuals who have been assigned to different treatment groups by natural circumstances rather than by random assignment or by self-selection (Lloyd, 1972). However, a comparison of two culturally different samples could be valid only if they are shown to be identical in all relevant aspects except for the independent variable of the study—that is, the amount of exposure to television. This approach differs significantly from the typical cross-cultural study, in which samples are taken from extremely different cultures, thus entailing numerous known and unknown differences. A comparison of the latter kind often fails to identify the specific cultural factors that may account for the observed differences (Goodnow, 1969). In this study, the cultural factor that was expected to affect skill-mastery was identified. Thus, the purpose of this study was to examine the extent to which mastery of specific mental skills could be ascribed to differences of exposure to a specific cultural medium, namely television, other factors being equal as much as possible.

The key factor of such a study is, of course the independent variable—*exposure to television*. But what does *exposure* mean in this context? Many cross-cultural studies use such terms as *experience* or *familiarity* (for example, Hudson, 1967; Harari and McDavid, 1966) with cultural tools or media to explain cross-cultural differences. Often, such terms remain ambiguous. Scribner and Cole (1978) argue that the specific kind of activity one applies to cultural phenomena affects the mastery of specific skills. Their study, mentioned earlier, clearly shows that the effects of literacy are closely connected to how people actually use it. What then does exposure to television mean in terms of the activities it entails?

According to the rationale presented in Chapters Three and Five, one needs to transform mentally (and, in some cases, to learn by observation) the coding elements of a message in the service of knowledge extraction. The recoding of a message's coding elements, which is the activity that may affect the mastery of mental skills, is but a means to the end of extracting knowledge.

Thus, exposure entails more than just looking at television programs. It entails the active extraction of knowledge and may be labeled *literate viewing* (not necessarily the same thing as *intelligent viewing*). It is a process of information extraction by the active negotiation of the coding elements of the message. More passive ways of televiewing, which do not result in any knowledge extraction, cannot be considered for these purposes as genuine exposure to the medium. (Measuring exposure in terms of, say, time devoted to watching specific programs is, of course, valid for other purposes, such as studying children's preferences.)

If exposure to television is defined in terms of the information extracted from it, then it becomes clear that the skills that facilitate information extraction are the ones whose mastery should be affected by viewing television. Other skills, such as verbal ability, which are either so general that they may serve information extraction from many symbol systems, regardless of medium, or which are unrelated to the extraction of knowledge from television, would not be uniquely affected by televiewing. Thus, we selected for measurement mainly those skills that we had previously associated with knowledge extraction from television.

I should emphasize that the focus of the study was not on the skills themselves but rather on the skill-cultivating effects of television. This study differs, therefore, from many cross-cultural or developmental studies, whose major concern is with specific skills or abilities. Focusing on what exposure does to the cultivation of mental skills enables us to choose a variety of different skills deemed to be relevant, regardless of their generality. Thus, many of the skills whose relevance to knowledge extraction from film and television was demonstrated in earlier studies were also tested for mastery in this study. We hypothesized that exposure to television, measured by the amount of the simplest possible kind of knowledge extracted from its programs (literate viewing), should be correlated with the mastery of specific mental skills. A second, closely related hypothesis was that children who are more heavily exposed to the medium should manifest better skill-mastery than those who are less exposed, in those skill areas that are related to literate viewing.

The hypothesized relations between literate viewing and skill-mastery could not be uniform across ages. Children whose cognitive development permits the extraction of only fragmented information units would not manifest strong relations between skill-mastery and exposure. Similarly, preadolescents might not manifest such relations either, since they may have already reached the level of skill-mastery necessary for the kind of information extraction they generally aim at. Only midschool-aged children would exhibit the kind of influence of exposure on skill-mastery that we wanted to study. Thus, we hypothesized that younger children (nine-year-olds) would manifest a stronger effect than older children (eleven-year-olds).

Method*

To test our hypotheses, we needed two kinds of samples. The first was a cross-cultural sample of children who have

*The study reported here was carried out in collaboration with Akiba A. Cohen of the Hebrew University of Jerusalem and David Feldman of Tufts University, Boston.

comparable levels of mental development, education, upbringing, and family background but differ with respect to the amounts of television they consume. The second kind of sample was across socioeconomic levels within a given culture, in which children consume television to a similar extent as the other samples but differ with respect to their general level of skill-mastery. Such samples should allow us to examine the relationship between literate viewing and skill-mastery within and across cultures, ages, and socioeconomic levels.

On the basis of available data (Greenberg and Dervin, 1970; Nielsen, 1977), we knew that American children are generally heavily exposed to television, so we turned to the United States for a sample of heavy television viewers. Israelis, who have available only one black-and-white noncommercial television channel, which broadcasts only a few hours each night, were the source for light television viewers. To allow comparability, the two samples needed to be of the same socioeconomic level with generally similar characteristics. Thus, we selected the two samples from known middle-class schools.

To these samples, a third sample of lower-class Israeli children was added. This addition allowed us to do cross-cultural comparisons between the American and Israeli middle-class groups and between the Israeli middle-class and lower-class groups.

Subjects

The subjects in the three samples were drawn from two age-groups, fourth-graders and sixth-graders. Whole classrooms were drawn from known middle-class and lower-class schools serving the Boston and Jerusalem districts. The breakdown into country, age, and socioeconomic groups is as follows: American sample (all middle-class Bostonians), 87 fourth-graders and 73 sixth-graders; Israeli middle-class sample (Jerusalem), 105 fourth-graders and 113 sixth-graders; Israeli lower-class sample (Jerusalem), 160 fourth-graders and 111 sixth-graders.

Procedure

The entire battery of measures used in the study consisted of three clusters (see details in next section): (1) background data secured from the children, their parents, and school files and records; (2) exposure to television, including televiewing habits, preferences over other media, amount of viewing done "yesterday," and, most importantly, amount of literate viewing (LV) done "yesterday"; (3) mastery of selected mental skills.

For the Israeli samples, the battery was divided into five parts of equal length and administered on five occasions to the two groups. In the United States, however, for practical and administrative reasons, the battery was divided into three parts and administered on three occasions. The Israeli battery included three additional reference tests, whose purpose was to aid in validating the skill measures. Since these tests were not included in the American battery, the testing load on each of the three occasions in the United States was identical to that in Israel.

Testing was carried out in the classrooms during regular school days. All tests were group-administered. Two to four trained students administered the battery in each classroom. Administration of the tests and other measures was done once a week on *randomly selected, unannounced* days. It took five weeks to complete the administration in Israel and three weeks in the United States.

Measures

All data except the information gathered from school files were obtained by means of tests and questionnaires. The latter served to obtain data pertaining to background and exposure variables.

Background Data. Background data obtained from each child dealt with after-school activities, movie-going, book-reading, helping at home, playing with games and toys, reading newspapers and magazines, and the like. Data obtained directly from the parents pertained to mother's and father's education and occupation, size of household, ownership of appliances, age at which child began formal education, and so forth.

Exposure. As discussed earlier, the exposure measure served as the major independent variable of the study. A number of different measures of exposure were obtained, including televiewing habits, preferences over other media, and amount viewed "yesterday." Each of these measures was obtained on at least two occasions, for reliability and validity purposes. However, the major measure of exposure was the literate-viewing measure (LV); it was obtained three times in the United States and five times in Israel.

The LV measure consisted of a series of content questions, one question pertaining to every fifteen-minute segment of broadcasting. The questions were extremely simple and called for the recognition of a highly salient feature that appeared in the corresponding fifteen mintues of the broadcast. Each question was followed by four alternative answers, only one of which was correct. There was also a possible response of "I didn't watch the program." A sample question follows.

On 'Hawaii Five-O' yesterday we saw:
1. A submarine
2. A horse race
3. A plane crash
4. A car accident

Correct responses to the LV questionnaire did not correlate with verbal intelligence, thus indicating that this measure did not tap intelligent viewing. It was reasoned that a child who could not answer the simple recognition questions included in the LV measure may have turned the television set on but did not extract any information from it. On the other hand, a child who answered the LV questions correctly was assumed to have attempted to extract information from it and thus was assumed to have recoded the symbolic carriers of the messages. Interestingly enough, LV correlated only about 0.50 with the self-reported number of hours of viewing "yesterday," suggesting that self-reports (particularly of the younger children) can be quite misleading. Alternatively, this unexpected low correlation suggests that viewing for the extraction of information is only part of what a child does while "watching television." As the correlation between children's self-reports and mothers' reports is 0.72 (Chapter Seven), we were inclined to prefer the alternative interpretation.

The LV questionnaire tapped the viewing of programs that were broadcasted the preceding afternoon and evening. A team of investigators watched *all* aired broadcasting between 4:00 and 10:00 P.M. and composed the twenty-four questions (in Israel) or the 192 questions (in the U.S.), one for each fifteen minutes of broadcasting. The whole questionnaire was typed and mimeographed the same night and administered the following morning. To avoid overload, each cluster of questions was identified by the time period it covered. A child who did not watch during that time period simply moved on without attempting to answer the questions on that page. The reliability of the measure was 0.76 in the Israeli sample and 0.82 in the American sample.

Tests of Mental Skills. Of the twelve tests we used, the following were adopted from the study reported in Chapter Four (values in parentheses indicate reliabilities): Detail and Concept (0.82), Detail and Whole (0.88), Closing Visual Gaps (0.80), Closing Verbal Gaps (0.80), Visual Memory (0.74), Space Construction (0.75), and Points of View (0.79).

The following new tests were added to the battery:

Picture Stories. The subject is shown three drawings depicting a sequence of events and has to provide a concise title (see Figure 12 for sample item). Two scores were given, one for conciseness and accuracy of the title (Titles) and one for degree of integration of the description (Content); the more the description dealt with each drawing separately, the lower the score. There were seven items (0.96 for Titles and 0.95 for Content).

Series completion. The original test was used. It was reasoned that the fragmented nature of many television programs calls for the skill measured by this test. There were fourteen items (0.88).

Interrupted series. This test was based on the known test of Series Completion. However, each series was interrupted by an irrelevant activity of twenty seconds, inserted between the presentation of a problem and the solution. The test had five items (0.79).

Stories. It was reasoned that literate viewing may strengthen one's ability to treat a mosaic of messages presented in

FIGURE 12. Sample Item from the Test of Picture Stories.

rapid succession as separate entities. Four half-page stories were read aloud (as well as presented in print), followed by five multiple-choice questions. The wrong alternative responses entailed mixed story-lines. (0.92).

Pairs. It was reasoned that literate viewing may affect one's *imagery*, either by calling on it and cultivating it or by supplanting and thus debilitating it. Twelve pairs of words, half of them concrete and half abstract, also divided into frequently and infrequently used ones, were read and presented in print. Subjects were urged to use imagery while attempting to memorize the pairs. Then they were given the response list, randomly ordered. In some pairs, the response member of the pair was missing; in others, the stimulus member was missing. This test was based on experimental treatments used in Paivio's experiments (1971). It was never used before as a test (0.93).

The Validity of the Tests

Attempts were made to gain better knowledge about the validity of the tests. Toward this end, three reference tests were added to the Israeli battery—Verbal Intelligence (MILTA), Field-Dependence (Embedded Figure Test-EFT; see Chapter Seven), and Spatial Rotations. The whole battery of fifteen tests was submitted to a factor analysis, and the resultant Varimax rotated factor solution yielded four factors with eigenvalues of more than 1.00.

A number of tests loaded heavily on the first factor. Most salient among them were the test of Closing Visual Gaps, Detail and Whole, Space Construction, and Series Completion. Tests with weaker loadings on this factor were Spatial Rotations, Pairs, Closing Verbal Gaps, Points of View, and Titles. It appears that this factor is a visual-spatial one. The fact that other tests, known to be mainly verbal (MILTA and Content), do not load on this factor strengthens this point.

The tests that were found to load heavily on the second factor were Content, Interrupted Series, MILTA, Series Completion, Pairs, Closing Verbal Gaps, and Spatial Rotations. It appears that this is a verbal factor. The fact that some of the spatial tests also load on this factor proves again the point often mentioned elsewhere that spatial problems are partly solved by verbal logic and internal speech. This does not apply to all spatial and visual tests, and it suggests that some of the tests (Closing Visual Gaps and Detail and Whole) are more purely visual, whereas the others also entail a verbal component (mainly Pairs, which is a test of verbal memorization aided by imagery, and Space Construction).

The third factor appears as a factor of memory. The following tests load heavily on it—Visual Memory, Detail and Concept, and Pairs. Two of these three tests were designed to measure memory, whereas the third, Detail and Concept, was not. It appears that the latter test, which was designed to measure one's ability to relate visual details to conceptual wholes and should therefore load on both the visual and the verbal factors, entails mainly visual memorization.

The fourth factor includes Witkin's test of Field-Dependence and to a lesser extent also Stories and Spatial Rotations. The fact that the Stories test loads on this factor and not on the verbal factor suggests that it taps one's analytic ability (indeed, a higher score was given to the child who succeeded in not confusing the four short stories presented) and thus measures the intended skill.

Generally, we found that the tests of Points of View, Closing Visual Gaps, and Detail and Whole are visual-spatial tests. The tests of Closing Verbal Gaps and Space Construction measure both spatial and verbal skills, whereas the test of Pairs also measures memory. The fact that it loads on the visual-spatial test is evidence that it apparently measures imagery, as intended. The test of Stories, as we have found, measures field-independence, as originally intended, and only the test of Detail and Concept fails to measure the intended skill. It will be recalled, however, that scores on this test correlated systematically with knowledge acquisition in most film versions in an earlier study (Chapter Four), and scores on its next of kin (Close-Up test) correlated highest with "Sesame Street" viewing. It thus appears to measure a skill of much relevance to the demands of film's and television's coding elements.

Results

The Samples

It was our intention to find Israeli and American samples of similar backgrounds, socioeconomic status, and home environment in addition to a lower-class Israeli sample. The two middle-class samples were expected to be similar on most relevant accounts but to differ in their amount of exposure to television; the two Israeli samples were expected to differ on most relevant accounts but to have similar amounts of exposure to the medium. Contrary to our expectations, there were small, yet significant, differences between the Israeli and American middle-class samples. Generally, it appeared that the Israeli sample represented a somewhat higher socioeconomic status than the American sample. Parents' levels of education and occupation were higher in the Israeli sample. Israeli children also started preschool education earlier and reported reading more books in the preceding months. They watched television and dined more often with other members of their families and had fewer siblings.

Comparison between the middle-class and lower-class Israeli samples revealed large and highly significant differences on all the background measures in the expected direction. Middle-class children had parents with higher levels of education and occupation, came from far smaller households, started preschool earlier, and read many more books. Lower-class children watched television and dined jointly with other family members more often. As expected, the middle-class Israeli group differed from the lower-class group on all accounts known to differentiate between the two socioeconomic levels.

The two comparisons have shown that, whereas the two Israeli samples represented the desired populations, the American sample deviated somewhat from our expectations, thus introducing undesirable differences from their Israeli counterparts.

A Major Surprise

As will be recalled, the American sample was chosen on the basis of the widely shared knowledge that American children, by and large, are among the heaviest known television consumers. Numerous surveys and field studies, using mainly self-reports, viewing diaries, or mothers' reports, have alleged time and again that the American child is an extremely dedicated viewer. Indeed, the American children reported viewing television for more than four hours daily and nearly three hours "yesterday." Israelis, as one would expect, reported watching only 3.5 hours daily and about two hours "yesterday." These differences are in line with the survey data of others. They are further corroborated by other findings. For example, 39 percent of the American children in our study report having three or more television sets at home! Israelis, on the average, have but one.

However, when children's LV scores were computed, a surprising finding emerged. Americans received *lower* LV scores than their Israeli counterparts. At fourth-grade elvel, the Israeli mean LV score (hours per day) was significantly higher than the American mean. ($\bar{X}$ = 1.06, SD = 0.57 and $\bar{X}$ = 0.86, SD = 0.7 respectively, t = 2.28, $p < 0.05$). At sixth-grade level, there was still a small difference in favor of the Israeli sample, but it failed to reach statistical significance ($\bar{X}$ = 1.29, SD = 0.59 and $\bar{X}$ = 1.23, SD = 0.79 respectively, t = 0.58, N.S.).

This finding is surprising indeed and raises questions as to the validity of the data. Could it be that the questions pertaining to literate viewing were more difficult for the American sample? If indeed they were, then the children's *attempts* to answer the questions, whether correctly answered or not, should be considered. Accordingly, a separate calculation was made in which all responses, *either correct or incorrect*, were scored as "watching," whereas only the response "I didn't watch the program" was scored as "not watching." The mean number of attempted answers for the Israeli fourth-graders when translated into daily hours of watching was 1.12 hours, and that of the American fourth-graders was 1.01 hours ($p < 0.05$). The mean for the Israeli sixth-grader was 1.31 hours, and that of the American sixth-grader was 1.27 hours (N.S.). Thus, even if all correct or incorrect responses are considered, the expected difference in favor of the American child does not appear. The correlations between LV (correct responses) and the number of attempted answers were 0.72 for Israel and 0.92 for the American sample.

Could it be that literate viewing actually measured *intelligent viewing,* and that, since the Israeli sample was of a slightly higher socioeconomic status than the American, this factor compensated for less actual television viewing? The findings did not support such a possibility either. Literate viewing correlated *negatively* with mothers' education and occupation (-0.22 to -0.25) in the fourth-grade groups and with *no* socioeconomic variable at all in the sixth-grade groups.

The same occurred when literate viewing was correlated with verbal intelligence (MILTA) in the Israeli smaple and with language scores in the American sample—no correlation was found. Correlations of LV with mathematics scores were similarly low, ranging from -0.07 to 0.15. Thus, the LV measure cannot be taken as a measure of intelligent viewing and hence cannot be considered as biased in favor of any sample. I will discuss the significance of this surprising finding later in this chapter.

Tests of the Hypotheses

We first tested the hypothesis that exposure to television, measured by the average LV score of each individual, correlated with mastery of what we considered to be relevant mental skills. As in the earlier study of "Sesame Street," we used multiple-regression techniques to partial out the contribution of the various background measures to skill-test variances. Following this, we introduced the LV measure to test the amount of *added* portions of skill-test variances it accounts for.

The first thing we noted in analyzing the American and the Israeli middle-class data was the relatively small amounts of skill-variances accounted for by the different background variaables included in the analyses as predictors. Clearly, the more homogeneous the subgroup of subjects, the smaller the contribution of background variables. Still, even when the whole sample was considered, the amounts of skill-variance accounted for by background did not exceed 34.8 percent. A similar finding was reported in our study on the cognitive effects of "Sesame Street" on Israeli children (Chapter Seven). This repeated finding suggests that other than socioeconomic or verbal-intelligence factors seem to affect the mastery of the measured skills. Television could possibly be one of those "other" factors. However, LV did not account for any significant portion of skill-mastery variance in the *combined* American-Israeli middle-class sample. Breaking the sample down into age subgroups showed that, within the fourth grade, LV accounted only for 3.91 percent of the variance on Detail and Concept ($p < 0.05$). In the sixth-grade group, LV accounted only for 3.9 percent of the Visual Memory variance ($p < 0.05$).

The breakdown according to country showed that LV accounted for *no* variance on any of the skill-mastery tests in the total *American* sample. It accounted for 3.4 percent of the Titles variance (N.S.) in the American sixth-grade group and negatively for 3.8 percent ($0.10 < p < 0.05$) of the imagery (Pairs) variance in the American fourth-grade group. In the Israeli middle-class sample, LV accounted for 2.86 percent ($p < 0.05$) of the variance of Detail and Concept and 4.85 percent ($p < 0.01$) of the Visual Memory variance. More specifically, in the sixth grade, LV accounted for 9.87 percent ($p < 0.001$) of the variance of Visual Memory; in the fourth grade, it accounted for 5.1 percent ($p < 0.01$) of the variance of Content and 6.3 percent ($p < 0.01$) of the variance of Series Completions. In all those cases, when the amount of variance accounted for by LV in one of the Israeli subgroups was compared with that in the *parallel* American subgroup, the differences of the b-weights were statistically significant at $p < 0.05$ or smaller. It thus appears that, *overall*, LV contributed to the variance of only a few tests, and that these contributions were only within the Israeli sample, a bit larger in the fourth grade than in sixth grade.

Analysis of the Israeli sample and its subgroups revealed a somewhat different picture. Within the total Israeli sample, LV significantly accounted for no more than 3.1 percent of the variance of the Stories test and less than 2 percent on Detail and

Concept, Detail and Whole, Series Completion, and Visual Memory. Although statistically significant, these contibutions were rather small.

The breakdown into subgroups was a bit more revealing. LV significantly accounted for between 2.3 percent and 3.8 percent of the variances of *six* tests in the fourth-grade group and 6.7 percent on only *one* test (Visual Memory) in the sixth-grade group. Similarly, LV accounted for 2.3 percent to 3.8 percent ($p<0.05$) on *five* tests in the lower-class group but only on *two* tests in the middle-class group. A further breakdown into social class and age-groups showed that, whereas LV accounted significantly for between 3.5 percent to 6.4 percent of the variance on *five* tests in the lower-class fourth-grade group, it accounted for 5.1 percent to 6.3 percent on *two* tests in the middle-class fourth-grade group. In the sixth grade, LV significantly accounted for 6.9 percent and 4.1 percent of the variance on *two* tests in the lower-class group and 9.8 percent of the variance on *one* test (Visual Memory) in the middle-class group. Comparison of the *b*-weights associated with LV between the two social classes of fourth-grade age and sixth-grade age showed that there were statistically significant differences of *b*-weights between the social-class subgroups in all cases in which LV accounted for significant portions of skill-mastery variances.

Two points emerge from these analyses. First, LV accounted for variances on more tests in some groups than in others. The group in which LV significantly accounted for variance on the largest number of tests was the *Israeli lower-class fourth-grade* group. Next came the Israeli middle-class fourth-grade group and the lower-class sixth-grade group. The point seems to be rather important, as it tends to suggest that LV is related to a larger number of mental skills among younger and less-advantaged (also verbally less-intelligent) children.

Second, LV accounted for different skills in the different groups. In the lower class, LV accounted for variances on tests that seem to measure mainly *analytic and visual abilities* (see the description of the tests' factor analysis). Thus, for example, the test of Stories (to whose variance LV accounted 3.0 percent in fourth grade and 4.18 percent in sixth grade, both $p < 0.05$)

loaded heavily on one factor together with Witkin's Figure-Embedded Test, clearly appearing as an analytic ability. Similarly, the tests of Detail and Concept, Closing Visual Gaps and Detail and Whole are more analytically oriented. The only exception is the test of imagery (Pairs), which is more a test of synthesis than a test of analysis. On all the analytic tests, LV accounted for significantly more variance in the lower-class group than in the middle-class group. At the same time, LV accounted in the middle-class group mainly for skills of *synthesis* —Content, in which the child had to synthesize different drawings to make one story out of them, and Visual Memory, in which one's performance is facilitated by chunking the items through categorizing them. LV accounted for variance on the Detail and Concept test in both groups, but it accounted for *more* variance ($p < 0.05$) in the lower-class group. Also, the test of Series Completion, in which superordinate concepts are to be inferred and integrated, was accounted for by LV in both groups. However, LV accounted for *more* of its variance ($p < 0.05$) in the middle-class group.

In general, then, literate viewing did not appear to be related to the mastery of mental skills in the American sample. It was related to a number of skills in the Israeli sample, to a larger extent in the younger and disadvantaged group and to a lesser extent in the older and more-advantaged group. Related to this is the finding that, whereas LV is related to skills of *analysis* in the younger and less-advantaged group, it is related to skills of *synthesis* in the *older and more-advantaged* group.

Next, we turn to a comparison between the mean test scores of the groups. Our hypothesis was that those who are more heavily exposed to television will also have better mastery of the relevant mental skills. We expected the American sample to show better skill-mastery than the Israeli sample because of (alleged) heavier exposure to the medium. However, as we discovered to our surprise, the Israeli fourth-grade sample was significantly more exposed to television than its parallel American group. In the sixth grade, we found the American and Israeli samples to be equally exposed to television. Thus, our hypothesis had to be changed—Israelis should have better mastery of the skills related to LV than the American parallel groups.

Comparisons revealed a number of significant differences between the mean scores of the different groups. The Israeli fourth-grade group achieved higher scores than the American group on Content, Detail and Concept, Visual Memory, Interrupted Series, and Stories; the American fourth-grade group performed better than the Israelis on Detail and Whole and on Series Completion. Similar but fewer differences were found when the two sixth-grade groups were compared.

These comparisons would be valid if the two national samples were identical on all other (background) variables, as we expected them to be. However, they were not. The Israeli sample appeared to come from a somewhat more favorable background, which could account for most of the differences between test scores. This possibility called for the partialling out of those intial background differences that were related to skill-mastery differences. We used multiple-regression methods, through which relevant variables were neutralized; the variable of country was entered as the last predictor.

Most of the differences between the American and Israeli fourth-grade groups observed earlier disappeared as a result of the covariance method used. Still, the variable of country accounted for significant differences in favor of the Israeli fourth-grade group on three tests—Content, Interrupted Series, and Series Completion. In other words, once relevant background variables are statistically controlled, the samples still differed on these three tests. Literate viewing accounted for significant portions of variance of *two* out of these three tests (Content, 5.12 percent, $p < 0.05$; Series Completion, 6.34 percent, $p < 0.01$). *It thus appears that on the tests for whose variance LV accounted significantly the group with higher LV scores also achieved higher skill-mastery scores.* This seems to be the rule, with one exception—Interrupted Series. The higher mean score achieved on it by the Israeli fourth-grade sample was not associated with differences of LV and must therefore be due to other, unknown factors. In the sixth grade, we observed a very similar pattern. Once differences due to background variables were partialled out, only three significant differences due to nationality remained—on the tests of Detail and Concept, Closing Verbal Gaps and Visual Memory. All significant differences were in favor of the Israeli sample.

It will be recalled that, although the American and Israeli sixth-grade samples were not found to differ in amount of literate viewing, LV significantly accounted for 9.87 percent ($p <$ 0.01) of the variance of Visual Memory and 3.18 percent (0.10 $> p <$ 0.05) on Detail and Concept in the Israeli sixth-grade group. These are also two of the three tests on which the Israeli sample received significantly higher scores. The only exception was the test of Closing Verbal Gaps, to which LV was not related, and yet the two samples differed on it. In sum, comparisons between countries, separately for each age-group, tend to support our hypothesis—when other things are made equal by statistical means, more LV is associated with better skill-mastery, or, as is the case in the sixth-grade sample, the group in which LV is related to skill-mastery also achieves higher scores on the same mastery tests.

Discussion

The purpose of this study was to examine the extent to which coding elements of a medium, in this case television, cultivate the mastery of mental skills when used under normal, natural conditions. Exposure to television, defined and measured as literate viewing (LV), was found to account for significant (but never large) portions of skill-variance in the Israeli sample but not in the American sample. Within the Israeli sample, LV accounted for the variance of more tests in the younger, lower-class group than in the older, middle-class group.

LV also accounted for skill-mastery variances in the middle-class group in skills of synthesis; the skills that LV accounted for in the lower-class group were mainly skills of analysis. This finding is strikingly similar to the one reported in the "Sesame Street" study. Using the crossed-lagged correlation technique with panel data, it was possible to show in the earlier study that improvement in analytic skills due to exposure to television *preceded* improvements taking place in skills of synthesis. When background variables were partialled out, the fourth-grade group with more LV (Israel, as we have found to our surprise) also achieved higher scores on two of the three tests whose variances were accounted for by LV. In sixth grade, a very similar pattern emerged. Thus, it can be concluded that more LV is associated with better skill-mastery scores.

Affected and Unaffected Skills

Our findings raise a number of questions. The first question is why LV was related to the mastery of some skills but unrelated to the mastery of the skills measured by the test of Points of View, Titles, Interrupted Series, and Closing Verbal Gaps. How can we explain this absence of any relation? The first three of these four tests were not used in our earlier study (Chapter Four), and we do not really know how relevant the skills measured by these tests are to the typical handling of television's symbol systems. Only the test of Closing Verbal Gaps was used in that study, where it was found to correlate with the extraction of general knowledge when logical gaps and close-ups were encountered. It is possible that the tests of Points of View, Titles, and Interrupted Series do not correlate with LV at all, simply because they measure skills that are not called for when typical television messages are encountered. However, this does not account for the Closing Verbal Gaps test, which was found to measure a relevant skill.

The most reasonable explanation seems to be that this test measures an entirely *verbal* skill, unlike its parallel test of Closing Visual Gaps (the two tests intercorrelate 0.40 to 0.50, but Closing Verbal Gaps also correlates 0.45 with Verbal Intelligence, while the visual test correlates with intelligence only 0.22). This is shown in the factor analysis of the test items—the verbal test of closing gaps loads heavily on the verbal factor, but the visual test does not. It stands to reason that verbal rearrangement of *visual* sequences is rarely called for under natural conditions of televiewing, unless one is required to perform such a task. Indeed, this test correlated in our earlier study only with general knowledge acquisition, which was measured by a logical-sequence-rearrangement test.

Direction of Effect

Another even more important issue concerns the directional interpretation of the findings. We have reasoned that the examination of the "net" amount of skill-mastery variance accounted for by LV would tell us how strongly exposure and matery are interrelated, and that mean differences would tell us the direction of that relationship. Indeed, it was found that, where LV accounted for more mastery-variance, mean mastery scores were also higher. Still, such findings could be interpreted in two ways. As deduced from our rationale, LV cultivates the mastery of specific mental skills, thus more LV leads to better skill-mastery. Alternatively, mastery of specific mental skills could be a necessary condition for literate consumption of television, and hence better skill-mastery would lead to more LV. Formulating this dilemma in terms analogous to a similar question in psycholinguistics, we would label the first interpretation as the hypothesis about the symbolic code input and the second as the cognitive-determinism hypothesis (Schlesinger, 1977a). The former hypothesis would assert that the child's mastery of the mental skills under investigation is determined, at least *in part*, by experience with the symbol systems of television. The latter hypothesis would assert that the child's literate viewing of television is determined by cognitive development.

There is no firm and unequivocal answer to this dilemma in the psycholinguistic literature, but there is good reason to believe that the two hypotheses pertain to different abilities and to different levels of development (see Chapter Five). The development of some abilities, or skills, must precede any activity of knowledge extraction from coded messages. However, that activity, in turn, further cultivates these skills.

Our findings lend indirect support to the hypothesis about the symbolic code input (that is, that LV leads to better skill-mastery). As we have found, mean differences on the mastery tests between American and Israeli same-age children were limited in four out of six cases to those tests whose variances LV accounted for significantly. The mastery scores of the groups did not differ on any of the *other* ten tests. According to the cognitive-determinism hypothesis, if LV is a function of general better skill-mastery, then the group with higher LV scores should manifest better skill-mastery across the board. That is, that group should have better mastery on *all* tests, not just those that are related to LV. However, since the groups differed nearly exclusively on only those tests that were related to LV, one may wonder why the Israeli groups excelled precisely on *those* tests and not on the others. It is therefore warranted to conclude that *LV led to better mastery of specific mental skills,* rather than the converse.

Cultural Differences

Next, there is the question as to why LV was found to be associated with skill-mastery in the Israeli sample but not the American sample. There was no evidence to show that any one of the (generally identical) tests or questionnaires had psychometric properties that differed from country to country. Nor were the testing conditions any different. Similarly, the background differences between the two samples cannot account for the finding that LV was unrelated to skill-mastery in the American sample, as these differences were statistically irrelevant anyway.

Let us go back to the study by Scribner and Cole (1978), in which they found literacy to cultivate skill through the specific qualitative functions it accomplished. May it not be that the qualitative nature of televiewing differs from one cultural environment to another? Consider, for instance, the fact that the American child selects a program from among several alternatives, whereas the Israeli child has but *one* channel to view. Goodhart, Ehrenberg, and Collins (1975) and Wakshlag (1977) have studied some patterns of televiewing and noted the relatively high rate of channel switching among American children. It stands to reason that the amount of time devoted to watching television may not be strongly affected by frequent channel switching, but literate viewing may be strongly affected by it.

Our data bear on this point. As will be recalled, one of the exposure measures employed was the children's self-reported amount of televiewing on the preceding day. This measure accounted *negatively* for up to 8.5 percent of skill-mastery variances in the American sample and for *no* variance at all in the Israeli sample. Although it is difficult to interpret this finding, it becomes quite evident that the qualitative nature of tele-viewing in a television-saturated country such as the United States differs from that of a television-hungry country such as Israel. Consider a few more findings. The mothers of our American sample liked television, on the average, significantly *less* than their Israeli counterparts. We have also found that the American children in the sample watch television jointly with parents or siblings significantly less than their Israeli counterparts. The latter observation is of particular interest in light of some previous findings of ours (Chapter Seven), which show that the coobservation of television by mother and child has a rather strong effect on cognitive change and knowledge acquisition. Finally, Israeli children were found to attach greater importance to the medium than their American counterparts.

These additional findings suggest that, in the face of great choice, commercial interruptions, low social regard for the medium, and little reinforcement to invest much mental effort in dealing with its messages, the American children define the tele-viewing task for themselves as mentally undemanding. The Israeli children, due to the absence of choice, the novelty, and positive social norms, define the task as requiring deeper processing of messages.

To the extent that Israelis process the messages more deeply, they can be expected to transform more coding elements into internal representations and to imitate those elements that model a process, so that they extract more knowledge from the messages. Thus, exposure to the medium has a stronger effect on their mastery of specific relevant mental skills. The American children, while devoting more time to the medium, process its messages more shallowly, thus negotiating fewer coding elements. Consequently, they are affected by the medium's symbol systems to a lesser extent, if at all.

Chapter Three explained amount of mental recoding as a function of the psychological difference between external and internal modes of representation, given a particular person, content, and task to be accomplished. The study reported in

Chapter Four suggested that the task children are required to perform determines the kind of information they extract and thus affects the coding elements they address. The results reported in Chapter Seven showed how cognitive development affects the choice of information to be extracted and how mother's coobservation changes the child's depth of processing. This study provides an additional element—namely, that socially defined demand-characteristics of the televiewing situation have a similar effect.

Stated more generally, when a social environment communicates to a child that a medium's messages are to be taken more seriously, the environment directs him to process the information quantitatively more and qualitatively more deeply. Under such circumstances, a child is more likely to encounter particular coding elements that he would not have bothered to deal with otherwise. Encountering them—that is, mentally transforming them in the service of extracting the desired information, may cultivate the pertinent skills.

But even under such conditions, a child is relatively free to choose his preferred depth of processing. As many of the known surveys show (for example, Goodhart, Ehrenberg, and Collins, 1975), children engage in many unrelated activities while watching television. Thus, the cognitive effects of watching television under normal conditions, even when the child is reinforced to "take television seriously," cannot be very large. This may explain the large difference betwen the cognitive effects observed in field studies and in experiments. Experimental television-viewing conditions turn children into temporarily more serious viewers, thus producing impressive effects. But these effects are rarely replicated in field studies where children are often much shallower processors of televised information.

Age Differences
		Finally, let us discuss the age differences found in the study. Literate viewing accounted for variance on more skill tests in the younger (fourth-grade) than in the older (sixth-grade) Israeli group. As one would have expected, the skill-mastery level of the sixth-graders was higher than that of the fourth-graders.

But this does not rule out the possibility of further cultivating the skill-mastery of eleven-year-olds. In effect, that may be the most responsive age to new cognitive challenges. Why then did LV account for more test-variance in the younger age-group?

Although sixth-graders can continue to acquire and cultivate skills, the kind of television programming they are typically exposed to continues to use the *same* symbolic elements. These elements do not provide new processing demands in concert with the general improvement of abilities, nor do they typically offer new modeling elements that can be internalized. Thus, children at the age of eleven may be said to process most coded television messages automatically, and like proficient readers, to apply mainly "top down" processes.

This, however, does not mean that no new skills can be developed by media's symbol systems at all. First, youngsters may still encounter new symbolic elements in other media, such as computers, avant-garde films, and the like. Second, as the youngsters' abilities develop, so do their information expectations. At age eleven, the task-perception of televiewing is likely to differ from that at age nine. Thus, elements that entailed no critical information and were not processed at one age may become a cognitive challenge later. Such elements then cannot be processed by automatic skills. Rather, they need to be dealt with by "controlled" processes, which in turn can be cultivated.

Indeed, the only skill-mastery that was strongly associated with literate viewing in the sixth-grade sample was that of chunking and synthesizing relatively large bodies of information (Visual Memory test). This finding should not surprise us. As television messages do not increase in complexity, and as the sixth-grader is capable of dealing with them effectively, he may want to acquire more information from dense messages offered by the medium and hence improve mastery of the chunking skill.

Summary

In a cross-cultural study, Israeli fourth- and sixth-graders were compared with a similar sample of American children for amount of television viewing and mastery of related mental skills. Viewing was defined as one's ability to answer extremely simple content questions pertaining to the programs shown on the preceding day (literate viewing). This measure correlated only about 0.50 with the more common measure of self-reports, and not at all with intelligence, socioeconomic level, or parents' education.

To our surprise, we found the Israeli children (particularly the fourth-graders) to exhibit significantly more literate viewing than their American counterparts, in spite of the fact that Israel has only one black-and-white channel and only six hours of broadcasting per day. Furthermore, 39 percent of the American children have three or more television sets at home, but Israeli homes average only one set. Additional data led to the conclusion that, for a variety of reasons (including the coobservation of parents), Israeli children view television at a deeper level. They invest more mental effort in processing its messages, and they retain more of its contents; their American counterparts spend more time at the screen but view programs in a cognitively shallower way. Frequent shifting from channel to channel and interruptions by commercials probably facilitate that effortless pattern of viewing.

Viewing, as we have reasoned, can affect the mastery of mental skills only to the extent that skills must be applied to symbolic elements in the service of knowledge extraction. The same would apply to codes that supplant skills. Thus, children who are more serious viewers—that is, invest more mental effort in knowledge extraction—should have a better mastery of the relevant skills than those who invest less mental effort. Indeed, the data corroborated this claim. Not only did the mastery of specific skills (for instance, series completion) correlate with viewing in the Israeli but not the American sample, but the Israelis showed better mastery of precisely those skills that correlated with literate viewing. Thus, it appears that more serious viewing requires more handling of the coded messages and allows for the cultivation of the relevant skills.

There were also noteworthy age and socioeconomic differences. Israeli fourth-graders were more strongly affected by televiewing than sixth-graders, in spite of the fact that the latter exhibited more literate viewing and had an overall better mastery of the tested skills. In addition, younger lower-class children were affected more in the skill area of analysis, and older middle-class children were more strongly affected in synthesis (integrative memory). These findings are in striking agreement with the ones obtained in the "Sesame Street" study.

The cognitive effects observed in this study were far smaller than those observed in the "Sesame Street" study; apparently, the program's novelty contributed to its strong effects. Viewing of less novel programs, even over extended periods of time, did not account for more than 6 to 9 percent of skill-mastery variance. But literate viewing accounted for skill-mastery mainly in the Israeli fourth-grade sample. Two factors seemed to have contributed to this observation—the child's perception of what televiewing entails or demands and the child's age.

Social setting and social norms pertaining to the medium can influence what one looks for in televised messages. Thus, it is not only what information a child *can* extract that determines what symbolic elements will be processed, but also his perception of the televiewing task. Attempting to get at more and deeper meaning implies the processing of more and more complex elements, resulting in stronger cognitive effects. Quite obvious educational implications follow from this finding.

Age moderated the relationship between literate viewing and skill-mastery in a different way. The older children, it appeared, had a sufficient mastery of the relevant skills to use them automatically. This was apparently enough for the kind of information extraction at which they aim. Television's symbol systems do not seem to keep up with children's growing capacities, except when more information can be obtained through improved chunking, and that was the only skill area that was related in the older age-group to literate viewing.

NINE

Interaction of Media, Cognition, and Learning: Summary and Reflections

⠟ ⠟ ⠟ ⠟ ⠟ ⠟ ⠟

I began this book hoping to move media research in education from its exploratory phase to a phase of disciplined search. But disciplined search must be based on more than just the accumulation of scattered propositions and empirical findings; it requires a relatively coherent, *if tentative*, network of constructs and relations among them. In this chapter, then, I recapitulate and summarize the major arguments, propositions, and findings that are scattered among the preceding chapters in an attempt to arrive at a somewhat more theoretical view of how media, cognition, and learning are related.

There are different ways to study the psychological effects of media. One way, for example, is to investigate what and how people learn from media; another way is to study what functions people attribute to media and what gratifications the media offer them. Still another way is to study how children become consumers of media and how their comprehension of mediated messages develops. Research on media in education generally follows parallel avenues. It asks whether more can be taught by a particular medium and how students' varying aptitudes interact with alternative media. Research is also being carried out with new technologies, particularly computers, in an attempt to develop better curricula and optimize learners' acquisition of knowledge.

However, the approach in this book deviates from these lines of research. The focus here is on media's modes of presentation, or symbol systems. The approach follows McLuhan's general gist but not his methodology or claims. The approach is further influenced by other recent research on the symbolic aspects of media. Some researchers have begun to investigate how children learn to deal with the symbolic aspects of television (Huston-Stein and Wright, 1977; Meringoff, 1978) and art (Carothers and Gardner, 1978), or how symbolic capacities develop in children (Gardner, Shotwell, and Wolf, 1977). Still others have begun to generate hypotheses pertaining to the relationships between media's symbol systems and learning (Olson and Bruner, 1974) or skill-cultivation (Greenfield, 1972; Scribner and Cole, 1978). My questions, although somewhat developmental, pertain mainly to how the symbol systems of the media interact with the cognitive functions of their users, and, by extension, what functions these can be made to serve in education. The difference between more developmental approaches and my approach is similar to the difference between the study of how literacy is acquired and the study of literacy's cognitive consequences. The core of my approach is more akin to the latter, although I could not overlook the former.

The research reported in this book pertained primarily to coding elements taken from the symbol systems of film and television. However, these coding elements were assumed to represent symbol systems in general; and the two media were assumed to represent media's symbol systems in general.

The central themes of this book can be summarized as

follows:

1.   Media's ways of structuring and presenting information—
     that is, their symbol systems—are media's most important
     attributes when learning and cognition are considered
     and thus should serve as our focus of inquiry.
2.   Symbol systems, the means by which messages are coded,
     address themselves to different aspects of content, and
     different symbol systems yield different meanings, when
     content is novel.
3.   Symbol systems vary with respect to the kinds of mental
     transformations (or recoding) that they require, and they
     vary with respect to the kinds of mental skills they acti-
     vate in the service of knowledge extraction. Thus, symbol
     systems in general, and coding elements in particular,
     vary as to the learners whose learning they facilitate.
4.   The kinds of information one *can, is required to*, or
     chooses to extract from a coded message determines the
     coding elements one deals with ("top-down" processes)
     and the kinds of mental processes that are called upon
     ("bottom-up" processes).
5.   The coding elements of a medium's blend of symbol sys-
     tems can be made to cultivate the mastery of specific
     mental skills by either activating or overtly supplanting
     the skills, in interaction with a learner's skill-mastery
     levels.
6.   Typical exposure to a medium's blend of symbol systems
     has similar but weaker skill-cultivating effects. The novel-
     ty of the encountered coding elements, the learner's
     cognitive makeup, and the amount of information
     extraction aimed at (the task) mediate these effects.

     The general premise on which my arguments are based is
that, for the two "systems," media and cognition, symbol systems serve as the most essential attribute; therefore, their
interrelations need to be explored. Because the acquisition of
knowledge is mediated by cognitive symbolic functions, media's

symbolic input may play an important differential role in learning. Since one's cognitive symbolic functions develop in interaction with societal inputs, media's symbol systems ought to be considered as part of such societal influences. Thus, my major propositions pertain to the differential role of media's symbol systems in the acquisition of knowledge and their functions as cultivators of mental skills. In this chapter, I will examine the issues of media's role in the acquisition of knowledge and in the cultivation of mental skills and then examine their interdependence.

Media's Symbol Systems and the Acquisition of Knowledge

Why should it matter whether knowledge is acquired by means of maps or aerial photos, films or scripts, a straightforward educational television production or a contrived one? The first and simplest answer is that different symbol systems represent different kinds of content. For example, by segmenting a dense quality such as simultaneous movement so that it fits a disjoint notational system such as a graph, some information is lost. However, another symbol system, film, may represent precisely that information which was lost when the information about movement was segmented. Thus, we say that film's symbol systems render the density of simultaneous movement, and that simultaneous movement is better suited to film than graphs.

However, symbol systems often overlap with respect to the essential aspects of content that they can convey. And yet, we would expect learning outcomes to differ with exposure to different media. I argued first that different symbol systems, even when representing the same content, differ with respect to the *amount* of mental translation from external symbol system to internal mode that they require. Second, I proposed that symbol systems differ with respect to the *kinds* of mental skills that they invoke in the process of knowledge extraction. *To the extent that symbol systems call on quantitatively and qualitatively different mental skills, knowledge-acquisition outcomes can be expected to vary respectively.*

Amounts of Mental Activity

The claim that symbol systems differ as to the *amount* of mental activity they require was based on the following reasoning. We use a variety of qualitatively different symbolic modes for the representation of information in thought. Some of the external modes of representing information, other things being equal, are less isomorphic or less congruent with the internal ones. Thus, some external symbolic modes, other things being equal, require more mental transformations (recoding) or more skills than others. It follows, for instance, that, for a person who is more inclined to represent internal information spatially, information presented cartographically would require a shorter chain of mental transformations than, say, presenting it verbally. There are many studies (see Chapter Three) whose findings can be interpreted to support these assumptions.

The important prediction that follows from these assumptions is that the amount of knowledge extracted from a particular coded message is a negative function of the "length" of the required mental chain of recodings or transformations. The more congruent the symbolic carriers of a message are with one's specific symbolic mode of internal representation, the less translation is needed, and the more information will be extracted and presumably learned. Some of the findings reported in Chapters Three and Four seem to support this contention.

On the basis of this argument, I offered a way to conceptualize differences between symbol systems to replace popular notions of resemblance between symbol and referent. I claimed that resemblance occurs between a symbol and a mental conception of the referent, not between a symbol and its referent. Hence, symbolic modes differ with respect to the amount of recoding (or number of recoding steps) one has to carry out to extract meaning from them. However, further examination of this contention suggests that congruity, resemblance, or isomorphism between external and internal representation cannot be conceived of as a simple dimension of "distance." As Gardner (1974a) correctly points out, the construct of resemblance in this context is as ambiguous as when discussed in a purely semiotic context, as Goodman (1968) does. For if we cannot easily define the nature of resemblance between symbol and physical referent, how can we define resemblance between symbol and internal template of conception?

If congruity of symbol and mental conception were a simple quantity, then some symbolic modes could be so congruent with internal conceptions that no recoding would be needed at all. This, of course, is certainly not the case, as even the most common symbolic messages require some skillful (although automatic) recoding. It is more reasonable to assume that congruity is not simply distance but a function of how well mastered the requisite recoding skills are. As was pointed out in Chapters Three and Four, well-mastered skills are automatically applied as part of one's appropriate anticipatory scheme. Automatic skills entail short-cuts that help to recode the message rapidly with little effort.

Thus, congruity is a function of automaticity of recoding skills. The observation reported in Chapter Four, that knowledge acquisition from the straightforward film version did not correlate with skill-mastery, indicates that all our subjects recoded the message automatically. Less congruity or resemblance between external and internal codes, which we deliberately edited into the other film versions in the same study, requires the utilization of less-well-mastered recoding skills, hence the observed correlations between skill-mastery and knowledge acquisition.

On the basis of these arguments, it becomes possible to speak of *ease* of extracting information from symbolically coded messages. One symbol system does not communicate better than another. It calls for better-mastered skills than another. And, the better mastered the requisite skills are, the better is the acquisition of knowledge from the coded message. Swanson (1978) shows similarly that poor readers often fail, even before mental elaboration of the printed material has begun, because they fail to integrate the verbal symbol with its imagery counterpart.

In other cases, one symbol system may call on better-mastered recoding skills than another. Chandler, Greenspan, and Barenboim (1973) tested six- and seven-year-olds' moral judgments either by verbally describing to them the traditional moral dilemmas or by displaying them on television. "Special care was exercised to ensure that no detail was present in the films which was not equally available in the written stories" (p. 316). Exposure to the verbally presented dilemmas yielded the traditional finding that children at that age center on action consequences but not on intentions. Contrary to traditional findings, exposure to the videotaped pictorial stories resulted in the childrens' centering on both intentions and consequences, thus exhibiting more advanced moral judgment for that age. Note how symbol-system dependent the results were. It can be argued that, as the recoding skills required by the verbally presented information were less well mastered, more information was lost or lost saliency. The video presentation called on better-mastered recoding skills; since its symbols were more congruent with the childrens' schemata than verbal descriptions were, television allowed subsequent elaboration of more of the information provided.

But note that the ease or difficulty of recoding is not a function of congruence, or resemblance to referents, inherent in (and thus a permanent attribute of) a symbol system. Ease or difficulty of recoding depends on how a learner prefers to, can, or is required to internally represent the material to be learned. Symbol systems differ as to their congruity with a learner's internal representations. Thus, some symbol systems call for better-mastered, more automatically executed recoding activities than others, given a particular task, content, and learner.

I have argued previously that dense depictions are often treated by our nervous system as if they are slight deviations from familiar perceptual events, and hence they are often automatically recoded. But the same would be true for expert cartographers when reading maps and for fluent readers when encountering text (as indeed was the case in the study of map reading versus text reading in Chapter Three). Thus, a given symbol system carrier of information (say, language) may be easier for recoding for a "verbalizer" than for a "visualizer"; and it will be more easily recoded when logical, propositional knowledge is to be extracted and more difficult when imagery is called for.

The ease or difficulty or processing coded information is not limited to differences among whole symbol systems. The choice of specific coding elements within a symbol system may affect the ease with which information is learned. Some coding elements can, as we have seen, save mental activity and thus ease the processing burden on unskilled learners.

There is an important distinction between the mental operation of *recoding* a message from its external symbolic form into its internal counterpart and the mental *elaboration* of the already recoded material. Recoding precedes elaboration (see, for example, Melton and Martin, 1972; Bower, 1975; Bandura, 1977). Bandura, Jeffery, and Bachicha (1974) show that internal elaboration (rehearsal) is applied to an already internally coded representation of an observed model. When that internal representation is meaningful—that is, well integrated into one's anticipatory schemata—elaboration adds little to learning. But elaboration becomes crucial when the observed model is recoded in a meaningless way. Craig and Tulving (1975) argue similarly that degree of (it seems, recoded) stimulus elaboration accounts for amount of learning, and Kane and Anderson (1978) found that asking subjects to complete the last word in a sentence led to better retention than simply reading the sentence.

Postrecoding elaboration is similar to depth of processing and is independent of the preceding act of recoding. The activities of elaboration can vary dramatically in amount and complexity. The more one elaborates the already recoded material, the more contact will this material make with other mental schemata, thereby leaving more memory traces as well as enriching the meanings accrued (Kintsch, 1977). Amount of elaboration is positively related to learning, particularly to long-term retention and comprehension (Kane and Anderson, 1978). But these outcomes are contingent upon one's mastery of the relevant skills. Attempts at deeper elaborations by an unskillful learner cannot result in better learning unless "instructional supports" (Tobias, 1976) are provided. The function of such supports is to save the learner the effort of attempting elaborations he cannot perform on his own.

Traditionally, amount of mental elaboration is a concept that is associated with instructional procedures, not symbol systems. Saving the learner from attempting to perform mental elaborations he cannot perform is not supposed to result from the choice of symbolic elements. But, as it turns out, such supports can be provided not only by pedagogical procedures but also by selection of appropriate coding elements. The zoom film (Chapter Four) overtly supplanted the process of relating parts to wholes and thus facilitated learning for those subjects who could not easily execute that process on their own. However, the same supplanting element *debilitated* learning of better-skilled subjects (Chapter Six, Experiment 2) apparently by interfering with their depth of processing.

Could facilitation also be achieved by coding elements that short-circuit processes of elaboration, thereby providing an unskilled learner with the *ready-made* results of elaboration? Recall Olson's (1970) theory, according to which each performatory act lets the learner encounter specific choice-points; selection among these requires that the learner acquire information. If an internal activity is short-circuited (rather than overtly modeled or supplanted), then no choice-points are encountered, and no information can be acquired. Thus, short-circuiting may save too much—it prevents elaboration altogether, whereas supplantation at least models it. Explicit modeling may show the choice-points to be encountered, thus permitting the learner to acquire the necessary information. Clearly, a coded message that neither short-circuits nor models but rather *activates* elaboration leads to the most learning. However, such activation favors the skilled learner.

Media's symbol systems play profound roles in mental activities. First, the choice of specific coding elements can put greater or lighter processing burdens on learners. Second, symbol systems differ with respect to the amounts and kinds of elaboration they *allow* or *require*. A flow chart of historical events may require the learner to use poorly mastered recoding skills, but after recoding has been accomplished, the flow chart allows little additional elaboration, as it is a sufficiently meaningful reductive internal code. The flow chart short-circuits the kinds of elaborations that a learner who is given a verbal exposition of the same information would have to carry out on his own to arrive at a summary arrangement of the historical facts.

Meringoff (1978), it may be recalled, compared childrens' understanding of a televised story versus a story read aloud. One of her findings was that children in the verbal condition generated more inferences on their own and connected the story more with their general knowledge than those in the television condition. It can be argued that the pictorial aspects of television are more congruent with children's internal symbolic modes of representation than sequential verbal messages, appear more lifelike, and hence require less recoding. As more of the original information is left intact after recoding, and since the children are not told how much elaboration they have to engage in, there is no need for them to elaborate the information much further. It is relatively meaningful to them as is and thus allows them to engage in less elaboration than a verbally presented equivalent.

Script messages demand more elaboration than pictorials. Script material "requires us to draw upon our own memories and fantasies, to take time to try to follow the drift of a writer, to conjure up by ourselves exotic settings, sights, and sounds" (Singer and others, 1977, p. 37). Krugman (1971, 1976) has found, on the basis of individual case studies, that the brain activity of reading is more extensive than that of television viewing. The implication is that the pictorial system of television *allows* (but does not require) shallower processing than a written story or a verbally told one. To generalize, some symbol systems may allow shallower mental processing, and others may demand deeper mental elaboration. The implied skeleton hypothesis is that, other things being equal, nonnotational systems, *when perceived as depicting lifelike messages, allow* shallower processing than notational symbol systems that describe their referents. The latter *demand* more elaboration, if meaning is to be accrued. It follows, for example, that television's nonnotational messages may be better recalled by young children than verbally described ones. However, where more mental elaboration is needed for, say, inferential learning, verbally described events will be better learned as they demand more elaboration. Clearly, however, this difference may disappear when children are not left to voluntarily choose amount of elaboration but are given specific tasks to be accomplished. In the latter case, amount of elaboration (but not of recoding) may be the same regardless of symbolic system of incoming information.

Kinds of Mental Activity

But the differential effect of symbol systems on the ease of recoding and elaboration does not exhaust their possible impacts on knowledge acquisition. After all, variations of ease of recoding and elaboration can be produced by varying learning tasks, by introducing noise, by varying instructional conditions, or by changing content complexity. The somewhat more unique contribution of symbol systems beyond the differences of ease of processing is that they also influence the *kind* of mental skills involved. The way one recodes a verbal description into an internal spatial representation is likely to differ from the way one recodes a drawing into internal propositions. Psychological and neuropsychological evidence (see Chapters Three and Four) tends to support this contention.

It is extremely difficult to determine exactly what kinds of recoding skills are required by what symbol systems. However, we can hypothesize that notational symbol systems require crystallized ability (G_c), based on verbal skills, and nonnotational systems require mainly fluid ability (G_f), based on spatial and perceptual skills (Hakstian and Cattell, 1978; Snow, 1978a). We know, for example, from the Koran, Snow, and McDonald (1971) study, that extraction of information from a video presentation calls for a skill labeled *film memory* (Snow, Tiffin, and Seibert, 1965). Mastery of this skill is irrelevant for learning from script, which is facilitated by the ability to deal with embedded figures; learning from a video presentation requires no such skill-mastery. Cronbach and Snow (1977) suggest that learning from visual (that is, nonnotational, dense) depictions is apparently dependent on such abilities as being able to abstract a class of concepts from exemplars, to discriminate visual objects by multiple cues, and the like.

It seems reasonable to argue that the more dissimilar coded messages are, the more dissimilar the required skills will be. Specifically, as more *unique* coding elements are used, more diversified skills are called into play, thus benefiting learners with a greater variety of skill-mastery.

The kinds of mental skills required and the resulting recoding and elaboration do not depend *only* on the symbolic nature of the information. The empirical results reported in Chapters Four, Seven, and Eight indicate that the nature of externally imposed, situationally defined, or self-selected tasks plays an important role as well. It seems as if symbol system and task compete with each other in determining the nature of the mental skills called into play, thereby jointly determining the outcomes of knowledge acquisition.

Recall the experiment reported in Chapter Four. The two learning tasks may have required the same amount of elaboration, but they did not require the same skills. The dominant coding element in each film version, together with the learning task, determined the types of mental skills that were called on. Consider also the effect of the coobserving mothers on children's learning from "Sesame Street" (Chapter Seven). The coobserving mothers increased their children's enjoyment of the program and served as "energizers." By redefining the viewing situation as a more pleasurable one, mothers caused their five-year-old children to elaborate the presented information in greater depth, relative to the control group. The difference between the Israeli and American ways of watching television (Chapter Eight) were interpreted in a similar way—because of social pressure and social desirability, Israelis tend to elaborate the presented material more deeply. These are examples of cases where changes in the task or in the perception of the task determined the types of skills that were used and the amount of elaboration performed on the material.

The observation (in Chapter Seven) that preschoolers virtually ignored novel coding elements of "Sesame Street," because they were not aiming at the information these elements carried, suggests a division of labor between what is determined by the task and what is determined by the symbol system. Cronbach and Snow (1977), while identifying abilities that may be related to the processing of visually presented information, also point out that the nature of specific skills called on in a given situation depends on the kind of information to be processed according to the specific task requirements. Thus, it can be argued that *the task to be performed determines what, how, and how much information is to be elaborated ("top-down" processes), whereas the symbol system determines what kinds of mental skills are to be employed ("bottom-up" processes).*

Further, we hypothesize that the acquisition of learning is maximized when the "top-down" processes (determined by the task) are compatible with the "bottom-up" processes (determined by the symbol system). In one study (Salomon and Sieber, 1970), a structural element—random editing of film segments—was so dominant as to override the effects of the task, thus activating mental skills (search for a plot line) that were dysfunctional for one of the tasks (cue attendance). The randomly spliced film employed a structure that was so incongruent with the subjects' schemata that much elaboration was needed, regardless of the task requirements. In the absence of an externally imposed learning task, children adapt their own task requirements (what they are looking for in a television show, a sculpture, or a map) to the kinds of mental skills they can successfully bring to the coding elements they encounter. For this reason, we can speak of differences between symbol systems with respect to the depth and shallowness of processing that they *allow*. In the absence of a predetermined task, the child who watches television at home (much like the occasional museum visitor) *can match the depth he aims at with the skills he can most easily apply to the coding elements he elects to encounter.*

To summarize, the symbol systems of media affect the acquisition of knowledge in a number of ways. First, they highlight different aspects of content. Second, they vary with respect to ease of recoding. Third, specific coding elements can save the learner from difficult mental elaborations by overtly supplanting or short-circuiting specific elaboration. Fourth, symbol systems differ with respect to how much processing they demand or allow. Fifth, symbol systems differ with respect to the kinds of mental processes they call on for recoding and elaboration. Thus, symbol systems partly determine who will acquire how much knowledge from what kinds of messages.

Media's Symbol Systems and the Cultivation of Mental Skills

The parallelism of symbol use in the media and in thought is quite striking. Bruner (1964, p. 1) believes "that the development of human intellectual functioning from infancy to such perfection as it may reach is shaped by a series of technological advances in the use of the mind. Growth depends upon the mastery of techniques and cannot be understood without reference to such mastery. These techniques are not, in the main, inventions of the individuals who are "growing up"; they are rather skills transmitted with varying efficiency and success by the culture—language being a prime example. Cognitive growth, then, is in a major way from the outside in as well as from the inside out."

Indeed, we cannot ignore the possible role media's symbol systems play in the cultivation of mental skill, not just as carriers of information *about* skills or as carriers of *skill-models*, but rather as the *mental-skills-to-be*. As Bruner argues (1964, p. 2), internal representation of the environment depends on learning "precisely the techniques that serve to amplify our acts, perceptions, and our ratiocinative activities." Media, to whose messages children are often heavily exposed, must surely be included among these techniques. We should first ask *where*, among the many other environmental elements, do media's symbol systems belong. Second, we should ask *how* media's symbol systems affect mental skills.

Media and Environment

Feldman (in press) proposes a continuum of developmental achievements ranging from universal through cultural

and disciplined to idiosyncratic and unique. The major difference among achievements ranked along this continuum is the
degree to which they are spontaneously achieved by all children. Thus, universal achievements, such as walking or conservation, are attained by all, but nonuniversal achievements
occur only under specialized environmental conditions (such as
instruction and appropriate technology). Developments in the
nonuniversal domains of achievement (ranging, for example,
from writing through map reading to violin playing) are neither
spontaneous nor inevitable.

Specifically, cultural achievements are the ones that all
individuals within a given culture are expected to acquire, such
as reading, understanding the political system, or fluency in the
prevailing language. In disciplined domains, such as chess,
mathematics, or aviation, levels of mastery are clearly set down,
as are criteria for attainment of levels (for example, Expert or
Master). Fewer individuals reach higher levels of achievement in
disciplined domains than in cultural domains. Idiosyncratic
achievements, such as one's speciality or hobby, are achieved by
even fewer individuals. Furthermore, they require more specific
environmental inputs than the other achievement domains.

Feldman also proposes a continuum of environments to
parallel that of achievements. These environments, or rather,
environmental conditions, range from the most universal (those
that appear in all human environments, such as three-dimensional objects, gravitation, and human interaction) to the most
unique (highly specific tutoring). In between, one finds cultural
conditions (use of tools) and disciplined conditions (specific
training).

The proposed relationship between the two continua is of
great importance to our discussion. Feldman postulates, first,
that some of the universal achievements are necessary for nonuniversal ones to occur. But not *all* universals need to be achieved before *any* culutural or disciplined mastery may take place.
Thus, for example, "It is not necessary . . . to have achieved the
full use of formal logic and reasoning to begin to learn to read,
nor is it necessary to have mastered reading to begin to play the
violin. It *is* necessary, however, to know that symbols can stand

for things or ideas (a universal) in order for reading to make any sense at all (Feldman, in press, p. 34). Feldman then postulates that universal conditions give rise to universal achievements, and provide some of the conditions requisite to cultural achievement. Cultural conditions give rise to cultural achievement and set the stage for disciplinary achievements, and so on.

This scheme is further elaborated by Snow (1978b). He offers an ogranizational scheme of abilities and aptitudes, which is based on recent analyses of large quantities of ability-test data. According to Snow, human abilities can be arranged from general (for instance, fluid analytic ability) to peripheral (for instance, film memory). The continuum from peripheral to general abilities implies, among other things, the processing of increasingly more complex information and a parallel increase in depth of cognitive processing.

Human abilities, aptitudes, or mental skills come into play upon situational demand. Some such skills (the general ones) are useful for a wider range of situations and stimuli than others. Crystallized ability may be relevant to most forms of education in the classroom in our culture, as it reflects skillful use of certain past experience in that situation (Snow, 1978b). Spatial skills may be relevant only when mental rotations or other such transformations are needed (Cronbach and Snow, 1977). Similarly, the cluster of skills identified as *film literacy* (Worth, 1968) is needed to enable learning from films (Snow, 1963), but skill in spatial reconstruction is relevant only when space is fragmented in films, as one of my experiments shows (Chapter Four).

On the basis of Feldman's theory and the assumption that human abilities come into play and are *cultivated* on situational demand, Snow then proposes a two-dimensional model. One dimension pertains to human abilities (achievements, according to Feldman); the other pertains to environmental conditions that give rise to them. The ability dimension ranges from the universally attained abilities (including those that are physiology-based, such as perceptual speed) to unique ones (painting). The environmental dimension ranges, likewise, from those conditions that can be found in all environments to the most specifically implemented ones. Note that a diagonal band is implied by this scheme, starting with the interaction of universal environments with universal achievements and gradually moving to the diagonally opposite corner, where highly specific environmental elements call for and cultivate specific mental skills.

The following examples of cognitive changes can be ranked along the diagonal, from those closer to the universal end to the ones closer to the unique end. When a whole socio-cultural environment exerts new demands, such as the collectivaization of Central Asian peasants, whole modes of thinking are reorganized (Luria, 1976). When only formal schooling is singled out for investigation (Scribner and Cole, 1973), more limited abilities, such as analytic thinking, are found to be affected. The influence of literacy without schooling affects even more specific skills (Scribner and Cole, 1978). Modeling of specific grammatical constructions, such as abstract questions or propositional and passive phrases, led to improved rule-governed language behavior (Rosenthal, Zimmerman, and During, 1970); Bandura and Harris, 1966). These skills have important transfer values, but they are more limited than the skills affected by literacy. The effects of using the abacus (Hatano, Miyake, and Binks, 1977) are even more restricted than those of modeling grammatical structures. Many other examples can be placed in this scheme.

Where do media's symbol systems belong? Media and the symbol systems they use seem to belong to the cultural region of this scheme. As Vygotzky (1978) argues, sign systems (language, numbers) are created by human societies over the course of history. The internalization of such sign systems leads to cognitive changes that bridge the gap between earlier and later stages of an individual's cognitive development.

But media's symbol systems, as we have seen (Chapter Two), vary with respect to their generality. Some symbol systems (gesture) are shared by a number of media and other, nonmedia acts of communication. Still other systems or combinations of systems are medium-specific (iconography or syntagms in film). Thus, media's symbol systems cannot be placed at one particular point in the achievement-environment scheme. Rather, symbol systems that are shared by several media and are also used outside media will be closer to the universal side of cultural conditions. Indeed, when a whole symbol system is newly introduced, more general abilities are apparently tapped, as was found by Elkind (1969), who studied the effects of first encounters with pictorials in an Indian tribe. On the other hand, specific coding elements within symbol systems would be placed somewhat closer to the unique side of the scheme.

It follows, for example, that all television shows tap some relatively general skills, partly shared by other symbol systems, but that televised commercials tap more specific skills; the zoom calls for even more specific skills. Thus, for example, one could expect the symbol system of cartography to affect more general spatial skills, but it would be unreasonable to expect *a particular* coding element (such as the representation of heights) to affect more than a specific skill. The cognitive effects of discovery-learning methods in schools (Egan and Greeno, 1973) are necessarily more limited than the effects of schooling in general.

Skill Activation and Supplantation

Having placed media's symbol systems in a wider context, we still need to ask how these symbol systems affect the mastery of cognitive skills. As Goodnow (1969) has argued, it is not enough to know that cultural factors affect cognition; the reseracher is challenged to identify *specific* links between cultural experiences and cognitive outcomes. I have postulated two mechanisms or procedures through which symbol systems and specific coding elements can affect cognition: They *call on*—that is, *activate*—mental skills, and, by exercising these skills, they cultivate skill-mastery. Or, they *overtly supplant* mental skills, and, by modeling these skills, the symbols are internalized. The findings reported in Chapters Seven and Eight support the general claim that a medium's coding elements cultivate skills, and the experiments reported in Chapter Six provide evidence to support the two-mechanism hypothesis.

Cultivation by activation can easily be seen as a specific

case of stretching a skill by its repeated application to new instances. Since the invoked skill serves to recode messages and/or to elaborate on them, successful information processing reinforces the skill. Much of the known research on instruction, as well as recent research on behavioral change through increasing people's self-efficacy and self-control (Bandura, 1978), converges to show that, when skills are successfully exercised, their mastery improves. For example, when the two-dimensionality of maps needs to be recoded into a three-dimensional image, or when a close-up/long-shot sequence in film needs to be elaborated so the segments become interrelated, or when the continuity in a television sequence needs to be maintained in the face of interruptions by commercials, skills are invoked, and their mastery can be gradually improved.

Cultivation by supplantation is a different kind of skill-cultivation, in which a particular internal process is overtly simulated, most likely by an equally dynamic external transformation of information that can serve as a model. When the model overtly supplants the internal process, it can be learned by observation or, following Vygotsky, be internalized. To the extent that a zoom shot in film or a mathematical transformation on paper simulates internal counterparts, they can be perceived as models and can be learned by observation.

At this point, however, a new problem arises. What exactly is the nature of the skills cultivated by activation, and what is the nature of the skills cultivated by supplantation? Are these skills of the same class? One may suspect that they are not. I propose that a coding element calls on mental skills for recoding purposes. If an element that is supposed to supplant does in fact supplant the *same* processes of recoding, then, unlike a skill-activating element, the supplanting element would not need to be recoded any more. However, there is no reason to assume that an element that overtly models an operation does not *itself* need to be recoded. Imagine a film in which a printed word transforms into a picture by means of some animation. First, the result of the modeled transformation—the picture—itself needs to be recoded. It may perhaps require better-mastered processes of recoding than the printed word, thus suggesting that recoding was partly short-circuited for the viewer but not really modeled. Second, the coding element through which the printed words were transformed into the picture *also* needs to be mentally recoded. Thus, it would not be reasonable to claim that recoding can be modeled, and certainly not that it can be supplanted. Rather, it is more reasonable to postulate that *all* coding elements to which one attends need to be recoded. Thus, all elements activate skills of recoding, whether they supplant something or not.

What then is supplanted by elements that are alleged to supplant or model a process? For example, what was modeled or supplanted by the zooms, the laying-out of objects, the camera movements around objects, or the rotation of cubes described in Chapter Six? Consider the findings of these experiments: Exposure to supplanting elements improved learners' mastery of singling items out from dense displays, improved visualization, improved skill in changing perspectives, and, in Rovet's study (1974), improved ability to imagine the results of spatial rotations.

The logical conclusion is that some coding elements can be made to model or supplant overtly specific processes of *elaboration*. The zoom in Experiments 1 and 2 in Chapter Six supplanted the process of relating parts to wholes, the model of laying-out objects supplanted the process of transforming an object in space, and so on. None of these supplanted processes were processes of recoding. In effect, supplanting components of elaboration by complex symbolic processes probably made recoding more demanding.

If such elements as the zoom or the changes of perspective model processes of elaboration, then one of two possibilities must be the case. Either there are other elements, not identified thus far, that *can* also model recoding processes, or modeling can pertain only to elaboration but not to recoding. The first possibility is logically inconsistent and empirically untestable. We are left with the second possibility—namely, that modeling and supplantation can pertain only to elaborations. Theoretically, this indeed is the only defensible possibility. For, if mental elaboration entails acts of comparing, analyzing, transforming, and other activities of manipulating information by symbolic means, then external symbolic counterparts could simulate some of these activities. The experiments reported in Chapter Six lend empirical support to this rationale. Thus, to the extent that a symbol system entails coding elements that simulate (or can be made to simulate) a hypothesized internal process of elaboration, it can supplant the process and become internalized for use as a mental tool.

It appears that two mechanisms can account for the way symbolic elements and symbol systems affect the mastery of mental skills. *All* elements, simple or compound, activate skills of recoding and of elaboration and can exercise them. And *some* skills, those that depict transformations, can model acts of elaboration (but not of recoding) and be learned by observation.

It could follow from here that only media whose symbol systems can *depict* transformations (that is, elaborations) are best suited to model them. Indeed, the studies reported in Chapters Six through Eight tested this possiblity only with the nonnotational systems of film and television. Yet, there is no theoretical reason to believe that overt modeling, or supplantation, of an elaborative transformation could not also be accomplished by nonnotational systems. To the extent that specific mental elaborations are of the logical-verbal rather than imagery type, nonnotational overt modeling should be capable of supplanting them and hence make them available to learning by observation, provided the necessary prerequisites are already mastered by the learner. The internalization of the arithmetic operations by the expert abacus users reported by Hatano, Miyake, and Binks (1977) is a case in point.

But learning by observation is surely not a simple act of copying or imitation. For one thing, learning must follow acts of recoding. For another, learning is based on certain prerequisite cognitive developments, as was suggested in Chapter Five—that is, it very likely requires previous mastery of constituent acts. It follows that, before one can learn by observation from a model or internalize it, one must skillfully recode it. This argument is very much in line with Bandura's (1977) analysis of how learning by observation occurs and with Vygotsky's (1978) description of how signs are internalized. Both Bandura and Vygotsky would agree in principle with Olson and Bruner (1974, p. 138) that learning from a model requires skill, as it "depends precisely on the capacity not so much to imitate directly as to construct behavior from already mastered constituent acts in order to match selected features of the model— a procedure more like paraphrasing than imitating."

If so much prerequisite mastery is demanded, why did our subjects with the *poorest* skill-mastery benefit *most* from supplantation in the experiments? These subjects, it should be noted, exhibited poor mastery of the elaboration skills that were either supplanted or activated, but they may have been quite skillful in recoding. More importantly, supplantation of one skill or another in all the experiments was aimed at children of appropriate age levels—that is, children who could be expected already to have mastered at least the constituent skills. For instance, cultivation of the skill of laying-out objects was directed at thirteen-year-olds, and the cultivation of changing prespectives was aimed at seven-year-olds. Attempting to cultivate the same skills in much younger children would probably have failed. The aptitude-treatment interactions systematically found in these and similar experiments, suggest that although modeling requires prior mastery of *constituent* skills, activation requires mastery of the *whole* skill. Therefore, cultivation by activation benefits the already skilled learner. Generalizing the case, I should conclude that media's symbol systems do not so much *generate* new skills as *cultivate existing ones*.

How congruent is this conclusion with the claim that symbol systems in communication (and art) can become "tools of thought" (Bruner, 1964) and serve for exploratory purposes (Olson, 1977)? For, if media's symbol systems, and specific coding elements thereof, only *aid* in the cultivation of mental skills, how can they be said to provide *new* mental tools? Recall Snow's (1978b) claim that human aptitudes are called into play by situational demand. Recall also Scribner and Cole's (1978) finding that certain literacy practices among the Vai produced intellectual outcomes closely tied to those practices, and that

neither literacy nor schooling had an all-or-none effect. Although these claims are true, the application of a skill that is
cultivated by specific situational or task demands (to write a
letter, to read a map, to understand a movie) need not be limited to the situation or task that originally demanded it.

Rosenthal, Zimmerman, and During (1970) modeled
adult-inquiry strategies to groups of disadvantaged children.
Some of the children saw a model that sought information
about the physical properties of objects. Others saw a model
that sought causal information, and still others saw a model that
sought information on functional usages. Later analyses of the
children's responses showed that they abstracted the learned-
inquiry strategies and generalized them to new instances.

As applied to the handling of coded messages, what may
initially be a skill used only for, say, the elaboration of slow-
motion may generalize to new instances as a result of practice.
The constituents need to be mastered before much cultivation
(let alone generalization) can take place, but the results of
cultivation can be relatively new. That is, the skill that has been
cultivated by one's handling of a symbol system ends up being
more generalizable and better integrated into one's mental
schemata than it would have been without such encounters.

Once generalized, the skill can be used in response to *new
and less*-specific situational demands (provided, or course, the
latter indeed demand such skill). For this reason, Feldman (in
press, p. 36) postulates that, over the history of a culture, more
personalized and unique skills become increasingly universal:
"A unique set of conditions gives rise to a unique mental
reorganization in one or a few human beings at some point in
time. If that reorganization is communicated or manifested in
a change in technology, it immediately becomes a dark horse
candidate for *universal* status."

More specifically, a symbolic element that cultivates a
skill through activation makes the skill's use more automatic—
that is, it shortens the routes of encoding or elaboration. *It
becomes part of one's mental schemata*, as these entail not only
stored knowledge but also operations of elaboration (Neisser,
1976). Thus, continuous exposure to a symbol system should

result in one's ability *to think in terms* of that symbol system.

Modeling or supplantation should yield such results much faster than activation, although with another type of symbolic elements—those that simulate an operation. And, as supplantation pertains to elaboration rather than to recoding, it should result in internalized mental tools whose constituents were mastered previously but whose integration results from exposure to a symbol system. Ultimately, then, the results of skill-activation and skill-supplantation should converge. Through both mechanisms, one should learn to think in terms of the symbolic forms afforded by media and by other cultural encounters. Indeed, the mechanisms of skill-activation and skill-supplantation may account for a variety of observed cultural effects on cognition. For example, the cognitive effects of literacy on the Vai (Scribner and Cole, 1978) seem to be best explained by the mechanism of mental skill-activation, and some of the cognitive effects of language, particularly its use as mental tools, can be explained in terms of overt supplantation and internalization.

But let us not overstate the case with media. First, typical exposure to media's symbol systems, unlike activities related to language, does not afford much interaction in terms of media's symbolic forms. Thus, unless specific symbolic elements are *made* to affect cognition under favorable conditions (Chapter Six), effects are not very strong (Chapter Eight). The difference between what *can be* affected and what is *typically* affected is particularly great for media that allow shallow processing.

Second, media's symbol systems are not the only messages to affect cognition, and not all of media's symbolic forms function in this capacity. Where, then, is media's unique contribution, and which of media's symbolic forms contribute uniquely to cognition? As the research to date warrants only speculation, I would propose the following: *To the extent that a medium's symbol systems (1) are sufficiently unique that is, do not easily map upon alternative forms or systems (as does the Morse Code with respect to language), and yield knowledge not fully represented by an alternative, (2) provide an organization of information not provided by an alternative medium* (there are few, if any, alternatives to a decision-making flow chart or to mathematical formulae), *and (3) contain a wide potential field of reference—to that extent it can contribute uniquely to one's mental schemata.*

Reciprocal Interaction

The differential effects of media's symbol systems on the acquisition of knowledge are related to their effects on the mastery of cognitive skills. The employment of skills in the service of knowledge acquisition allows their gradual cultivation, while the latter leads to the acquisition of more and different kinds of knowledge. This proposition is borne out in part by the observation (Chapter Seven) that, as the heavy "Sesame Street" viewers attempted to extract knowledge from the program, their skill-mastery improved, leading to increased knowledge acquisition.

Such interdependence can be described more formally as occurring among three focal points:

1. Environmental factors: Media's symbol systems, the information they carry, and the learning task one is to perform.
2. Personological factors: The learner's capabilities, mental schemata, and information preferences.
3. Behavioral factors: The specific actions or behaviors one carries out while handling coded information.

We might label the three factors as Environment (E), Person (P), and Behaviors (B). Much of the discussion thus far has focused on how cognitive skills are affected by media's symbol systems. As the Feldman scheme suggests, symbol systems are part of one's cultural environment, thus E→P. We also discussed how mental behaviors, such as recoding, mediate between the two, thus E→B→P. We have also seen that children's abilities influence how they perceive task-demands and what skills they bring to bear on coded messages, thus: P→B→E. Finally, the successful employment of skills leads to changes in one's mental schemata and to changes in the perception of the information to be dealt with, thus

FIGURE 13. Bandura's scheme of reciprocal determinism.

It should be apparent, then, that no unidirectional effects are implied by this scheme. Thus, I feel confident in following Bandura's (1978) scheme (Figure 13) of reciprocal determinism, which suggests that behavior (internal or external), personal factors (including abilities), and environments (coded messages, tasks) all operate as interlocking determinants of each other.

Bandura's scheme entails both Person and Behavior, not because they are completely independent of each other, but because one operates on coded messages through *specific* skills that are drawn from a larger cognitive storage. Environment is also interlocked with P and B, as individuals "play an active role in what information they extract from ongoing events and when and how they use the acquired skills" (Bandura, 1978, p. 351). Environment changes as abilities grow.

This scheme can describe, for example, my arguments about similarity and resemblance between symbolic depictions and referents (Chapter Two). Although I agreed with Goodman (1968) that, *logically*, no symbol bears any intrinsic similarity to its referent, I submitted that *psychologically*, people seek out resemblances in dense, nonnotational symbol systems, even when such perceived resemblances are erroneous. Objects in one's environment (E), whether real or represented in some symbolic form, are recoded and elaborated (B) in terms of one's mental schemata (P). New information yields a conception or forms of internal representation, which change to some degree one's schemata (P), which is then expressed in other recoding and elaboration activities (B), and results in an altered perception of the object (E). When a later encounter with a symbolic representation of the object is easily recoded and requires little change of schemata, the person judges the representation to "resemble" the object, although in effect it resembles the stored image in his schemata. Judgment of resemblance determines, in turn, the application of, say, a "pictorial standard" of recoding by the person (Roupas, 1977).

The three factors, P, B, and E, are not always equally powerful. As Bandura points out, sometimes environmental conditions are so powerful that they override the other factors. For instance, when a coded message greatly deviates from one's schemata, as was the case in the Salomon-Sieber (1970) randomly spliced movie, most same-age subjects engaged in the same mental activities regardless of differences in task or cognitive make-up. The same applies when extremely demanding tasks are imposed on learners, such as the learning requirements in the experiments reported in Chapter Six. On the other hand, when children are exposed to coded messages and no task is imposed on them, cognitive make-up dominates. Recall the differences between what was learned from "Sesame Street" by lower-class versus middle-class children (Chapter Seven) and what was learned from television by younger versus older children (Chapter Eight).

In light of the discussion earlier in this chapter, it is desirable to add a developmental dimension to Bandura's scheme. The extended model is presented in Figure 14. The developmental aspect is an "upward" dimension, implying that the tridirectional reciprocal determinism is a *spiral*; as one's cognition develops, the same three factors undergo changes. As one's cognitive apparatus grows, skill-mastery improves, and the environmental inputs are perceived differently. As coding elements become internalized, enriching one's cognition, the newly acquired mental tools afford new ways of exploring the environment (Olson, 1977b).

The extended model can now describe, among other things, the relationships between the nature of a coded message, one's differential utilization and cultivation of skills, and the resultant acquisition of knowledge. A coded message (E) is encountered, and information is extracted in accordance with

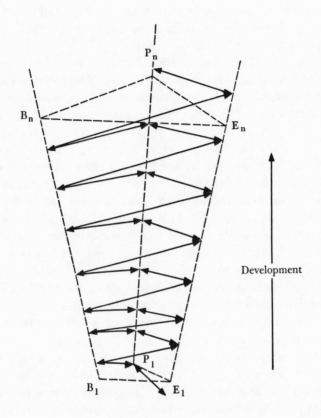

FIGURE 14: Schematic representation of Extended Developmental Reciprocal Determinism (Modified from Bandura, 1978).

one's abilities, expectations, and preferences (P→E); these determine the kinds of skills one *can* apply (P→B→E) and is *required* to apply by the symbolic nature of the material (E→B→P). But, as knowledge is acquired from the message's content, skill is being cultivated by the message's symbolic form. As skills are cultivated, *new* information can possibly be acquired from coded messages that were not dealt with before. Moreover, as symbolic modes are internalized, they equip one's cognitive apparatus with new tools, or more varied ways of handling more information. If paraphrasing within one symbol system underlies comprehension, then one's comprehension should improve even more when knowledge encoded in one internal symbolic mode is mapped onto other symbolic modes.

Olson (1978) distinguishes between two functions of symbols in cognition—the *representational* function (the expression and explication of already stored ideas and feelings) and an *epistemological* function (the acquisition of new knowledge about one's self and one's environment). The representational function is exemplified by a child's learning how to label for himself an already experienced event, the epistemological function is exemplified by a child's learning to examine a territory through newly acquired ways to represent spatial relations (this is where the claim about mental-tools seems to fit).

Olson goes on to suggest that the expressive function of symbols in thought precedes the epistemological function, thus implying reciprocal determinism of the kind presented in Figure 14. Encounters with a symbol system allow the child to translate implicit knowledge into more concise and more explicit form. This affords him new forms of mental activity—for example, a new classification scheme. Having such a new tool, the child can now use it as part of his anticipatory schemata to examine new events and acquire information he was unable to acquire earlier. The internalization of cultural symbolic forms, although initially serving only the explicationary function, may later serve the epistemological function.

We may derive a number of skeleton hypotheses from our model. These hypotheses are concerned with reciprocal interactions of media, cognition, and learning, although specific questions that result from them are more limited. One such hypothesis is based on findings that younger children fail to integrate narrative material, for example, from television—that is, they fail to make necessary inferences as to plot logic, motives, and similar connections (Collins, in press)—while using fantasy and imaginary connections (Winner, Rosenstiel, and Gardner, 1976; Gardner, Kircher, Winner, and Perkins, 1975).

If younger children address themselves to discrete, unrelated segments of a presentation, disregarding conventional boundaries of experience and language, then exposure to a medium's symbol systems would not be expected to affect their cognitive skill-mastery in significant ways. Thus, more general (more universal) cognitive development needs to precede skill-cultivation by a medium such as television. However, early exposure to such a medium could begin to have skill-cultivating effects if tutoring (say, mother's coobservation) would lead the child to seek out somewhat more integrative information and to address himself to symbolic modes he would tend to ignore otherwise. Indeed, Gardner (1972) studied how style sensitivity develops in children of varying ages (style in paintings, for instance, is part of the symbol system employed and is to be distinguished from the figural contents of the paintings). He found that, in the absence of training, only high school and college students can group works of art by style rather than by figurative content only. When training is introduced, even seven-year-olds succeed in grouping paintings by style, and ten-to-twelve-year-olds do even better.

Another hypothesis is that, to the extent that the media a child encounters emphasize unique symbolic forms, the child acquires unique ways of representing internal knowledge. If these new forms are applicable to other new instances, then richness and variety of encountered symbol systems should allow the child to discover new properties and to afford new interpretations of the world. Thus, rather than using media as alternative technologies to convey the same information, they should be used as unique sources of symbolic forms, which are potential candidates for adoption as mental tools. For example, television can be used not only as an entertaining equivalent to verbal instruction but as a source of potentially learnable symbolic forms, including split-screen for acts of comparison, zoom-ins for acts of perceptual scrutiny, or camera movements around objects for acts of changing perspectives. It follows, then, that active exposure to more symbol systems should enrich a child's cognitive apparatus.

Another hypothesis, somewhat at odds with the preceding one, is that the cultivation of mental skills by means of one symbol system may come at the expense of other skills cultivated by another symbol system. Mayo, Hornik, and McAnany

(1976) found instructional television in El Salvador to affect mainly children's *nonverbal* abilities. However, Hornik (1978), examining parts of the same data, found that the introduction of television had a consistent negative effect on reading abilities. Such effects, claims Hornik, cannot be attributed to simple time displacement or missed homework assignments. It is possible that, as the children acquired new nonverbal skills from the nonnotational elements of the medium, notational skills that need to be overlearned to serve reading were not exercised (see also Harnischfeger and Wiley, 1976, for a similar hypothesis to account for the decline of SAT scores).

Still another skeleton hypothesis is that, if a symbol system used by a medium allows relatively easy recoding of messages, then it may not cultivate much skill. Thus, although the medium may facilitate knowledge acquisition by poor skill-masterers, it may become increasingly attractive to them and keep them away from more intellectually demanding symbol systems. To the extent that nonnotational systems (and the media that use them) require less mental recoding than notational ones, poorly skilled learners may be drawn to use them more than other systems. Indeed, Morgan and Gross (1978) found that the viewing of television is preferred by boys with particularly low IQ, whose reading comprehension consequently declines. The resultant preference for mentally less-demanding symbol systems may lead to failure to cultivate the skills related to that symbol system as well as skills related to the more demanding symbol systems that such learners shun.

From the research reported in preceding chapters, it is possible to hypothesize that the symbol systems of the media can be made to be mentally demanding, even if they initially allow shallow processing (recall the effects of the coobserving mothers in Chapter Seven and the social pressures in Chapter Eight); symbol systems can be made to affect one's mastery of mental skills; thus, one can use the unique symbolic features of media to enrich the variety of symbolic modes in children's cognitive make-up. To the extent that symbolic forms *are* unique and do not map upon each other, we would expect that skills would be differentially cultivated and lead to the acquisition of otherwise inaccessible information. However, the conception of spiral reciprocal determinism warns us against simplistic unidirectional hypotheses. We know that the effects of media's contents are influenced by what a child brings with him to the encounter with media. We also know that the same applies to the way the structure of a medium's messages affect a child's comprehension of the message (Collins, in press). We are not clear as yet how a child's symbolic capabilities and preferences interact with his way of handling the symbolic nature of media's messages, nor in what specific ways they affect his cognitive abilities. Having generated general propositions and launched a series of studies, we are only now beginning to come to grips with a new and complex territory.

The propositions discussed in the book cannot supply all the answers to our questions about media, symbol systems, cognition, and learning or the more general issues of media use in education. Focusing on one aspect of a complex phenomenon, justified as it may be, may not only create entirely new problems but also may overshadow other equally important aspects. Still, I hope that the propositions offered here are useful and can generate renewed interest in media in education as well as some fruitful research and discussion.

References

❉ ❉ ❉ ❉ ❉ ❉ ❉

Anderson, J. R. "Arguments Concerning Representations for Mental Imagery."*Psychological Review*, 1978, *85*, 249-277.

Anderson, R. C., and others. "Frameworks for Comprehending Discourse." *American Educational Research Journal*, 1977, *14*, 367-383.

Arnheim, R. *Film as Art.* Berkeley: University of California Press, 1957.

Arnheim, R. "Painted Skies and Unicorns." *Science*, 1969, *164*, 697-698.

Atkin, C. K. *The Effects of Television Advertising on Children: First Year Experimental Evidence.* Final report submitted to the Office of Child Development. Washington, D.C.: Department of Health, Education, and Welfare, 1975.

Atkin, C. K., and Wood, C. "Effects of Realistic Versus Fictional Television on Aggression." Paper presented at the Association for Education in Journalism, College Park, Maryland, August 1974.

Baddley, A. D. "The Trouble with Levels: A Reexamination of Craik and Lockhart's Framework for Memory Research." *Psychological Review*, 1978, *85*, 139-152.

Ball, S., and Bogatz, G. A. *The First Year of "Sesame Street": An Evaluation*. Princeton, N.J.: Educational Testing Service, 1970.

Bandura, A. *Aggression: A Social Learning Analysis*. Englewood Cliffs, N.J.: Prentice-Hall, 1973.

Bandura, A. *Social Learning Theory*. Englewood Cliffs, N.J.: Prentice-Hall, 1977.

Bandura, A. "The Self System in Reciprocal Determinism." *American Psychologist*, 1978, *33*, 344-358.

Bandura, A., Grusec, J. E., and Menlove, F. L. "Observational Learning as a Function of Symbolization and Inventive Set." *Child Development*, 1966, *37*, 499-506.

Bandura, A., and Harris, M. B. "Modification of Syntactic Style." *Journal of Experimental Child Psychology*, 1966, *4*, 341-352.

Bandura, A., Jeffery, R., and Bachicha, D. L. "Analysis of Memory Codes and Cumulative Rehearsal in Observational Learning." *Journal of Research in Personality*, 1974, *7*, 295-305.

Bem, D., and Allen, A. "On Predicting Some of the People Some of the Time: The Search for Cross-Situational Consistencies in Behavior." *Psychological Review*, 1974, *81*, 506-520.

Bender, B. G., and Levin, J. R. "Pictures, Imagery, and Retarded Children's Prose Learning." *Journal of Educational Psychology*, 1978, *70*, 583-588.

Berliner, D. C. "Aptitude-Treatment Interaction in Two Studies of Learning from Lecture Instruction." Paper presented at the annual meeting of the American Educational Research Association, New York, April 1971.

Berlyne, D. E. *Structure and Direction in Thinking*. New York: Wiley, 1965.

Bernstein, L. J. "Design Attributes of "Sesame Street" and the Visual Attention of Preschool Children." Unpublished doctoral dissertation, Columbia University, 1978.

Bever, T. G. "The Cognitive Basis for Linguistic Structures." In J. R. Hayes (Ed.), *Cognition and the Development of Language*. New York: Wiley, 1970.

Blank, M., and Solomon, F. "A Tutorial Language Program to Develop Abstract Thinking in Socially Disadvantaged Preschool Children." *Child Development*, 1968, *39*, 379-389.

Bloom, L., Hood, L., and Lightbown, P. "Imitation in Language Development: If, When, and Why." *Cognitive Psychology*, 1974, *6*, 380-420.

Blumler, J. G., and Katz, E. (Eds.). *The Uses of Mass Communication.* Vol. 3. Beverly Hills, Calif.: Sage, 1974.

Bobrow, S. A., and Bower, G. H. "Comprehension and Recall of Sentences." *Journal of Experimental Psychology*, 1969, *80*, 455-461.

Borke, H. "Piaget's Mountains Revisited: Changes in the Egocentric Landscape." *Developmental Psychology*, 1975, *11*, 240-243.

Bower, G. H. "Cognitive Psychology: An Introduction." In W. K. Esten (Ed.), *Handbook of Learning and Cognitive Processes.* Vol. 1. Hillsdale, N.J.: Erlbaum, 1975.

Bower, G. H. "Comprehending and Recalling Stories." Division Three Presidential Address, American Psychological Association, Washington, D.C., September 1976.

Brooks, L. "The Suppression of Visualization by Reading." *Quarterly Journal of Experimental Psychology*, 1967, *19*, 289-299.

Brooks, L. "Spatial and Verbal Components of the Act of Recall." *Canadian Journal of Psychology*, 1968, *22*, 349-368.

Brown, I., Jr. "Modeling Processes and Language Acquisition: The Role of Referents." *Journal of Personality and Social Psychology*, 1965, *2*, 278-282.

Brown, I., Jr. "The Role of Referent Concreteness in the Acquisition of Passive Sentence Comprehension Through Abstract Modeling." *Journal of Experimental Child Psychology*, 1976, *22*, 185-199.

Brown, R. *Words and Things.* New York: Free Press, 1958.

Brown, R. *Social Psychology.* New York: Free Press, 1965.

Brown, R., and Lennenberg, E. H. "A Study of Language and Cognition." *Journal of Abnormal and Social Psychology*, 1954, *49*, 454-462.

Bruner, J. S. "The Course of Cognitive Growth." *American Psychologist*, 1964, *19*, 1-15.

Bruner, J. S., Olver, R. R., and Greenfield, P.M. *Studies in Cognitive Growth.* New York: Wiley, 1966.

Calfee, R., and Drum, P. "Learning to Read: Theory, Research, and Practice." *Curriculum Inquiry,* 1978, *8,* 183-249.

Carothers, T. J., and Gardner, H. "When Children's Drawings Become Art: The Emergence of Aesthetic Production and Perception." Unpublished paper, Harvard Project Zero and Psychology Service, Boston Veterans Administration Hospital, 1978.

Carpenter, E. "The New Languages." In E. Carpenter and M. McLuhan (Eds.), *Explorations in Communication.* Boston: Beacon Press, 1960.

Carroll, J. B. "The Potentials and Limitations of Print as a Medium of Instruction." In D. R. Olson (Ed.), *Media and Symbols: The Forms of Expression, Communciation, and Education.* 73rd Yearbook of the National Society for the Study of Education. Chicago: University of Chicago Press, 1974.

Carroll, J. B., and Casagrande, J. B. "The Function of Language Classifications in Behavior." In E. E. Maccoby, T. M. Newcomb, and E. L. Hartley (Eds.), *Readings in Social Psychology.* New York: Holt, Rinehart and Winston, 1958.

Chaffee, S. M., McLeod, J. M., and Atkin, C. K. "Parental Influence on Adolescent Media Use." *American Behavioral Scientist,* 1971, *14,* 323-340.

Chandler, M. J., Greenspan, S., and Barenboim, C. "Judgments of Intentionality in Response to Videotaped and Verbally Presented Moral Dilemmas: The Medium is the Message." *Child Development,* 1973, *44,* 315-320.

Chapanis, A. "Men, Machines, and Models." *American Psychologist,* 1961, *16,* 113-131.

Charmonte, N. "On Image and Word." In L. Jacobs (Ed.), *The Movies as a Medium.* New York: Farrar, Straus & Giroux, 1970.

Chomsky, N. *Reflections on Language.* New York: Random House, 1975.

Clark, H. H., and Clark, E. V. *Psychology and Language.* New York: Harcourt Brace Jovanovich, 1977.

Cohen, A. A., and Salomon, G. "Children's Literate Television

Watching: Some Empirical Surprises and Possible Explanations." Unpublished report, Hebrew University, Jerusalem,
1978.

Cole, M., and Scribner, S. *Culture and Thought.* New York:
Wiley, 1974.

Cole, M., and others. "Linguistic Structure and Transposition."
Science, 1969, *164,* 90-91.

Collins, W. A. "The Effect of Temporal Separation Between
Motivation, Aggression, and Consequences: A Developmental
Study." *Developmental Psychology,* 1973, *8,* 215-221.

Collins, W. A. "The Developing Child as a Viewer." *Journal of
Communication,* 1975, *25,* 35-44.

Collins, W. A. "Children's Comprehension of Television Content." In E. Wartella (Ed.), *Development of Children's Com-
municative Behavior.* Vol. 8. The Sage Annual Review of
Communication Research. Beverly Hills, Calif.: Sage, in press.

Columbia Broadcasting System, Office of Social Research. *A
Study of Messages Received by Children Who Viewed an Epi-
sode of Fat Albert and the Cosby Kids.* New York: Columbia
Broadcasting System, 1974.

Comstock, G., and others. *Television and Human Behavior.*
Santa Monica, Calif.: Rand Corporation, 1978.

Cook, T. D., and others. *"Sesame Street" Revisited.* New York:
Russell Sage, 1975.

Craik, F. I. M., and Lockhart, R. S. "Levels of Processing: A
Framework for Memory Research." *Journal of Verbal Learning and Verbal Behavior,* 1972, *11,* 671-684.

Craik, F. I. M., and Tulving, E. "Depth of Processing and the
Retention of Words in Episodic Memory." *Journal of Experimental Psychology: General,* 1975, *104,* 268-294.

Cronbach, L. J. "The Two Disciplines of Scientific Psychology."
American Psychologist, 1957, *12,* 671-684.

Cronbach, L. J. "The Role of the University in Improving Education." *Phi Delta Kappan,* June 1966, pp. 539-545.

Cronbach, L. J. "Beyond the Two Disciplines of Scientific
Psychology." *American Psychologist,* 1975, *30,* 116-126.

Cronbach, L. J., and Snow, R. E. *Aptitudes and Instructional
Methods: A Handbook of Research on Interactions.* New
York: Irvington, 1977.

DeFleur, M., and Ball-Rokeach, S. *Theories of Mass Communication.* (3rd ed.). New York: McKay, 1975.

Deregowski, J. B. "Difficulties in Pictorial Depth Perception in Africa." *British Journal of Psychology,* 1968, *59,* 195-204.

Dorr, A. "When I Was a Child, I Thought as a Child." In *Social Science Research Council Committee on Television and Social Behavior* (Ed.), book in press.

Dyk, R. B., and Witkin, H. A. "Family Experiences Related to the Development of Differentiation in Children." *Child Development,* 1965, *30,* 21-55.

Egan, D. E., and Greeno, J. G. "Acquiring Cognitive Structure by Discovery and Rule Learning." *Journal of Educational Psychology,* 1973, *64,* 85-97.

Eisner, E. W. "Media, Expression, and the Arts." In G. Salomon and R. E. Snow (Eds.), *Commentaries on Research in Instructional Media.* Bloomington: Indiana University, 1970.

Eisner, E. W. "Reading and the Creation of Meaning." In M. Douglass (Ed.), *Claremont Reading Conference, 49th Yearbook.* Claremont, Calif.: Claremont Graduate School, 1976.

Eisner, E. W. "The Impoverished Mind." *Educational Leadership,* 1978, *35,* 615-623.

Elkind, D. "Developmental Studies of Figural Perception." In L. Lipsitt and H. Reese (Eds.), *Advances in Child Development and Behavior,* 1969, whole no. 4.

Epps, E. G., and others. "Effects of Race of Comparison Referent and Motives on Negro Cognitive Performance." *Journal of Educational Psychology,* 1971, *62,* 201-208.

Feldman, D. H. "Map Understanding as a Possible Crystalizer of Cognitive Structures." *American Educational Research Journal,* 1971, *8,* 485-503.

Feldman, D. H. *Beyond Universals in Intellectual Development: Six Interpretive Essays.* New York: Praeger, in press.

Ferguson, E. S. "The Mind's Eye: Nonverbal Thought in Technology." *Science,* 1977, *197,* 827-836.

Fillenbaum, S. "On Coping with Ordered and Unordered Conjunctive Sentences." *Journal of Experimental Psychology,* 1971, *87,* 93-98.

Fillenbaum, S. "Pragmatic Normalization: Further Results for

Some Conjunctive and Disjunctive Sentences." *Journal of Experimental Psychology*, 1974, *102*, 574-578.

Fishbein, H. D., Lewis, S., and Keiffer, K. "Children's Understanding of Spatial Relations: Coordination of Perspectives." *Developmental Psychology*, 1972, *7*, 21-33.

Flavell, J. H. "Stage-Related Properties of Cognitive Development." *Cognitive Psychology*, 1971, *2*, 421-453.

Flavell, J. H. *Cognitive Development*. Englewood Cliffs, N.J.: Prentice-Hall, 1977.

Fodor, J. A. *The Language of Thought*. New York: Crowell, 1975.

French, J. W., Ekstrom, R. B., and Price, L. A. *Manual for Kit of Reference Tests for Cognitive Factors*. Princeton, N.J.: Educational Testing Service, 1963.

Furth, J. G. *Thinking Without Language: Psychological Implications of Deafness*. New York: Free Press, 1966.

Gardner, H. "Style Sensitivity in Children." *Human Development*, 1972, *15*, 325-338.

Gardner, H. "A Psychological Investigation of Nelson Goodman's Theory of Symbols." *The Monist*, 1974a, *58*, 317-326.

Gardner, H. *The Shattered Mind*. New York: Vantage Books, 1974b.

Gardner, H. "Senses, Symbols, Operations: An Organization of Artistry." In D. Perkins and B. Leondar (Eds.), *The Arts and Cognition*. Baltimore: Johns Hopkins University Press, 1977.

Gardner, H. "Developmental Psychology After Piaget: An Approach in Terms of Symbol Systems." Unpublished paper, Harvard Project Zero and Aphasia Research Center, Boston Veterans Administration Hospital, 1978.

Gardner, H., Howard, V. A., and Perkins, D. "Symbol Systems: A Philosophical, Psychological, and Educational Investigation." In D. R. Olson (Ed.), *Media and Symbols: The Forms of Expression, Communication, and Education*. 73rd Yearbook of the National Society for the Study of Education. Chicago: University of Chicago Press, 1974.

Gardner, H., Shotwell, J. M., and Wolf, D. "Exploring Early Symbolization: Styles of Achievement." Paper presented at the Symposium on Fundamentals of Symbolism, Burg Wartenstein, Austria, July 1977.

Gardner, H., and Wolf, D. "First Drawings: Notes on the Relationships Between Perception and Production in the Visual Arts." Paper presented at the Symposium on "What Is a Painting?" Philadelphia, April 1978.

Gardner, H. and others "Children's Metaphoric Productions and Preferences." *Journal of Child Language*, 1975, *2*, 125–141.

Gazzaniga, M. S. "Cerebral Dominance Viewed as a Decisive System." In S. J. Dimond and J. G. Beaumont (Eds.), *Hemispheric Functions in the Human Brain.* New York: Wiley, 1974.

Gerbner, G., and others. "TV Violence Profile Number Eight: The Highlights." *Journal of Communication*, 1977, *27*, 171–180.

Gombrich, E. H. *Art and Illusion.* (2nd ed.). New York: Bollinger Foundation, 1960.

Gombrich, E. H. "The Visual Image." In D. R. Olson (Ed.), *Media and Symbols: The Forms of Expression, Communication, and Education.* 73rd Yearbook of the National Society for the Study of Education. Chicago: University of Chicago Press, 1974.

Goodhart, G. J., Ehrenberg, A. S. C., and Collins, W. A. *The Television Audience: Patterns of Viewing.* Westmead, England: Saxon House, 1975.

Goodman, K. S., and Goodman, Y. M. "Learning About Psycholinguistic Processes by Analyzing Oral Reading." *Harvard Educational Review*, 1977, *47*, 317–333.

Goodman, N. *The Languages of Art.* Indianapolis: Hackett, 1968.

Goodman, N. "When Is Art?" In D. Perkins and B. Leondar (Eds.), *The Arts and Cognition.* Baltimore: Johns Hopkins University Press, 1977.

Goodnow, J. J. "Cultural Variations in Cognitive Skill." In D. R. Price-Williams (Ed.), *Cross-Cultural Studies.* Middlesex, England: Penguin Books, 1969.

Gordon, G. N. *The Languages of Communication.* New York: Hastings House, 1969.

Gough, P. B., and Cosky, M. J. "One Second of Reading Again." In N. J. Castellan, Jr., D. B. Pisoni, and G. R. Potts (Eds.), *Cognitive Theory.* Vol. 2. Hillsdale, N.J.: Erlbaum, 1977.

Gray, S. "The Child's First Teacher." *Childhood Education*, 1971, *48*, 3.

Greenberg, B. S., and Dervin, B. *Uses of the Mass Media by the Urban Poor.* New York: Praeger, 1970.

Greenfield, P. "Oral or Written Language: The Consequences for Cognitive Development in Africa, the United States, and England." *Language and Speech*, 1972, *15*, 169-178.

Greeno, J. G. "Language Understanding and Learning." Paper presented at the Symposium on Individual Differences, Cognition, and Learning, American Association for the Advancement of Science, Denver, Colo., 1977.

Gross, L. "Modes of Communication and the acquisition of Symbolic Competence." In D. R. Olson (Ed.), *Media and Symbols: The Forms of Expression, Communication, and Education.* 73rd Yearbook of the National Society for the Study of Education. Chicago: University of Chicago Press, 1974.

Guttmann, J., Levin, J. R., and Pressley, G. M. "Pictures, Partial Pictures, and Young Children's Oral Prose Learning." *Journal of Educational Psychology*, 1977, *69*, 473-480.

Hakstian, A. R., and Cattell, R. B. "Higher-Stratum Ability Structures on a Basis of Twenty Primary Abilities." *Journal of Educational Psychology*, 1978, *70*, 657-669.

Hamilton, V. J., and Gordon, D. A. "Teacher-Child Interactions in Preschool and Task Persistence." *American Educational Research Journal*, 1978, *15*, 459-466.

Harari, H., and McDavid, J. "Cultural Influence on Retention of Logical and Symbolic Material." *Journal of Educational Psychology*, 1966, *57*, 18-22.

Harnischfeger, A., and Wiley, D. "Achievement Test Scores Drop. So What?" *Educational Researcher*, 1976, *5*, 5-12.

Hatano, G., Miyake, Y., and Binks, M. G. "Performance of Expert Abacus Operators." *Cognition*, 1977, *5*, 57-71.

Hayes-Roth, B. "Evolution of Cognitive Structures and Processes." *Psychological Review*, 1977, *84*, 260-278.

Heider, E. R. "Universals in Color Naming and Memory." *Journal of Experimental Psychology*, 1972, *93*, 10-20.

Heider, E. R., and Olivier, D. C. "The Structure of the Color

Space in Naming and Memory for Two Languages." *Cognitive Psychology*, 1972, *3*, 337-355.

Holton, G. "Influences on Einstein's Early Work in Relativity Theory." *American Scholar*, 1968, *37*, 14-28.

Hornik, R. C. "Television Access and the Slowing of Cognitive Growth." *American Educational Research Journal*, 1978, *15*, 1-16.

Hudson, W. "Pictorial Perception and Educational Adaptation in Africa." *Psychologica Africana*, 1962, *9*, 226-239.

Hudson, W. "The Study of the Problem of Pictorial Perception Among Unacculturated Groups." *International Journal of Psychology*, 1967, *2*, 89-107.

Huston-Stein, A., and Wright, J. C. "Modeling the Medium: Effects of Formal Properties of Children's Television Programs." Paper presented at the biennial meeting of the Society for Research in Child Development, New Orleans, March 1977.

Huttenlocher, J. "Language and Thought." In G. A. Miller (Ed.), *Communication, Language, and Meaning*. New York: Basic Books, 1973.

Huttenlocher, J., and Presson, C. "Mental Rotation and the Perspective Problem." *Cognitive Psychology*, 1973, *4*, 277-299.

Huttenlocher, J., and Higgins, E. T. "Issues in the Study of Symbolic Development." In A. Collins (Ed.), *Minnesota Symposia on Child Psychology*. Vol. 10. New York: Crowell, in press.

Jackson, P., and Kieslar, S. B. "Fundamental Research and Education." *Educational Researcher*, 1977, *6*, 13-18.

Jacobs, L. (Ed.). *The Movies as a Medium*. New York: Farrar, Straus & Giroux, 1970.

Jamison, D., Suppes, P., and Wells, S. "The Effectiveness of Alternative Instructional Media: A Survey." *Review of Educational Research*, 1974, *44*, 1-68.

Johnston, P. K. "Relationship Between Perceptual Style, Achievement, and Child Rearing Practices in Elementary School Boys and Girls." Unpublished doctoral dissertation, University of Southern California, 1974.

Jones, S. "The Effect of a Negative Qualifier in an Instruction."

Journal of Verbal Learning and Verbal Behavior, 1966, *5*, 495-501.

Kahneman, D., and Tversky, A. "On the Psychology of Prediction." *Psychological Review,* 1973, *80*, 237-251.

Kane, J. M., and Anderson, R. C. "Depth of Processing and Interference Effects in the Learning and Remembering of Sentences." *Journal of Educational Psychology,* 1978, *70*, 626-635.

Karnes, M. B., and others. "Educational Intervention at Home by Mothers of Disadvantaged Infants." *Child Development,* 1970, *41*, 925-935.

Karp, S. A., and Konstadt, N. "The Children's Embedded Figures Test (CEFT)." In H. A. Witkin and others (Eds.), *Manual for Embedded Figures Test.* Palo Alto, Calif.: Consulting Psychologists Press, 1971.

Katz, E. *Social Research on Broadcasting: Proposals for Further Development.* London: British Broadcasting Corporation, 1977.

Katzman, N. *The Impact of Communication Technology: Some Theoretical Premises and Their Implications.* Report for the National Institute of Health Information Science Training Colloquium, Stanford University, Stanford, Calif., Spring 1973.

Katzman, N., and Nyenhuis, J. "Color Versus Black-and-White Effects in Learning, Opinion, and Attention." *AV Communication Review,* 1972, *20*, 16-28.

Kendler, H. H., and Kendler, T. S. "Vertical and Horizontal Processes in Problem Solving." *Psychological Review,* 1962, *69*, 1-16.

Kerlinger, F. N. "The Influence of Research on Education Practice." *Educational Researcher,* 1977, *6*, 5-12.

Kintsch, W. *Memory and Cognition.* New York: Wiley, 1977.

Kjørup, S. "Film as a Meeting Place of Multiple Codes." In D. Perkins and B. Leondar (Eds.), *The Arts and Cognition.* Baltimore: Johns Hopkins University Press, 1977.

Kolers, P. A. "Reading a Year Later." *Journal of Experimental Psychology: Human Learning and Memory,* 1976, *2*, 554-565.

Kolers, P. A. "Reading Pictures and Reading Text." In D. Perkins and B. Leondar: *The Arts and Cognition.* Baltimore: Johns Hopkins University Press, 1977.

Koran, M. L., Snow, R. E., and McDonald, F. J. "Teacher Aptitude and Observational Learning of a Teaching Skill." *Journal of Educational Psychology,* 1971, *62,* 219-228.

Kosslyn, S., and Pomerantz, J. "Imagery, Propositions, and the Form of Internal Representations." *Cognitive Psychology,* 1977, *9,* 52-76.

Kracauer, S. *Theory of Film.* New York: Oxford University Press, 1960.

Krugman, H. E. "Brain Wave Measures of Media Involvement." *Journal of Advertising Research,* 1971, *11,* 3-9.

Krugman, H. E. "Long-Range Social Implications of the New Developments in Television Technology." Paper presented at the American Association of Public Opinion Research, Asheville, N.C., 1976.

LaBerge, D., and Samuels, S. J. "Toward a Theory of Automatic Information Processing in Reading." *Cognitive Psychology,* 1974, *6,* 293-323.

Langer, S. K. *Philosophy in a New Key.* Cambridge, Mass.: Harvard University Press, 1942.

Langer, S. K. *Problems of Art.* New York: Scribner's, 1957.

Leifer, A. D. "Teaching with Television and Film." In N. L. Gage (Ed.), *The Psychology of Teaching Methods.* Chicago: University of Chicago Press, 1976.

Leifer, A. D., and others. "Developmental Aspects of Variables Relevant to Observational Learning." *Child Development,* 1971, *42,* 1509-1516.

Lennenberg, E. H. "Color Naming, Color Recognition, Color Discrimination: A Reappraisal." *Perceptual and Motor Skills,* 1961, *12,* 375-382.

Lennenberg, E. H., and Roberts, J. "The Language of Experience, A Study in Methodology." Memoir 13. *International Journal of American Linguistics,* 1956.

Lesser, G. S. *Children and Television: Lessons from "Sesame Street."* New York: Random House, 1974.

Levenstein, P. "Cognitive Growth in Preschoolers Through Verbal Interaction with Mothers." *American Journal of Orthopsychiatry*, 1970, *40*, 3-17.

Levie, W. H., and Dickie, K. E. "The Analysis and Application of Media." In R. M. W. Travers (Ed.), *The Second Handbook of Research on Teaching*. Chicago: Rand McNally, 1973.

Lloyd, B. B. *Perception and Cognition: A Cross-Cultural Perspective*. Middlesex, England: Penguin Books, 1972.

Luria, A. R. *The Role of Speech in the Regulation of Normal and Abnormal Behavior*. New York: Pergamon Press, 1961.

Luria, A. R. "Towards the Problem of the Historical Nature of Psychological Processes." *International Journal of Psychology*, 1971, *6*, 259-272.

Luria, A. R. *Cognitive Development—Its Cultural and Social Foundations*. Cambridge, Mass.: Harvard University Press, 1976.

McCandless, B. R., Roberts, A., and Starnes, T. "Teachers' Marks, Achievement Test Scores, and Aptitude Relations with Respect to Social Class, Race, and Sex." *Journal of Educational Psychology*, 1972, *63*, 153-160.

McCombs, M., and Shaw, D. "The Agenda Setting Function of the Mass Media." *Public Opinion Quarterly*, 1972, *36*, 176-187.

McConkie, G. W., and Rayner, K. "Identifying the Span of the Effective Stimulus in Reading: Literature Review and Theories of Reading." In H. Singer and R. B. Ruddell (Eds.), *Theoretical Models and Processes of Reading*. (2nd ed.). Newark, Del.: International Reading Association, 1976.

McLuhan, M. *Understanding Media: The Extension of Man*. New York: McGraw-Hill, 1965.

Mahoney, M. J. "Reflections on the Cognitive-Learning Trend in Psychotherapy." *American Psychologist*, 1977, *32*, 5-13.

Mandler, J. M., and Johnson, N. S. "Remembrance of Things Parsed: Story Structure and Recall." *Cognitive Psychology*, 1977, *9*, 111-151.

Marantz, S., and Dowaliby, F. J. "Individual Differences in Learning from Pictorial and Verbal Instruction." Unpublished report, University of Massachusetts, 1973.

Mast, G. *Film, Cinema, Movie.* New York: Harper & Row, 1977.

Mayo, J. K., Hornik, R. C., and McAnany, E. G. *Educational Reform with Television: The El Salvador Experience.* Stanford, Calif.: Stanford University Press, 1976.

Melton, A. W., and Martin, E. *Coding Processes in Human Memory.* Washington, D.C.: Winston, 1972.

Meringoff, L. "A Story A Story: The Influence of the Medium on Children's Apprehension of Stories." Unpublished doctoral dissertation, Harvard University, 1978.

Metz, C. *Language and Cinema.* The Hague: Mouton, 1974.

Metzler, J., and Shepard, R. N. "Transformational Studies of the Internal Representation of Three-Dimensional Objects." In R. Solso (Ed.), *Theories in Cognitive Psychology: The Loyola Symposium.* Potomac, Md.: Earlbaum, 1974, 147-201.

Mialaret, G. *The Psychology of the Use of Audio-Visual Aids in Primary Education.* London: Harrap, 1966.

Mielke, K. W. "Questioning the Questions of ETV Research." *Educational Broadcasting Review,* 1968, *2,* 6-15.

Miller, S. H., Shelton, J., and Flavell, J. H. "A Test of Luria's Hypothesis Concerning the Development of Verbal Self-Regulation." *Child Development,* 1970, *41,* 651-665.

Mischell, R. W. "On the Future of Personality Measurement." *American Psychologist,* 1977, *32,* 246-255.

Morgan, M., and Gross, L. "Reading, Writing, and Watching: Television Viewing, I.Q., and Academic Achievement." Unpublished report, Annenberg School of Communcation, University of Pennsylvania, 1978.

Münsterberg, H. *The Film: A Psychological Study.* New York: Dover, 1970. (Originally published 1916.)

Neisser, U. *Cognition and Reality.* San Francisco: Freeman, 1976.

Nielsen Company. *Nielsen Television—1977.* Chicago: Nielsen, 1977.

Noble, G. *Children in Front of the Small Screen.* Beverly Hills, Calif.: Sage Publications, 1975.

Norman, D. A., and Rumelhart, D. E. *Explorations in Cognition.* San Francisco: W. H. Freeman, 1975.

Oettinger, A. G., and Zapol, N. *Will Technology Help Learning?*

Report prepared for the Carnegie Commission on Higher Education, December 1971.

Olson, D. R. *Cognitive Development*. New York: Academic Press, 1970.

Olson, D. R. "What Is Worth Knowing and What Can Be Taught." *School Review*, 1973, *82*, 27-43.

Olson, D. R. "Introduction." In D. R. Olson (Ed.), *Media and Symbols: The Forms of Expression, Communication, and Education.* 73rd Yearbook of the National Society for the Study of Education. Chicago: University of Chicago Press, 1974.

Olson, D. R. "The Languages of Experience: On Natural Language and Formal Education." *Bulletin of the British Psychological Society*, 1975, *28*, 363-373.

Olson, D. R. "Towards a Theory of Instructional Means." *Educational Psychologist*, 1976, *12*, 14-35.

Olson, D. R. "From Utterance to Text: The Bias of Language in Speech and Writing." *Harvard Educational Review*, 1977a, *47*, 257-281.

Olson, D. R. "The Arts as Basic Skills: Three Cognitive Functions of Symbols." Paper presented at the Conference on Arts, Cognition, and Basic Skills, Aspen, Colo., June 1977b.

Olson, D. R. "Three Cognitive Functions of Symbols." Paper presented at the Terman Memorial Conference, Stanford University, Stanford, Calif., October 1978.

Olson, D. R., and Bruner, J. S. "Learning Through Experience and Learning Through Media." In D. R. Olson (Ed.), *Media and Symbols: The Forms of Expression, Communication, and Education.* 73rd Yearbook of the National Society for the Study of Education. Chicago: University of Chicago Press, 1974.

Olson, D. R., and Filby, N. "On the Comprehension of Active and Passive Sentences." *Cognitive Psychology*, 1972, *3*, 361-381.

Paivio, A. *Imagery and Verbal Processes*. New York: Holt, Rinehart and Winston, 1971.

Palmer, S. E. "Visual Perception and World Knowledge: Notes on a Model of Sensory-Cognitive Interaction." In D. A. Norman and D. E. Rumelhart (Eds.), *Explorations in Cognition*. San Francisco: W. H. Freeman, 1975.

Palmer, S. E. "Hierarchical Structure in Perceptual Representation." *Cognitive Psychology*, 1977, *9*, 441-474.

Perkins, D., and Leondar, B. (Eds.). *The Arts and Cognition*. Baltimore: Johns Hopkins University Press, 1977.

Pichert, J. W., and Anderson, R. C. "Taking Different Perspectives on a Story." *Journal of Educational Psychology*, 1977, *69*, 309-315.

Pressley, M. "Imagery and Children's Learning: Putting the Picture in Developmental Perspective." *Review of Educational Research*, 1977, *47*, 585-622.

Pressley, M., and Levin, J. R. "Task Parameters Affecting the Efficacy of a Visual Imagery Learning Strategy in Younger and Older Children." *Journal of Experimental Child Psychology*, 1977, *24*, 53-59.

Pryluck, C., and Snow, R. E. "Toward a Psycholinguistics of Cinema." *AV Communication Review*, 1967, *15*, 54-75.

Putnam, H. "The Meaning of 'Meaning.'" *Mind, Language, and Reality*. (Philosophical Papers, Vol. 2). Cambridge, England: Cambridge University Press, 1975.

Pylyshyn, Z. "What the Mind's Eye Tells the Mind's Brain: A Critique of Mental Imagery." *Psychological Bulletin*, 1973, *80*, 1-24.

Rapoport, A. "Discussant II." In J. R. Royce (Ed.), *Psychology and the Symbol: An Interdisciplinary Symposium*. New York: Random House, 1965.

Rohwer, W. D., Jr. "Images and Pictures in Children's Learning: Research Results and Educational Implications." *Psychological Bulletin*, 1970, *73*, 393-403.

Rosch, E. "Cognitive Representations of Semantic Categories." *Journal of Experimental Psychology: General*, 1975, *104*, 192-233.

Rosch, E. "Human Categorization." In N. Warren (Ed.), *Advances in Cross-Cultural Psychology*. Vol. 1. London: Academic Press, 1977.

Rosch, E., and Mervis, C. B. "Family Resemblances: Studies in the Internal Structure of Categories." *Cognitive Psychology*, 1975, *7*, 573-605.

Rosenberg, S., and Simon, H. "Modeling Semantic Memory: Effects of Presenting Semantic Information in Different Modalities." *Cognitive Psychology*, 1977, *9*, 293-325.

Rosenthal, T. L., and Zimmerman, B. J. *Social Learning and Cognition.* New York: Academic Press, 1978.

Rosenthal, T. L., Zimmerman, B. J., and During, K. "Observational-Induced Changes in Children's Interrogative Classes." *Journal of Personality and Social Psychology*, 1970, *16*, 681-688.

Roupas, T. G. "Information and Pictorial Representation." In D. Perkins and B. Leondar (Eds.), *The Arts and Cognition.* Baltimore: Johns Hopkins University Press, 1977.

Rovet, J. "Can Spatial Skills Be Acquired via Film? An Analysis of the Cognitive Consequences of Visual Media." Unpublished doctoral dissertation, University of Toronto, 1974.

Saettler, P. "Design and Selection Factors." *Review of Educational Research: Instructional Materials: Educational Media and Technology*, 1968, *38*, 115-128.

Salomon, G. "Cross-Cultural Differences in Map Reading." Paper presented at the annual meeting of the American Educational Research Association, Chicago, February 1968.

Salomon, G. "Heuristic Models for the Generation of Aptitude-Treatment Interaction Hypotheses." *Review of Educational Research*, 1971, *42*, 327-343.

Salomon, G. "What Is Learned and How It Is Taught: The Interaction Between Media, Message, Task, and Learner." In D. R. Olson (Ed.), *Media and Symbols: The Forms of Expression, Communication, and Education.* 73rd Yearbook of the National Society for the Study of Education. Chicago: University of Chicago Press, 1974a.

Salomon, G. "Internalization of Filmic Schematic Operations in Interaction with Learners' Aptitudes." *Journal of Educational Psychology*, 1974b, *66*, 499-511.

Salomon, G. "Cognitive Skill Learning Across Cultures." *Journal of Communication*, 1976, *26*, 138-145.

Salomon, G. "Effects of Encouraging Israeli Mothers to Co-observe "Sesame Street" with Their Five-Year-Olds." *Child Development*, 1977, *48*, 1146-1151.

Salomon, G., and Clark, R. E. "Reexamining the Methodology of Research on Media and Technology in Education." *Review of Educational Research*, 1977, *47*, 99-120.

Salomon, G., and Cohen, A. A. "Television Formats, Mastery of Mental Skills, and the Acquisition of Knowledge." *Journal of Educational Psychology*, 1977, *69*, 612-619.

Salomon, G., and Cohen, A. A. "On the Meaning and Validity of Television Viewing." *Journal of Human Communication Research*, 1978, *4*, 265-270.

Salomon, G., and Sieber, J. "Relevant Subjective Response Uncertainty as a Function of Stimulus-Task Interaction." *American Educational Research Journal*, 1970, *7*, 337-349.

Salomon, G., and Sieber-Suppes, J. "Learning to Generate Subjective Uncertainty." *Journal of Personality and Social Psychology*, 1972, *23*, 163-174.

Salomon, G., and others. *"Sesame Street" in Israel: Its Instructional and Psychological Effects on Children.* Jerusalem: Hebrew University, 1974.

Samuels, S. J. "Effects of Pictures in Learning to Read, Comprehension, and Attitudes." *Review of Educational Research*, 1970, *40*, 397-407.

Savin, H. B., and Perchonock, E. "Grammatical Structure and the Immediate Recall of English Sentences." *Journal of Verbal Learning and Verbal Behavior*, 1965, *4*, 348-353.

Schlesinger, I. M. "The Language We Learn and the Language We Think In." Unpublished paper, Hebrew University, Jerusalem, 1977a.

Schlesinger, I. M. "The Role of Cognitive Development and Linguistic Input in Language Acquisition." *Journal of Child Language*, 1977b, *4*, 153-169.

Schneider, W., and Shiffrin, R. M. "Controlled and Automatic Human Information Processing: I. Detection, Search, and Attention." *Psychological Review*, 1977, *84*, 1-68.

Schramm, W. *Big Media, Little Media.* Beverly Hills, Calif.: Sage, 1977.

Scribner, S., and Cole, M. "Cognitive Consequences of Formal and Informal Education." *Science*, 1973, *182*, 553-559.

Scribner, S., and Cole, M. *Literacy Without Schooling: Testing for Intellectual Effects.* Vai Literacy Project, Working Paper No. 2. New York: Rockefeller University, 1978.

Segall, M. H., Campbell, D. T., and Herskovitz, M. J. *The Influence of Culture on Visual Perception.* Chicago: Bobbs-Merrill, 1966.

Seibert, W. F. and Snow, R. E. "Cine-Psychometry." *AV Communication Review*, 1965, *13*, 140-158.

Selman, R. L., and Byrne, D. R. "A Structural Developmental Analysis of Levels of Role Taking in Middle Childhood." *Child Development*, 1974, *45*, 803-806.

Shepard, R. N. "The Mental Image." *American Psychologist*, 1978a, *33*, 125-137.

Shepard, R. N. "Externalization of Mental Images and the Act of Creation." In B. S. Randhava and W. E. Coffman (Eds.), *Visual Learning, Thinking, and Communication.* New York: Academic Press, 1978b.

Shiffrin, R. M., and Schneider, W. "Controlled and Automatic Human Information Processing: II. Perceptual Learning, Automatic Attention, and A General Theory." *Psychological Review*, 1977, *84*, 127-190.

Shimmerlik, S. M. "Organization Theory and Memory for Prose: A Review of the Literature." *Review of Educational Research*, 1978, *48*, 103-120.

Sieber, J. "A Paradigm for Experimental Modification of the Effects of Test Anxiety on Cognitive Processes." *American Educational Research Journal*, 1969, *6*, 46-61.

Sieber, J., and Lanzetta, J. "Some Determinants of Individual Differences in Predecision Information-Processing Behavior." *Journal of Personality and Social Psychology*, 1966, *4*, 561-571.

Sinclair de Zwart, H. *Acquisition du language et development de la pensée: Sous-systemes linguistiques et operation concretes.* Paris: Dunod, 1967.

Singer, J. L., "The Powers and Limitations of Television." In P. Tannenbaum (Ed.), *The Entertainment Function of Tele-*

vision. Hillsdale, N.J.: Erlbaum, in press.

Singer, J. L., and others. "A Preschooler's Comprehension and Play Behavior Following Viewing of 'Mr. Rogers' and 'Sesame Street.'" Paper presented at the annual meeting of the American Psychological Association, San Francisco, August 1977.

Snow, R. E. *The Importance of Selected Audience and Film Characteristics as Determiners of the Effectiveness of Instructional Films.* Lafayette, Ind.: Audio Visual Center, Purdue University, 1963.

Snow, R. E. "Individual Differences and Instructional Theory." *Educational Researcher,* 1977a, *6,* 11-15.

Snow, R. E. "Research on Aptitudes: A Progress Report." In L. Shulman (Ed.), *Review of Research in Education.* Vol. 4. Itasca, Ill.: Peacock, 1977b.

Snow, R. E. "Aptitude Processes." Paper presented at the Conference on Aptitude, Learning, and Instruction: Cognitive Process Analysis, San Diego, Calif., March 1978a.

Snow, R. E. "Toward a Theory of Aptitude." Paper presented at the annual meeting of the American Educational Research Association, Toronto, March 1978b.

Snow, R. E., and Salomon, G. "Aptitudes and Instructional Media." *A V Communication Review,* 1968, *16,* 341-358.

Snow, R. E., Tiffin, J., and Seibert, W. F. "Individual Differences and Instructional Film Effects." *Journal of Educational Psychology,* 1965, *56,* 315-326.

Sontag, S. *On Photography.* New York: Farrar, Straus & Giroux, 1978.

Stefflre, V., Vales, V., and Morley, L. "Language and Cognition in Yucatan: A Cross-Cultural Replication." *Journal of Personality and Social Psychology,* 1966, *4,* 112-115.

Stein, N. L., and Glenn, C. G. "A Developmental Study of Children's Recall of Story Material." Paper presented at the annual meeting of the Society for Research in Child Development, Denver, Colo., April 1975.

Sternberg, R. J. *Intelligence, Information Processing, and Analogical Reasoning: The Componential Analysis of Human Abilities.* New York: Wiley, 1977.

Swanson, L. "Verbal Encoding Effects on the Visual Short-Term Memory of Learning Disabled and Normal Readers." *Journal of Educational Psychology*, 1978, *70*, 539-544.

Tannenbaum, P. H., and Zillman, D. "Emotional Arousal in the Facilitation of Aggression Through Communication." *Advances in Experimental Social Psychology*, 1975, *8*, 149-192.

Thorndyke, P. W. "Cognitive Structures in Comprehension and Memory of Narrative Discourse." *Cognitive Psychology*, 1977, *9*, 77-110.

Tikomirov, O. K. "Man and Computer: The Impact of Computer Technology on the Development of Psychological Processes." In D. R. Olson (Ed.), *Media and Symbols: The Forms of Expression, Communication, and Education*. 73rd Yearbook of the National Society for the Study of Education. Chicago: University of Chicago Press, 1974.

Tobias, S. "Achievement Treatment Interactions." *Review of Educational Research*, 1976, *46*, 61-74.

Tulving, E., and Thomson, D. M. "Encoding Specificity and Retrieval Processes in Episodic Memory." *Psychological Review*, 1973, *80*, 352-373.

Tversky, A. "Features of Similarity." *Psychological Review*, 1977, *84*, 327-352.

Tyler, P. *The Hollywood Hallucination*. New York: Simon & Schuster, 1970.

Urberg, K. A., and Docherty, E. M. "Development of Role-Taking Skills in Young Children." *Developmental Psychology*, 1976, *12*, 3, 198-203.

Von Bertalanffy, L. "On the Definition of the Symbol." In J. R. Royce (Ed.), *Psychology and the Symbol*. New York: Random House, 1965.

Vygotsky, L. S. *Thought and Language*. Cambridge, Mass.: M.I.T. Press, 1962.

Vygotsky, L. S. *Mind in Society: The Development of Higher Psychological Processes*. (M. Cole and others, Eds.) Cambridge, Mass.: Harvard University Press, 1978.

Wakshlag, J. J. "Programming Strategies and the Popularity of Television Programs for Children." Unpublished doctoral dissertation, Michigan State University, East Lansing, 1977.

Wanner, E. "On Remembering, Forgetting, and Understanding Sentences: A Study of the Deep Structure Hypothesis." Unpublished doctoral dissertation, Harvard University, 1968.

White, K. R. "The Relationship Between Socioeconomic Status and Academic Achievement." Unpublished doctoral dissertation, University of Colorado, 1976.

Whorf, B. L. *Language, Thought, and Reality.* Cambridge, Mass.: M.I.T. Press; New York: Wiley, 1956.

Willows, D. M. "A Picture Is Not Always Worth a Thousand Words: Pictures as Distractors in Reading." *Journal of Educational Psychology*, 1978, *70*, 255-262.

Winner, E., Rosenstiel, A. K., and Gardner, H. "The Development of Metaphoric Understanding." *Developmental Psychology*, 1976, *12*, 289-297.

Winograd, T. *Understanding Natural Language.* New York: Academic Press, 1972.

Wolf, T. "Reading Reconsidered." *Harvard Educational Review*, 1977, *47*, 411-429.

Worth, S. "Cognitive Aspects of Sequence in Visual Communication." *AV Communication Review*, 1968, *16*, 11-25.

Worth, S. "The Development of a Semiotic of Film." *Semiotica*, 1969, *16*, 282-321.

Wright, J. C., and Vliestra, A. G. "The Development of Selective Attention: From Perceptual Exploration to Logical Search." In H. W. Reese (Ed.), *Advances in Child Development and Behavior*. Vol. 10. New York: Academic Press, 1975.

Zajonc, R. B. "Attitudinal Effects of Mere Exposure." *Journal of Personality and Social Psychology*, 1968, *9*, 45-49.

Name Index

❈ ❈ ❈ ❈ ❈ ❈ ❈

A

Allen, A., 7, 247
Anderson, R. C., 44, 67, 91, 107, 221, 246, 256, 261
Arnheim, R., 44, 52n, 246
Atkin, C. K., 19, 63, 246, 249

B

Bachicha, D. L., 221, 247
Baddley, A. D., 247
Ball, S., 140, 161, 176–177, 247
Ball-Rokeach, S., 20, 251
Bandura, A., 129, 130, 131, 221, 230, 232, 234–235, 239, 240, 241, 247
Barenboim, C., 219–220, 249
Bem, D., 7, 247
Bender, B. G., 247
Berkeley, G., 29
Berliner, D. C., 13, 247
Berlyne, D. E. 247
Bernstein, L. J., 160n, 247
Bever, T. G., 91, 247

B (continued)

Binks, M. G., 127, 230, 234, 254
Blank, M., 116, 248
Bloom, L., 129, 248
Blumler, J. G., 81, 248
Bobrow, S. A., 248
Bogatz, G. A., 140, 161, 176–177, 247
Borke, H., 152, 248
Bower, G. H., 26, 221, 248
Brooks, L., 68, 248
Brown, I., Jr., 130, 248
Brown, R., 62, 116, 119, 248
Bruner, J. S., 3, 16, 27, 72, 76, 78–79, 81, 83, 84, 113, 116–117, 126, 135, 215, 227, 235, 248–249, 260
Byrne, D. R., 153, 264

C

Calfee, R., 108, 249
Campbell, D. T., 85, 264
Carothers, T. J., 50, 215, 249
Carpenter, E., 23, 249
Carroll, J. B., 120, 121, 122, 249

269

Casagrande, J. B., 120, 249
Cattell, J. M., 75
Cattell, R. B., 224, 254
Chaffee, S. M., 19, 249
Chandler, M. J., 219-220, 249
Chapanis, A., 36, 249
Charmonte, N., 54, 249
Chomsky, N., 249
Clark, E. V., 76, 77, 123, 249
Clark, H. H., 76, 77, 123, 249
Clark, R. E., 16, 263
Cohen, A. A., 8, 15, 92n, 190n,
    249-250, 263
Cole, M., 77, 80, 120, 131, 135,
    136, 157-158, 189, 208, 215,
    230, 235, 237, 250, 264
Collins, W. A., 18, 56, 65, 171,
    184, 208, 210, 242, 245, 250,
    253
Comstock, G., 6, 250
Cook, T. D., 140, 168, 177, 250
Cosky, M. J., 108, 253
Craik, F. I. M., 221, 250
Cronbach, L. J., 4, 11, 12, 70, 71,
    102, 110, 126, 132, 224, 226,
    229, 250

D

DeFleur, M., 20, 251
Deregowski, J. B., 76, 133, 188,
    251
Dervin, B., 191, 253
Dickie, K. E., 10, 258
Docherty, E. M., 152, 266
Dorr, A., 43, 56, 251
Dowaliby, F. J., 9, 258
Drum, P., 108, 249
During, K., 230, 236, 262
Dyk, R. B., 180, 251

E

Eagelstein, S., 160n
Eco, U., 53
Egan, D. E., 231, 251
Ehrenberg, A. S. C., 208, 210, 253
Einstein, A., 71-72
Eisner, E. W., 3, 22, 31, 37, 62, 65,
    86, 114, 115-116, 251
Ekstrom, R. B., 149, 252
Elkind, D., 82, 231, 251
Ellul, J., 16
Epps, E. G., 179, 251

F

Faraday, M., 72
Feldman, D. H., 16, 62, 63, 190n,
    227-229, 236, 238, 251
Ferguson, E. S., 62, 251
Filby, N., 69, 260
Fillenbaum, S., 69, 251-252
Fishbein, H. D., 154, 252
Flavell, J. H., 7, 126, 252, 259
Fodor, J. A., 106, 121-122, 125,
    252
French, J. W., 149, 252
Furth, J. G., 126, 129, 252

G

Gardner, H., 26, 33, 42, 50-51, 59,
    63, 76, 77, 79, 184, 215, 218,
    242, 243, 249, 252-253, 267
Gazzaniga, M. S., 76, 253
Gerbner, G., 55, 253
Glenn, C. G., 265
Gombrich, E. H., 40, 46, 47, 57,
    62, 66, 76, 253
Goodhart, G. J., 208, 210, 253
Goodman, K. S., 108, 253
Goodman, N., 3, 13, 20, 25, 26, 29,
    32, 33, 34, 35, 36, 38, 39, 40,
    41, 42, 43, 44, 48, 52, 58, 59,
    62, 112, 218, 239, 253
Goodman, Y. M., 108, 253
Goodnow, J. J., 188, 231, 253
Gordon, D. A., 181, 185, 254
Gordon, G. N., 15, 16, 253
Gough, P. B., 108, 253
Gray, S., 180, 254
Greenberg, B. S., 191, 253
Greenfield, P., 113, 116-117, 126,
    215, 249, 254
Greeno, J. G., 80, 81, 90, 231, 251,
    253
Greenspan, S., 219-220, 249
Gross, L., 20, 21, 244, 253, 259

Grusec, J. E., 129, 247
Guttmann, J., 70, 254

H

Hakstian, A. R., 224, 254
Hamilton, V. J., 181, 185, 254
Harari, H., 189, 254
Harnischfeger, A., 244, 254
Harris, M. B., 230, 247
Hatano, G., 127, 230, 234, 254
Hayes-Roth, B., 90, 254
Heider, E. R., 64-65, 120, 254-255
Herskovitz, M. J., 85, 264
Higgins, E. T., 43, 117-118, 255
Holton, G., 71-72, 255
Hood, H., 129, 248
Hornik, R. C., 10, 15, 243-244,
  255, 259
Howard, V. A., 33, 252
Hudson, W., 76, 189, 255
Huston-Stein, A., 109, 215, 255
Huttenlocher, J., 43, 48, 68, 116,
  117-118, 154, 255

J

Jackson, P., 10, 255
Jacobs, L., 52n, 255
Jamison, D., 2, 255
Jeffery, R., 221, 247
Johnson, N. S., 258
Johnston, P. K., 180, 255
Jones, S., 69, 256

K

Kahneman, D., 46, 256
Kane, J. M., 221, 256
Karnes, M. B., 177, 256
Karp, S. A., 161, 256
Katz, E., 6, 81, 248, 256
Katzman, N., 11, 15, 256
Keiffer, K., 154, 252
Kendler, H. H., 122, 256
Kendler, T. S., 122, 256
Kerlinger, F. N., 11, 256
Kieslar, S. B., 10, 255
Kintsch, W., 67, 68-69, 90, 105,

221, 256
Kjørup, S., 21, 29, 52, 53, 55, 57,
  58, 60, 61, 256
Kolers, P. A., 76, 114, 136, 256-257
Konstadt, N., 161, 256
Koran, M. L., 102, 110, 224, 257
Kosslyn, S., 48, 67, 79, 257
Kracauer, S., 52n, 257
Krugman, H. E., 223, 257

L

LaBerge, D., 77, 90, 257
Langer, S. K., 13, 62, 257
Lanzetta, J., 156, 264
Leifer, A. D., 2, 257
Lennenberg, E. H., 119, 248, 257
Leondar, B., 76, 261
Lesser, G. S., 84, 117, 158, 257
Levenstein, P., 180, 258
Levie, W. H., 10, 258
Levin, J. R., 63, 67, 70, 247, 254,
  261
Lewis, S., 154, 252
Lightbown, P., 129, 248
Lloyd, B. B., 188, 258
Lockhart, R. S., 250
Luria, A. R., 122, 124-125, 126,
  230, 258

M

McAnany, E. G., 10, 15, 243-244,
  259
McCandless, B. R., 175, 258
McCombs, M., 5, 258
McConkie, G. W., 108, 258
McDavid, J., 189, 254
McDonald, F. J., 102, 110, 224,
  257
McLeod, J. M., 19, 249
McLuhan, M., 22, 23, 30, 215, 258
Mahoney, M. J., 258
Malve, D., 160n
Mandler, J. M., 258
Marantz, S., 9, 258
Martin, E., 221, 259
Mast, G., 52n, 53, 58, 259
Mayo, J. K., 10, 15, 243-244, 259

Melton, A. W., 221, 259
Menlove, F. L., 129, 247
Meringoff, L., 82, 99, 215, 223, 259
Mervis, C. B., 24, 123, 262
Metz, C., 52, 53, 57, 259
Metzler, J., 116, 259
Mialaret, G., 19, 259
Mielke, K. W., 4. 16, 259
Miller, S. H., 126, 259
Mintzberg, A., 160n
Mischell, R. W., 7, 12, 259
Miyake, Y., 127, 230, 234, 254
Morgan, M., 244, 259
Morley, L., 119, 265
Münsterberg, H., 32, 52n, 54, 58, 259

N

Napoleon, 30
Neisser, U., 46, 47, 62, 75, 78, 79, 90, 236, 259
Noble, G., 259
Norman, D. A., 62, 67, 259
Nyenhuis, J., 11, 256

O

Oettinger, A. G., 2, 259-260
Olivier, D. C., 64-65, 254-255
Olson, D. R., 2, 3, 10, 21, 22, 27, 57, 69, 72, 75, 76, 77, 78-79, 81, 83, 84, 85, 104, 105-106, 108, 116, 122, 125, 128, 135, 215, 222, 235, 240, 242, 260
Olver, R. R., 113, 116--117, 126, 249

P

Paivio, A., 196, 260
Palmer, S. E., 45, 46, 67, 260-261
Perchonock, E., 69, 263
Perkins, D., 33, 76, 252, 261
Piaget, J., 62, 79, 122, 125, 128, 130, 152
Pichert, J. W., 107, 261
Plato, 16

Pomerantz, J., 48, 67, 79, 257
Pressley, G. M., 70, 254
Pressley, M., 63, 67, 261
Presson, C., 154, 255
Price, L. A., 149, 252
Pryluck, C., 9, 261
Putnam, H., 44, 261
Pylyshyn, Z., 66, 261

R

Rapoport, A., 3, 261
Rayner, K., 108, 258
Roberts, A., 175, 258
Roberts, J., 257
Rohwer, W. D., Jr., 67, 261
Rosch, E., 24, 43, 69, 123, 261-262
Rosenberg, S., 67, 79, 82, 88, 261
Rosenstiel, A. K., 26, 242, 267
Rosenthal, T. L., 3, 130, 230, 236, 262
Roupas, T. G., 29, 39, 40, 43, 112, 240, 262
Rovet, J., 155, 233, 262
Rumelhart, D. E., 62, 67, 259

S

Saettler, P., 8, 262
Salomon, G., 4, 6, 8, 15, 16, 49, 63, 77, 92n, 107, 109, 110, 141, 143, 156, 160n, 176n, 226, 240, 249-250, 262-263, 265
Samuels, S. J., 77, 83, 90, 257, 263
Sapir, E., 113
Savin, H. B., 69, 263
Schlesinger, I. M., 121-122, 123-124, 207, 263
Schneider, W., 114-115, 263, 264
Schramm, W., 6, 7, 10, 263
Scribner, S., 77, 135, 157-158, 189, 208, 215, 230, 235, 237, 250, 264
Segall, M. H., 85, 264
Seibert, F. M., 264
Seibert, W. E., 89, 224, 265
Selman, R. L., 153, 264
Shaw, D., 5, 258
Shelton, J., 126, 259

Shepard, R. N., 47, 48, 55, 67, 72, 85, 116, 126, 259, 264
Shiffrin, R. M., 114-115, 263, 264
Shimmerlik, S. M., 264
Shotwell, J. M., 215, 252
Sieber, J., 6, 13, 107, 109, 156, 226, 240, 263, 264
Sieber-Suppes, J., 143, 156, 263
Simon, H., 67, 79, 82, 88, 261
Sinclair de Zwart, H., 122, 133, 264
Singer, J. L., 17, 19, 36, 63, 71, 81, 117, 223, 264-265
Snow, R. E., 4, 9, 12, 13, 67, 70, 71, 75, 89, 102, 110, 126, 224, 226, 229, 235, 250, 257, 261, 264, 265
Solomon, F., 116, 248
Sontag, S., 38, 55, 265
Starnes, T., 175, 258
Steffler, V., 119, 265
Stein, N. L., 265
Sternberg, R. J., 71, 265
Suppes, P., 2, 255
Swanson, L., 219, 266

T

Tannenbaum, P. H., 62, 266
Thomson, D. M., 72, 266
Thorndyke, P. W., 26, 91, 266
Tiffin, J., 89, 224, 265
Tikomirov, O. K., 114, 266
Tobias, S., 221, 266
Tulving, E., 72, 221, 250, 266
Tversky, A., 24, 44-45, 46, 256, 266
Tyler, P., 54, 266

U

Urberg, K. A., 152, 266

V

Vales, B., 119, 265
Vliestra, A. G., 2, 267
Von Bertalanffy, L., 9, 84, 116, 266
Vygotsky, L. S., 84, 124, 125, 126, 127, 129, 131, 230, 232, 234-235, 266

W

Wakshlag, J. J., 208, 266
Wanner, E., 107, 267
Watson, J., 72
Wells, S., 2, 255
Welner, L., 160n
White, K. R., 175, 267
Whorf, B. L., 118-119, 120, 123, 126, 267
Wiley, D., 244, 254
Willows, D. M., 267
Winner, E., 26, 242, 267
Winograd, T., 267
Witkin, H. A., 180, 251
Wolf, D., 184, 215, 252-253
Wolf, T., 21, 22, 76, 267
Wood, C., 246
Worth, S., 31, 52n, 229, 267
Wright, J. C., 2, 109, 215, 255, 267

Z

Zajonc, R. B., 179, 267
Zapol, N., 2, 259-260
Zillman, D., 63, 266
Zimmerman, B. J., 3, 130, 230, 236, 262

Subject Index

‚Ç ‚Ç ‚Ç ‚Ç ‚Ç ‚Ç ‚Ç

A

Achievements, universal through cultural continuum of, 227-231, 236, 238

Activation: of mental skills, through filmic codes, 141, 142, 143, 145, 146, 148-149, 153, 154, 155; and skill cultivation, 222, 231-238

Analog: concept of, 47-48; as symbol system characteristic, 36, 47

Analogy, as symbol system dimension, 25

Analysis, skills of, and television impact, 170-171, 173-174, 203, 205-206, 213

Anticipatory schemata: and codes, 133, 135; and cognition, 75, 78, 79; and mental skills, 90-91, 105. *See also* Internal representation

Aptitude-treatment interaction

(ATI): of film and mental skills, 143, 146, 147, 150, 154, 155; and information processing, 126; and mental skills, 112; and research assumptions, 4-7

Asia, Central, internalization of language in, 124-125, 230

ATI. *See* Aptitude-treatment interaction

B

Behavioral factors, and symbol systems, 238-242

Brain, and information processing, 67-68

C

CEFT. *See* Children's Embedded Figure Test

Changing Points of View, and "Sesame Street," 161-162, 164, 173-181. *See also* Perspective,

275

changing; Points of View test
Children: literate viewing by, 189–213; preschool knowledge and skills of, 167–171, 184; second- and third-graders, knowledge and skills of, 171–175; socioeconomic status of, and literate viewing, 198, 202, 203, 205, 213; socioeconomic status of, and television impact, 165–167, 168–169, 171, 172–173, 174–175, 177–180, 184; television-naive, and "Sesame Street," 157–186
Children's Embedded Figure Test (CEFT), and "Sesame Street," 161, 162, 168, 169, 171, 173–174, 176, 178, 179, 180, 181
Classification test, and "Sesame Street," 161, 162, 167, 168, 169, 170, 171, 172, 173, 174, 175, 176
Close-Up Test: Detail and Concept test correlated with, 183, 197; and "Sesame Street," 162, 172, 173, 176, 181, 183
Closing Verbal Gaps test: and literate viewing, 194, 196, 197, 205, 106; as mental skills test, 94, 101
Closing Visual Gaps test, and literate viewing, 194, 196, 197, 203, 206; as mental skills test, 94, 95, 101
Codes: mental functions of, 131–135; observational learning of, 130; sizes of, 52–53, 56, 136; stationary and transformational, 132–134
Coding elements: choice of, by learner, 184–185; and recoding, 232–234; of television, and learning, 182–186; transformation of, and literate viewing, 209–210, 212
Cognition: concept of, 3; cross-cultural effects of television exposure on, 187–213; and

symbol system, reciprocal interaction of, 238–245; symbol systems related to, 61–87; 237–238; theoretical view of interaction with media and learning by, 214–245
Cognitive development: exploration and search in, 2; and information processing, 71; stages of, 7
Cognitive preference, and information processing, 71
Coherence, prescription distinct from, 30
Color, language and thought related to, 119–120
Compensation, hypothesis of, 69–70
Construed meanings, and symbol systems, 78–82
Contents of media: centrality of, assumed, 1, 2, 4, 7; contribution of, 16–18; knowledge related to, 27; as media attribute, 14
Correlation, concept of, 32
Cross-cultural studies: of cognitive effects of television exposure, 187–213; of media's functions, 6
Cue-attendance: uncertainty related to, 156; and verbal mediation, 144–149; and zooming, experiment on, 142–149, 155

D

Density: and film, 55, 57; as symbol system characteristic, 25, 34–35, 40, 41, 43, 47, 48, 49, 50
Depiction: description distinct from, 36, 38–40, 59; description and expression related to, 36–42
Description: depiction distinct from, 36, 38–40, 59; depiction and expression related to, 36–42
Detail and Concept test: Close-Up test correlated with, 183, 194; and literate viewing, 194, 197, 201–202, 203, 204, 205; as mental skills test, 94, 97, 101
Detail and Whole test: and literate viewing, 194, 196, 197, 202,

203, 204; as mental skills test, 94, 98, 101
Digitalness, as symbol system dimension, 25

E

EFT. *See* Embedded Figure Test
El Salvador, television in, 10, 15, 244
Elaboration: and nonnotational systems, 234; and symbol systems, 221-224, 233-234
Embedded Figure Test (EFT), and literate viewing, 196, 197, 203
Environment: and media, 227-231; and symbol systems, 238-242
Expression: description and depiction related to, 36-42; metaphorical possession related to, 41-42, 49, 59

F

Field-dependence and -independence, and television viewing, 161, 180. *See also* Children's Embedded Figure Test; Embedded Figure Test
Fields of reference: and films, 54-55; and symbol systems, 3, 31-32, 58
Figure and Ground test, and "Sesame Street," 162, 172, 173, 181
Film: analyzed as symbol system, 51-58, 60; compositional syntax in, 53; compounding of messages in, 52; and density, 55, 57; development of, 21; and fields of reference, 54-55; metaphors in, 57-58; and notationality, 55, 56-57; and perception, 55; and repleteness, 55; skill cultivation through, 139-156; and symbol schemes, 52-54; transformation conventions in, 54. *See also* Television
Form Board test, and visualization, 149

G

The Godfather: as television or novel, 9; transformation conventions in, 54
The Gold Rush, metaphor in, 57

H

Hidden Figures Test, and analytic skills, 9
Hypotheses. *See* Skeleton hypotheses

I

Iconicity, as symbol system characteristic, 29, 36, 37, 49, 60
Information processing: and the brain, 67-68; and cognitive development, 71; and cognitive preference, 71; and content of symbol systems, 64-74; and task to be performed, 72; unimodal or multiple, 66-67
Internal representation: as coded within symbol system, 3; and information processing, 66; psychologically, 46-50; and symbol systems, 3, 46-49, 221. *See also* Anticipatory schemata
Internalization: of language, 124-129; through observational learning, 129-131
Interrupted Series test, and literate viewing, 194, 196, 204, 206
Israel: literate viewing in, 191-213, 225; map symbols in, 63; "Sesame Street" in, 14-15, 157-186
Israeli Standardized Verbal Ability Test (MILTA), 145, 146-148, 196, 200, 206

K

Knowlege: acquisition of, and skills,

correlated, 105–106; acquisition of, and symbol systems, 217; acquisition of, and transformations 218; extraction of, ease of, 219–221; extraction of, and literate viewing of television, 189; skill compared with, 75, 175–176
Korea, television in, 10
Kpelle, language structure of, 120

L

Language: internalization of, 124–129; and symbol systems, analogy between, 127–128; thought related to, 118–124
Laying out, and visualization skills, 149–153, 155
Learning: individual differences in, 4, 110–111; observational internalization through, 129–131; task and symbol system compatibility related to, 226; theoretical view of interaction with media and cognition by, 214–245
Letter Matching test, and "Sesame Street," 161, 167, 168, 169–170
Liberia: Kpelle of, 120; Vai of, and literacy, 77, 135, 235, 237
Literate viewing (LV): age differences in, 210–211, 212–213; concept of, 189, 212; cross-cultural results on, 199–200; cross-culutral study of, 187–213; and cultural differences, 208–210; direction of effect of, 207–208; measure of, 193–104; and skill mastery, 201–208; skills affected and unaffected by, 206
LV. See Literate viewing

M

Maps: development of, 30; and notationality, 34–35; temporal representations on, 64
Media: as alternative means to same ends, 5, 8–10; attributes of, 14–26; as complex entities, 1; conception of, 25, 61–62; conceptions of, and educational research, 1–27; content of, assumed central in, 1, 2, 4, 7; differing dimensions of, 7–8; and environment, 227–231; family resemblances among products of, 24; impact and effects of, 2; invariant nature of, 5–8; learning effected by, 2, 4, 6; potential contribution to learning of, 6; relative effectiveness in teaching of, 4, 5, 7; state of the art in, summarized, 2; structural elements of, 63; symbol systems central to, 13–26; task interaction with, 81–82; theoretical view of interaction with cognition and learning by, 214–245. See also Symbol systems
Media research. See Research
Medium-stimulus, as invariant, 5–6
Memory, active and long-term, 117–118
Mental skills: achievements as, universal through cultural continuum of, 227–231, 236, 238; activation of, through filmic codes, 141, 142, 143, 145, 146, 148–149, 153, 154, 155; activation of, and skill cultivation, 222, 231–238; and analysis and synthesis, and literate viewing, 203, 205–206, 213; of analysis and synthesis, and television impact, 170, 171, 173–174; automatic use of, 90; code-specific, 76; concept of, 75; differential uses of, 3, 88–112; experiment concerning, 89–112; generalizability of, 236; hypotheses about, 92; and knowledge acquisition, correlated, 105–106; knowlege related to, 75, 175–176; modeling of, and skill cultivation, 222, 234–235; modeling of, through filmic

codes, 141, 142, 143, 144, 145, 146, 147-148, 149, 150, 151-152, 153, 154, 155; performatory skills distinct from, 128-129; range of stimuli related to, 106; rationale for, 89-92; short circuiting of, through filmic codes, 141, 142, 143, 149, 150, 153, 154; short circuiting of, and skill cultivation, 222, 223; and situational demands, 229-230; supplantation of, 222, 231-238; and tasks to be performed, 107-111; transfer of cultivated, 135-147, 156. *See also* Skill cultivation
Mentalese, concept of, 121-122
Metaphors, in film, 57-58
MILTA. *See* Israeli Standardized Verbal Ability Test
"Mr. Rogers' Neighborhood," learning from, 63
Modeling: of mental skills, through filmic codes, 141, 142, 143, 144, 145, 146, 147-148, 149, 150, 151-152, 153, 154, 155; observational learning of, 129-131; and skill cultivation, 222, 234-235
Modes of appearance. *See* Symbol systems
Moral judgment, and symbol system effects, 220
Mothers, coobservation of television by, 176-180, 185, 209, 212, 225

N

Nielsen Company, 191, 259
Nonnotational systems, and elaboration, 234
Notationality: and film, 55, 56-57; illustrations of, 34-35; as symbol system dimension, 25; in symbol systems, 33-36, 39, 49, 58-59
Number Matching test, and "Sesame Street," 161, 167, 168, 169-170

O

Organization, verbal mediation and, in cue-attendance, 145, 147-148

P

Paintings, and style sensitivity, 243
Pairs test, and literate viewing, 196, 197, 201, 203
Paper Folding test, and visualization, 149, 150
Parts of the Whole test, and "Sesame Street," 161, 172, 167, 168, 169, 170, 171, 172, 173, 174, 176, 178, 183
Perception: and anticipatory schemata, 46-47; and film, 55
Performatory skills, mental skills distinct from, 128-129
Perseverance, and "Sesame Street," 181, 182, 185-186
Personality research, 7
Personological factors, and symbol systems, 238-242
Perspective, changing: and cultivation of mental skills, 152-154, 155; structural and content components of, 152. *See also* Changing Points of View test; Points of View test
Picture-Number Matching test, and "Sesame Street," 161, 168, 169-170
Picture Ordering test, and "Sesame Street," 161, 162, 163, 168, 169, 171, 173, 175, 176, 178, 181
Picture Stories test, and literate viewing, 194, 195, 196, 201, 203, 204, 206
Points of View test, and literate viewing, 194, 196, 197. *See also* Changing Points of View test; Perspective, changing
Potemkin, metaphor in, 57
Prescription, coherence distinct from, 30

R

Reading, code processing in, 108-109, 114-115
Recoding: of coding element, 232-234; as skill, 75
Relational Concepts test, and "Sesame Street," 161, 168, 169-170, 171
Repleteness: and film, 55; as symbol system characteristic, 36, 39-40, 41, 50, 59
Representation. *See* Internal representation
Research: assumptions in, 4-13; as basis for practice, 10-13; educational, and conceptions of media, 1-27; generalizing conclusions from, 6; holistic approach to, 1, 2; on instructional and mass effects, 6-7; on interactions, 11-13; potential-extracting versus natural-phenomena, 139-141; on skill cultivation, 139-156; on television impact, 157-213
Resemblance: and information processing, 66; psychologically, 43-46; role of, 218-219, 239-240; as symbol system characteristic, 37-39, 50, 59-60

S

Series Completion test, and literate viewing, 194, 196, 201, 202, 203, 204, 212
"Sesame Street": adventure films compared with, 181-182; attention to, 63; attributes of, 14-15; effects of, in Israel, 157-186, 238; encouragement to coobserve, 140, 176-180, 225; longitudinal study of, 160-167; and perspective changing, 152; symbol system of, 159
Short circuiting: of mental skills, through filmic codes, 141, 142, 143, 149, 150, 153, 154; and skill cultivation, 222, 223

Sign, Concept of, 37
Similarity: perceived, 44-46; as symbol system characteristic, 49, 59-60, 218
Situations: contributions of, 18-19; as media attribute, 14
Skeleton hypotheses: on codes, 134; on instructional treatment, 12; on processing of nonnotational systems, 223; on range of stimuli, 106; on reciprocal interactions, 242; on recoding, 244
Skill cultivation: through activation and practice, 114-115; cross-cultural effects of television exposure on, 187-213; through filmic codes, 141-155; through films, 139-156; through supplantation, 222, 234-235; through symbol systems, 3, 82-85, 113-156, 227-245; through television, 157-186. *See also* Mental skills
Skills. *See* Mental skills; Skill cultivation
Socioeconomic status: and literate viewing, 198, 202, 203, 205, 213; and television impact, 165-167, 168-169, 171, 172-173, 174-175, 177-180, 184
Space Construction test: and literate viewing, 194, 196, 197; as mental skills test, 94, 96, 101, 102
Spatial Rotations test, and literate viewing, 196, 197
Stationary codes, 132-134
Stories, conceptual treatment of, 26
Stories test, and literate viewing, 194, 196, 197, 201, 202-203, 204
Supplantation, 222, 234-235; through filmic codes, 141-155
Surface Development test, and visualization, 149, 150
Symbol schemes: atomic elements in, 30-31; and film, 52-54;

prescription and coherence in, 30-31, 58; syntax of, 30-31

Symbol systems: and amounts of mental activity, 218-224; availability and actuality of, 23-24; and behavioral factors, 238-242; characteristics of, 28-60; cognition effected by, naturally and potentially, 139-141; and cognition, reciprocal interaction of, 238-245; and cognitive functions, 215; and construed meanings, 78-82; content of, and ease of processing, 64-74; cultural rather than universal, 230-231; defined, 3, 19-20; differential effects of, 3, 62-63; dimensions of, 25; effects and effectiveness of, 110; elementary, 20; and environmental factors, 238-242; as essential in thinking and cognition, 3; field of reference related to, 3, 31-32, 58; importance of, 3, 26-27; and individual differences of learners, 4, 110-111; interaction of internal and communicational, 3-4; and internal representation, 3, 46-49, 221; internalization of, 126-129; kaleidoscopic, 186; and kinds of mental activity, 224-227; and knowledge acquisition, 217; knowledge specified through, 78; logical analysis of, 29-42; as media attribute, 3, 14; and mental elaboration, 221-224, 233-234; mental skills required for, 74-78; notationality in, 33-36, 39, 49, 58-59; and personological factors, 238-242; propositions concerning, 64, 68, 71, 72-73, 77, 80, 81, 82, 84, 86-87; psychological considerations of, 42-51; as research focus, 1-4; skill activation and supplantation by, 231-238; skills cultivated by, 3, 82-85, 113-156, 227-245; skills related to, 27; syntactic and semantic components of, 32; and tasks, 225-226; and technology, 19-26; theses on interactions of, 216-217; as tools of thought, 84-85, 235; translations of messages to, 68-71; unique contributions of, to cognition, 237-238; and user interaction, 49-51. See also Media

Symbolic code input, hypothesis of, 207-208

Symbolic processes, symbol and signification in, 117-118

Symbols: classes of, 37; combinations of, 32; communication and thought functions of, 116-117; connotative, 37; conventional, 37; logical analysis of 29-42; qualitative, 37; representational, 37; representational and epistemological functions of, 242; as tools of thought, 115-118

Syntagms, film role of, 52, 53, 56, 57

Syntax: compositional, in film, 53; of symbol scheme, 30-31

Synthesis, skills of, and television impact, 170-171, 173-174, 203, 205-206, 213

T

Task requirement: and cue-attendance, 143; and mental skills, 107-111

Technology: contribution of, 15-16; as media atrribute, 14; and symbol systems, 19-26

Television: affective factors of, and skill cultivation, 162, 165, 166, 178, 179; close-ups/long-shots in, 93, 94, 100, 101, 102, 103, 104, 105, 133; coding elements of, and learning, findings on, 182-186; cognitive factors of, 165, 166-167, 178, 179; coobservation of, by mothers, 176-180, 185, 209, 212, 225; effects of, on naive children,

157-186; exposure to, cross-cultural cognitive effects of, 187-213; exposure to, defined, 189; exposure to, measure of, 192-194; exposure to, and mental skills, 162, 165, 166, 167-168, 172, 178, 200-205; fragmentation of space in, 93, 94, 100, 101, 102, 103; literate viewing of, 189-213; logical gaps in, 93, 94, 100, 101, 102, 103, 104; and mental skills experiment, 92-106; news from, as agenda setting, 17; reading ability negatively affected by, 244; and social environment, 209-210, 213, 225; straightforward version of, 93, 101, 102, 103, 104, 105; and violence, 17-18; and violence, "realistic" versus "fictional," 63; zoom-ins and -outs in, 93, 101, 102, 103, 104, 105, 144. *See also* Film; Literate viewing
Thought: language related to, 118-124; linguistic and non-linguistic, 123; tools of, 84-85, 115-118, 235
Three Mountain problem, and points of view, 152
Tools of thought: symbol systems as, 84-85, 235; symbols as, 115-118
Transformational codes, 132-134

U

United States: educational stimulation in, 175; literate viewing in, 191-213, 225; map symbols in, 63; messages from television in, 180; "Sesame Street" in, 14-15

V

Vai, and literacy, 77, 135, 235, 237
Verbal mediation: and cue-attendance, 144-149; and visualization, 150-151
Verbal messages, elaboration demanded by, 223
Visual Memory test: and literate viewing, 194, 197, 201, 202, 203, 204, 205, 211; as mental skills test, 94, 99, 100, 101
Visualization: and language ability, 150-151; skills in, and laying out, 149-153, 155

Z

Zambia, graphic perspective in, 133, 188
Zooming: assumption about, 141-142; and cue-attendance, experiment on, 142-149
Zuni Indians, and Whorfian hypothesis, 119